Chris!

Transactional Analysis Counselling

Phil Lapworth
Charlotte Sills
Sue Fish

HELPING PEOPLE CHANGE:
THE ESSENTIAL
COUNSELLING SERIES

Transactional Analysis Counselling

Phil Lapworth
Charlotte Sills
Sue Fish

WINSLOW PRESS
Telford Road, Bicester, Oxon OX6 0TS

First published in 1993 by
Winslow Press Limited, Telford Road, Bicester, Oxon OX6 0TS,
United Kingdom
www.winslow-press.co.uk
Reprinted 1994, 1996, 1998, 2000

Typeset by The Comp-Room, Aylesbury, Bucks

002–1720/Printed in Great Britain/2000

British Library Cataloguing in Publication Data
Lapworth, Phil
Transactional Analysis Counselling.-
(Helping People Change: The Essential Counselling Series)
I. Title II. Bailey, Roy III. Series
158

ISBN 0 86388 119 X

CONTENTS

Phil Lapworth Cert Ed Dip Counselling Skills Dip Systemic Integrative Psychotherapy is a BAC accredited counsellor and Certified Transactional Analyst (ITAA). He came to counselling and psychotherapy through his work in Special Education in London (as Deputy Headteacher in a school for children with learning disorders and as Senior Teacher at the Maudsley Psychiatric Hospital). For many years the Director of Clinical Services at **metanoia** Psychotherapy Training Institute, he currently runs a psychotherapy and supervisory practice in West London and in Bath.

Charlotte Sills MA Cert Ed Dip Systemic Integrative Psychotherapy is a Certified Teaching and Supervising Transactional Analyst (ITAA). She works as a counsellor and psychotherapist in private practice and as a trainer and supervisor in a variety of mental health settings. She has a particular interest in bereavement counselling, as well as using transactional analysis in her work with individuals, couples, groups and organizations. She is the Director of TA Training at **metanoia** Psychotherapy Training Institute.

Sue Fish BSocSc Dip Ed Dip Speech & Drama Dip NLP & Counselling is a Certified Teaching and Supervising Transactional Analyst (ITAA) and a Teaching Member of the Gestalt Psychotherapy Training Institute of Great Britain. She has extensive training and experience in remedial and therapeutic work with children and young people, including several years as the head of a unit for disturbed adolescents. She is a founder Director of **metanoia** Psychotherapy Training Institute, where she practises psychotherapy with children, families and adults, as well as training and supervising in TA and Gestalt.

PREFACE TO THE SERIES

Welcome to *Helping People Change: the Essential Counselling Series.* Counselling skills are now becoming more and more recognized as an essential part of effective helping. Nowhere is this more true than in social services, education, the health care professions and their associates. In publishing this series Winslow has produced a range of books on different approaches to counselling that should be of immediate practical benefit to anyone in the 'people business'. Each book in the series is written by experienced counsellors respected in their own field. Each title reveals a different way in which you can develop your counselling skills with your clients. I hope you will find them a welcome and close companion in your work.

ROY BAILEY
Series Editor

ACKNOWLEDGEMENTS

We would like to thank our friends and colleagues: Roy Bailey, Series Editor; Petruska Clarkson for encouraging us to write this book. We have been enriched by the knowledge, skills and creativity she has shared with us and taught us over the years. Her development of theory has been an important influence in the world of TA. It is this and the work of metanoia (which she co-founded with Sue Fish) which provides much of the foundation of this book. Thanks also to: Maria Gilbert, who has further enhanced our learning with a precision and clarity we hope is well reflected in these pages, of which she was our 'expert reader'; Barbara Porter for providing us with the case material for the client example in Chapter 11; Leo Lapworth for his computer-graphic skills and his patient provision of all the figures.

Special thanks go to Stephen Karpman, Marilyn J. Zalcman and Muriel James for their kind permission to reproduce the diagrams in Figures 16, 18 and 22.

The authors would also like to thank each other for staying co-operative, creative and cheerful throughout the writing of this book. Sue and Charlotte would like to give special thanks to Phil for his role as main author, which entailed enormous extra work with regard both to the content of the book and to the process of co-ordinating its writing.

We would like to extend our appreciation and respect to our clients, trainees and supervisees who have taught us more about counselling than any book can possibly teach and to whom this book is dedicated.

PREFACE

A Brief History of TA

Eric Berne (1910–70), the originator of transactional analysis, was a Canadian-born psychiatrist who began his psychoanalytic training in 1941 at the New York Psychoanalytic Institute. His analyst was Paul Federn, a student of Freud's. Before he came to write about transactional analysis, his writing was more psychoanalytic in nature, as in *The Mind in Action* (London: John Lehmann, 1949).

In 1943, Berne's studies were interrupted by service in the army. It was here that he began practising group psychotherapy and developing his intuitive and observational skills which were later to appear as observations and definitions of ego states. Between 1949 and 1962, he developed these ideas and presented them in several journals; these articles were later to be compiled as *Intuition and Ego States* (ed P. McCormick, San Francisco: TA Press, 1977). It was in 1958 that his ideas were first published in the *American Journal of Psychotherapy*, under the title, 'Transactional Analysis: A New and Effective Method of Group Therapy'. He went on to publish eight books and numerous articles on the subject of transactional analysis. His final book, *What Do You Say After You Say Hello?*, rated by some as his most erudite and comprehensive work, was published posthumously, in 1972. It certainly combines the creativity, originality, wit and wisdom of the author into a book of enormous popular appeal.

After his work in the army, Berne pursued his psychoanalytic training at the San Francisco Psychoanalytic Institute and went into analysis with Eric Erikson. But, perhaps because of his unorthodox and innovative ideas (especially the idea that people could be helped to change much more quickly than by traditional psychoanalysis), he never gained recognition as a member of the psychoanalytic establishment. Clearly, Berne was attracted to psychoanalysis — much of his work testifies to the respect and esteem he had for psychoanalytic thought — yet he found it too rigid, too cumbersome, too complicated, too precious; above all, too slow. In response, he devoted his energy to combining individual and social psychiatry into a unified system he was to call transactional analysis (TA).

Around the time of his first TA publication, in 1958, Berne began to hold seminars to discuss and develop ideas on transactional analysis. They were called the San Francisco Social Psychiatry Seminars. Six people attended the first meeting. By the end of the first year, attendance and established TA theory had grown so much that there was both an introductory course — known as a 101, which continues to this day as a basic introductory course — and an advanced seminar, known as a 202. By 1962, the first quarterly *Transactional Analysis Bulletin* (*TAB*), later to become the *Transactional Analysis Journal* (*TAJ*), was published and the following year the first annual summer conference was held. In the mid-1960s the San Francisco Seminar was renamed the International Transactional Analysis Association (ITAA). Throughout this time, and until his death in 1970, Berne continued to develop TA theory.

The ITAA now has a membership of over 8,000 worldwide and has been further complemented by the formation, in 1976, of the European Association for Transactional Analysis (EATA) which now has responsibility for training standards and certification throughout Europe. Both associations have their own respective examining bodies and are dedicated to the continuance of the development and enhancement of TA theory, organizational development and maintaining the standards of journals and conferences.

Britain has its own Institute of Transactional Analysis (ITA) which produces a thrice-yearly magazine, the *ITA News*, monitors the professional and ethical practice of TA in Britain and organizes an annual conference.

Note: Many of the case examples in this book are derived from practical counselling sessions. The real identities of these cases have been removed and examples changed in the interests of protecting the clients.

Chapter 1

AN INTRODUCTION TO TRANSACTIONAL ANALYSIS

In this first chapter we will give an overview of TA in order to place it in a general context. In the chapters that follow we will introduce some basic TA concepts for you to explore and experiment with for yourself and in your work with others. In each chapter we will give a definition or description of the concept, some everyday examples to clarify the concept, suggestions as to how the concept may be usefully applied, a clinical example and some exercises for you to practise for yourself and with your clients. At the end of the book we provide a reading list of TA books and addresses of TA organisations for those of you who are interested in furthering your knowledge and skills in counselling with transactional analysis.

The debate concerning the distinction between 'counselling' and 'psychotherapy' is a long-standing one. What seems to be agreed by most of the discussants is that counselling and psychotherapy overlap considerably. What remains contentious is where the overlap begins and ends. It is not our intention to enter the debate in this book. We believe that the TA concepts and techniques presented here may be used by counsellors or psychotherapists working with non-psychotic clients and whose practices are sufficiently supervised and monitored by more senior practitioners.

An Introductory Overview

What is Transactional Analysis?

Transactional analysis is a theory of personality based on the study of specific ego states, a theory of social interaction or communication based on the analysis of interpersonal transactions and a system of group and/or individual psychotherapy used as a tool for personal growth and personal change. It involves four methods of analysis — structural, transactional, games and script — and has taken its name from the second of these, though it clearly comprises all four.

Transactional Analysis (commonly called TA) is a way of looking at what goes on between people and inside people in order to help them make changes. The transactional aspect is exactly what it says: a two-way communication, an exchange, a transaction. This may be of spoken words, expressed feelings, physical behaviours, shared thoughts, stated opinions or beliefs and so on. A transaction may be a raised eyebrow that is responded to with a smile. It may be a comforting hug when another is crying, or it may be a silence at the other end of the telephone following some unexpected news. We may look at and analyse what goes on between people in terms of the words that they are using or the gestures they are making or the beliefs they are expressing and learn something of each of these people. But how does this apply 'inside' people? How can one person transact? Here is an incident as described by a client:

> "I was really scared when the lift stopped between floors. I said to myself, 'Don't panic whatever you do!' But this didn't help much. In fact, I started to panic more. So I said, 'I'm really scared,' and I told myself this was all right. I felt a lot better knowing this and got myself thinking about how to deal with the situation. I told myself I could feel scared and still think of what to do. Of course, it was simple, I just pressed the alarm button. A man on the intercom reassured me I'd be out soon. The lift started to move while he was still talking. 'Well done,' I said to myself, 'A year ago you'd have been a gibbering wreck.' "

This person is simply doing what we all do: he is talking to himself. Notice that sometimes he refers to himself as 'I' and sometimes as 'you'. In this way, though he is still one person, he can hold an internal dialogue between different parts of himself. He is transacting internally.

TA provides a model which defines these parts of oneself as different ego states. Whether it is thoughts, feelings or behaviours that are being exchanged externally or internally — usually it is all three, whether we are aware of this or not — they will be coming from one of three types of ego state, the Parent, the Adult or the Child ego state. Early in this book, we will introduce the concept of ego states and will return to the concept many times, as these ego states are the building-blocks of TA theory.

This three-part model is both simple and profound. Unfortunately, like many good ideas which have immediate appeal, the model is open to misuse. It can be seen in a rather simplistic way and used manipulatively for selfish and exploitative ends. Eric Berne, the originator of the model, was astute enough to recognize this possibility and in his catalogue of psychological 'games people play' included one called 'Transactional Analysis', which is when people use TA to belittle themselves or others. The simplicity and usefulness of the TA model lies, not only in the colloquial language adopted to describe the various and often complicated concepts, but in the ease of understanding and identification people tend to show in response to TA theory. It is not uncommon to hear people using ego state language adeptly and creatively within minutes of its introduction. The profundity of the TA model lies in the depth and breadth of its psychological understanding and exploration. The list of contents of this book, including Ego States, Transactions, Functional and Transactional Options, Life Script, and Assessment and the Process of Change, indicates the range to which this three-part model may be applied. We hope this introductory book will show some of the depth and breadth of understanding that TA can bring to many aspects of life, living, relating and communicating and, especially, to counselling.

Since its introduction and development by Eric Berne and others who will be mentioned in this book, many people from varied professional backgrounds have been attracted to TA and found in it something useful and exciting. Clearly, they still do. What is it about TA that has attracted psychotherapists, counsellors, psychologists, doctors, social workers, nurses, teachers, children and others over the years? Here are some of the reasons we think TA is so popular:

- The basics of TA theory are expressed in simple, colloquial and easily understood language with words like 'games', 'scripts' and 'strokes' (a term that has now been included in several English dictionaries as well as being commonly found in pop songs and TV programmes).

- Though there is now common reference to the 'inner child' both in popular and in mainstream psychology, counselling and psychotherapy literature, the term 'Child' and the concept of part of oneself remaining phenomenologically alive as a child throughout one's adult life has been a central tenet in TA — a concept that is appealing and experientially validated and validating for many people.
- TA concepts are often shared with clients, so there is a talking *with* rather than talking *at* clients. In this way the content and process of psychotherapy and counselling are demystified and developed into a shared endeavour.
- TA lays stress on personal responsibility for one's experience and in so doing puts the client in a central, proactive and therefore potentially powerful role in the counselling situation. In this respect, TA is referred to as a decisional model. If we are personally responsible for our own experience, we must be responsible for the choices and decisions that we make about how we behave, how we feel, how we think and what we believe, even though many of these decisions may not be made in awareness. Even as children we made such decisions in response to the environments of home, school and society. Clearly, some of these decisions were misinformed, misperceived, skewed by immaturity, but nonetheless the best we could manage in those early circumstances. Hope lies in the fact that new and reparative decisions can be made in the present to replace the now dysfunctional and maladaptive decisions of the past.
- The appeal of TA to some may also be due to its embracing and integrating the three main streams of psychology within its theoretical model: the psychoanalytic, the behavioural and the humanistic/existential. As mentioned earlier, Berne's formative training was in psychoanalysis. TA theory owes much to the psychoanalytic thinking and experience with which Berne was familiar — to Freud, Klein, Fairbairn, Federn and Erikson, to name but a few — and to the concepts belonging to traditional psychoanalysis, ego psychology, social psychology and object

relations, particularly intrapsychic phenomenological structures. Though Parent, Adult and Child ego states are not the Superego, Ego and Id of psychoanalysis, there is no denying that they are derivatives. It is also clear that the Freudian concept of the repetition compulsion was developed by Berne into one of the central notions of TA, that of the Life Script and the repetitive games and rackets that support it. An example of the inclusion of behavioural concepts is the emphasis given in TA to the effect of positive and negative reinforcement (operant conditioning) or 'stroking' as an important element of script formation. Our hunger for strokes influences how we adapt to the perceived wishes of others in terms of the feelings we feel or show, the thoughts we have, the beliefs we hold and the behaviours we exhibit. This adaptation will be based particularly upon our experience of our parents when we were little and how they responded to our hunger for strokes. The humanistic/existential component has already been touched upon. TA emphasizes personal responsibility, growth, self-awareness and choice; even when circumstances are not chosen, people can still choose their attitude towards these circumstances in a positive and creative way.

TA Philosophy

Much of what has been written above touches upon the philosophical underpinnings of transactional analysis. The first of the three philosophical beliefs central to TA is the notion that people are born OK. The second is that people with emotional difficulties are nevertheless full human beings and the third is that all emotional problems, given adequate knowledge and resources, are curable. These beliefs mean that all people have a fundamental worth and as such should be valued and respected. This does not mean that we necessarily accept and approve of a person's behaviour but that beneath the behaviour we see the person and value that person's humanity. In counselling this involves working with the person from a position described by Carl Rogers as 'unconditional positive regard'. We need to hold ourselves in the same regard if we are to approach another person with human equality. Thus the existential position of I'M OK — YOU'RE OK is paramount in TA. As counsellors (and people) if we are coming from a position of I'M OK — YOU'RE NOT OK or I'M NOT OK — YOU ARE OK or I'M NOT OK — YOU'RE NOT OK, we are coming from a position of inequality (or, in the last instance, equal hopelessness) which cannot be conducive to growth and change.

Implicit within the I'M OK — YOU'RE OK philosophical position is the belief that our core selves are lovable and creative and that our intentions are positive and constructive, even when our behaviour is unattractive, undesirable, misguided or destructive. We think the following anonymous quotation with which we end this chapter expresses well this essential philosophical attitude towards ourselves and others:

> Every single human being,
> when the entire situation is taken into account,
> has always, at every moment of the past,
> done the very best that he or she could do,
> and so deserves neither blame nor reproach
> from anyone, including self.
> This, in particular, is true of you.

Chapter 2

CONTRACTS

The practice of TA involves the use of contracts. A contract is an agreement between two or more people. Its purpose is to clarify matters so that there is no confusion about what everyone expects of themselves and other people. TA counsellors make contracts with their clients about how they will work together, what is to be expected and what goals the person wants to achieve through the process of counselling.

Eric Berne first developed his ideas at a time when psychotherapy and counselling usually followed the 'medical model' where counsellors, like doctors, were considered to be the experts with all the learning and skill. They employed this expertise to 'cure' the patient who was regarded as having the problem and as being in the position of weakness or 'illness'. Berne felt very strongly that this was a position that could not effect lasting change. It disempowered the patients, making them reliant on the helper. He also thought it was disrespectful as it implied an inequality between human beings, categorizing them as the well and the sick. He, therefore, used a language understandable to his clients and encouraged them to read books and to study the theory. He believed that most people can take responsibility for themselves and, therefore, have the ability and the right to decide what they want in their lives. Consequently, he would ask his clients what they saw as the problem, what they wanted to change in their lives and what they wanted from him. He would explain to them how he worked and then together they would decide if and how he could be helpful to them in achieving what they wanted for themselves. From this position a client would make a contract, an agreement, not only about the time and duration of sessions, fees to be paid and so on (the *business contract*), but also about the specific change the client wanted to make (the *treatment contract*).

In what follows concerning counselling contracts, we want to stress that such contracts are made in the service of the people involved, that they are made to enable, not to bind or restrict. They are not made so that later one person can take another to a court of law and prove how bad that person is for not having met the contract or for wanting to change it. They are made in order for both parties to feel safe and clear about what they are going to do together. The only exception to this is where there is some breach of the ethical or professional practice guidelines relating to the counselling body to which each counsellor should belong.

The Initial Contact/the Initial Contract

The initial contact between counsellor and client is often over the telephone when the counsellor may offer the client an initial assessment interview. Apart from the time and the place, the client will need to know how long the session will last and how much it will cost. This is an initial business contract for that session.

When clients first come to see a counsellor, many will almost certainly be feeling anxious. They will probably be experiencing some sort of unhappiness in their lives which has caused them to seek help and they are coming with a mixture of fear and hope. It may be distressing for them to talk about what is painful. They may not know what is going to happen. They may consider that the counsellor will think them silly or bad or they may see themselves as having failed in some way in needing to see a counsellor. Equally, they are really hoping that a counsellor will help: maybe counselling can work magic and turn their lives around. In any case, they will need two things: one is to feel that the counsellor is sufficiently caring and trustworthy for them to risk spending their time — and probably money — coming to talk about very private things; the other is a clear idea of what is going to happen. Later in the book we will be writing about 'structure hunger' and how anxious people can become if they do not have enough order in their lives. This includes clear expectations. If you think back to the last time you went somewhere new, where the people and surroundings were unfamiliar to you, you can probably remember what your initial concerns were. For example, who were the other people? Where were the relevant rooms? Where were the cloakrooms? What time would lunch be? What were the rules? It is the same for your clients.

In order for counsellors to be experienced as caring, trustworthy and interested, they have to give their clients space to talk and be listened to. The most important thing is that, from the first moment of the relationship, clients feel encouraged to trust that the consulting room is a place where they can bring all their concerns in an atmosphere of support and safety. For that atmosphere to feel supportive and safe, the counsellor will need to be experienced by the client as providing protection and potency and, to achieve this, there must be a clear structure — a contract. This initial contract will be a business contract. Counsellor and client will make an agreement about the length, timing, regularity and frequency of the sessions, with agreement about what arrangements will be made if a session cannot be attended by either party, the possibility of rescheduling, advance notice of holidays, and so on. A fee (if any) will need to be agreed upon which is acceptable to the counsellor and the client.

Once the business contract is made, counsellor and client will also make an agreement about what they will be doing together. This initial counselling contract — a mutual commitment to a particular focus — is sometimes referred to as the treatment contract.

The Treatment Contract

From the start, some clients like, or are able, to be very specific about what they want to change in their lives. For example, 'I want to make a good relationship with a woman — up to now my partners seem to get bored with me', or 'I've been depressed all year since I was made redundant and I want to start enjoying my life', or 'I want to discover how I keep getting into arguments with my friends and find better ways of communicating with them.' With people like this, there are some useful formats for clarifying treatment contracts which we will discuss later.

Many clients, however, do not have a clear idea about what they want from the counselling. They are conscious of their distress, anxiety or depression but may not be aware of the reasons for feeling this way or what they can do about it. They may have some vague feeling of unease or they may be aware that there is something missing in their lives. With these clients, it would be wrong to insist upon getting what is sometimes referred to as a 'hard' contract. At the very least, it is a waste of time. At worst, it could be abusive, as the client might receive the impression that they have to know everything about themselves before they start or that they are being asked to restrict what they talk about.

In his book *Till We Have Faces* (London: Fount Paperbacks, 1978), C.S. Lewis wrote, 'How can we meet the gods face to face until we have faces?' Broadly, he meant that we cannot attain a higher understanding of anything until we know who we are. He was talking about spiritual growth, but the same truth obtains in counselling. We cannot know exactly what it is that we might want to change about ourselves until we know and accept ourselves the way we are at the moment. For these clients, the initial contract may consist of loosely naming the problem and making a commitment to focus on understanding and exploring until such a time as the goal can be clarified. Even then, this may be a gradual process, with the contract being updated sensitively as time goes on. For example, at the start of counselling, Andrew said, "I've been feeling low for months. I don't know why. I'm successful at work — I just feel low." The initial contract was to explore this. After several weeks of counselling, Andrew said, "I realize now that I'm living my life as if to please my mother. I need to start living it for me." The counsellor agreed and for the next few weeks they worked together to fully understand the implications and significance of this. It was not long before Andrew discovered that "Living my life for me is harder than I thought. I don't really even know what I want to do." The contract then became for him to learn to listen to his own feelings and needs and to figure out what he could do to get them met. Yet later, after Andrew had spent a painful and exciting time truly getting to know himself — including some of the feelings he had shut out of his awareness over the years — he began to be more in touch with what was missing in his life. He had found his own 'face' and was ready to make decisions for his future. He was now able to identify behavioural changes that he wanted to make in his life in terms of how he spent his time and how he related to people. This was the focus of his counselling which ended when he achieved intimate, enjoyable and interdependent relationships in which he could express his feelings, ask for his needs to be met, have fun and reciprocate from an I'm OK — You're OK position.

To sum up so far, there are many benefits to contract-making when this is sensitively undertaken:

1 Contracts stress the equality and respect inherent in a working relationship in which the client has the right to say what they want from the counselling situation.

2 They encourage self-responsibility, in that clients not only have the right to say what is wanted but are asked to fully 'own' that want, to be aware that they have some control of their own lives, that they have options and that only they can change their lives.

3 They provide clarity of focus and, in naming a goal, give both client and counsellor something to aim for. Another meaning of the word 'contract' is 'to make smaller'. In this sense, the clarity of goal can mean economy of time and energy for client and counsellor. The time spent in clarifying a contract constitutes an important part of the total work to be done. Furthermore, the contract acts as a 'mind set' such that the client not only moves towards the goal consciously but also holds it as an internal frame of reference.

4 They help to avoid misunderstandings: for instance, they challenge the belief that the counsellor has some magic potion that is kept in a secret drawer and handed out to any client who has the password. Specifically, they avoid what in TA are called 'games'. These will be discussed later in the book. Games are partly the result of lack of clarity and hidden agendas — hidden to all parties — which would seriously impede or prevent effective counselling.

5 Contracts provide a useful yardstick for measuring the effectiveness of the counselling. This is essential if we are to work ethically with our clients. If contracts are not being achieved, either they are the wrong contracts — in which case, the focus of the work needs to shift — or the client and the counsellor are not suited — in which case, the counselling will need to be brought to an end and the client referred elsewhere.

6 The achievement of a contract instills hope and optimism in a client, along with a sense of power. This can be a fine foundation for future changes.

The disadvantages of contracts, especially when used in a rigid way, are:

1 Clients may experience themselves as not being listened to or seen in all their dark and hidden parts but only in the specific area they have named.
2 Contracts can sometimes feel like homework assignments to some clients. For instance, Cleo, who has spent her life being 'good', getting things right, always achieving 'A' grades and so on, may feel as if this is another test and that the counsellor will be marking her on her performance.
3 Clients who 'don't know' what they want can feel inadequate, 'bad', despondent or hopeless when asked to name their goal. Some may comply with the expectation and invent something to please the counsellor, while others may be rebellious in response.
4 Contracts may seem to exclude spontaneous other work or issues.

These disadvantages can be avoided if the counsellor sees contract-making not as static but as a flexible, growing process in which the counsellor and client together are aware of the journey they are making and are responsive to the changing needs and goals of that journey.

In practice, therefore, TA counselling starts with an initial contract comprising the business agreement and the named focus. This is what our colleague Sonia Mathias calls the 'ticket to counselling' which states the commitment that both counsellor and client are there to help bring out the best in the client. After this, there is an unfolding process wherein the initial agreement is explored. The client and the counsellor find out what the agreement means, clarify it, agree it and decide what needs to be done.

Application

Sometimes it is useful to contract in a formal way. Martha and William Holloway (*The Monograph Series*, Midwest Institute for Human Understanding Inc, 1973) identify two kinds of contract: the Social Control Contract (which we prefer to call the Social Change Contract) and the Autonomy Contract. Contracts for social change involve some specific aspect of change in thought, feeling or behaviour. Autonomy contracts involve a wider change in the person's life and their intra-psychic structure. In theory, counsellors will normally make social change contracts with their clients. In practice, however, the fulfilment of such contracts often has far-reaching effects. Contracts, according to the Holloways, answer two questions:

- What do you want to change?
- How will you and I know you have made those changes?

Sometimes the answer to the second question is a subjective one; for instance, the client will feel relaxed instead of tense and worried. However, TA counsellors often prefer to ensure clarity by making contracts for observable change. Even if the desired change is of thought or feeling, this can be translated into behavioural terms that are verifiable. In the example of someone wanting to feel relaxed instead of worried, this may be observable in their body posture, their breathing and their problem-solving behaviour, all of which will be very different if they are feeling relaxed rather than tense and worried.

Some examples of contracts for social change could include the following:

- A mother who is miserable and angry makes a contract to stop smacking her children and do something enjoyable with them every day.
- A lonely man makes a contract to make three new friends.
- An anxious and housebound person makes a contract to travel, gradually increasing distances outside the house week by week.

Though these contracts emphasize an observable, behavioural change, they are likely to involve the client in exploration as to why they are respectively miserable and angry, lonely or anxious and what they are doing, or not doing, to keep it that way.

There are many formats for making contracts that have been suggested by different TA practitioners. We include two of them here. In her book, *Techniques in Transactional Analysis* (Reading, Mass., Addison-Wesley, 1977), Muriel James provides a list of contracting questions which have been expanded by our colleagues, Petruska Clarkson and Shona Ward:

1 What do you want that would enhance your life?
2 What do you need to change to achieve this?
3 What would you be willing to do to effect this change?
4 How would other people know when the change has been made?
5 How might you sabotage yourself?
6 How will you prevent sabotage?
7 How will you reward yourself on completion?
8 How are you going to spend your time when you have changed?
9 Where and how will you get your strokes, now that you have changed?

Allen & Allen (New York: Medical Examination Pub. Co., 1984), offer some simple questions to focus the client:

1 What will you be doing when you are well that you are not doing now? (It is interesting to note that they use the word 'well', which suggests a medical model of illness and health. However, we think they intend 'well' to mean having a sense of 'well-being' within yourself.)
2 What are you doing now that you will not be doing when you are well?
3 How will we both know when you are well?

The answers that two clients gave to this last set of questions demonstrate the flexible way in which they can be used. Ann answered without hesitation. She had thought a lot about what she wanted from her life. To the first question she replied, "I will have friends who I will see regularly. I will sing in a choir and I will be training as a counsellor." To the second question she responded with, "I'm having panic attacks when I go out and I certainly won't be having those any more." There was no need for the third question, as it had been answered implicitly in the first two. But Sally was different. She needed a long time to explore the implications of the questions and she spread them over several sessions in her exploration. She needed to understand what it was that lay beneath her general feeling of malaise in order to start to let herself know what she wanted to change in her life. Eventually, she knew that what she would be doing when she was well was expressing her feelings, asking for what she wanted and managing creatively those situations in which she could not have what she wanted. What she decided she would not be doing was telling herself that she was not important and that others should come first. She said we would both know when she was well when she looked, acted and sounded more energetic and had taken up a new hobby — she was not yet sure what. (The 'new hobby', incidentally, turned out to be several, including a regular aerobics class and squash. She also started a new relationship.)

So far, we have looked at ways in which contracts may be formally made by TA counsellors. Just as important are the small, regular agreements that counsellor and client make together. Contracting, or clarifying, may be used as a friendly tool for making sure that both parties are remembering that they are separate human beings who will need to check the course of the counselling rather than go by assumptions. Thus, when Beth is spending her time in the session talking about her daughter rather than herself, the counsellor may wonder if this is useful to the client and may say to Beth, "You seem to want to tell me the story of your daughter today, is that right?" To which Beth answers, "Yes, really. I don't know why but I want to tell you about her." This is a contract. It has clarified the situation for the counsellor. It has also highlighted it for Beth. It tells her that she has charge of the session in the sense of choosing what she talks about. She is, therefore, more likely to be aware of when she wants to change the focus. If, later, she discovers that talking about her daughter was not useful after all, she has the option of exploring this with the counsellor in order to understand how or why she did this and how to do it differently next time. However, it may be that in talking about her daughter something very important emerged for her which might have been lost if the counsellor had been in the habit of starting the session by immediately requiring her to name something that she wanted to do that day that would have an observable outcome for her.

Contracts to Stay Alive, Non-harmful and Sane

The Holloways (*The Monograph Series*, Midwest Institute for Human Understanding Inc, 1973) introduced TA practitioners to the idea of what they refer to as Escape Hatches. By this they mean that many people have an idea of what they would do if 'things got really bad'. The common escapes are (1) to commit suicide, (2) to harm or kill someone else, and (3) to go crazy.

Sometimes people, experiencing their life situation as already being 'really bad', present themselves in the counselling situation clearly feeling suicidal, murderous or on the verge of 'going crazy'. Often, however, people are unaware of making such a desperate plan. Most have not reached this extreme. However, in the course of the counselling, people start to give up ways of being that have at least kept them going all their lives, even if they have not been happy. The stress experienced due to loss of structure and the attendant disorientation can result in the surfacing of one or more of these means of escape. The counsellor must be vigilant to notice whether this is the case by being alert to comments that imply self-destructiveness, real threat to others or belief that the client may 'go crazy'. Whether the intention is overt or covert, the counsellor will seek to close these escape hatches by asking clients to make a contract to keep themselves safe from harm and not to injure anyone else. This contract should be made unequivocally. If a client cannot agree to make it for life, it should be made for specified periods within the counselling, at the end of which the situation can be reviewed and re-contracting take place where needed. For example, Mary, who is very distressed and depressed, will not agree to a long-term, self-safety contract but assents to keeping herself safe between her current session and the next session a week later. The counsellor sensibly makes an addendum that, should they be prevented from meeting for the next session, the safety contract stands until they next meet. Mary willingly agrees. If the client will not do this then the feasibility of counselling must be reconsidered and further assistance should be sought from the counsellor's supervisor. In some instances, the client may need the protection of in-patient care for the crisis period.

This process of closing the escape hatches, as with other contracts, is a behavioural contract. The client is contracting not to *act upon* their feelings or thoughts of, for example, suicide. However, there is a danger that, in making such a contract, the client may infer that sharing their feelings and thoughts of suicide is now prohibited, particularly if the counsellor rushes to make a contract when they do. Clearly, this situation must be avoided. If the client does not feel permitted to share such thoughts and feelings and to explore them with the counsellor, it is unlikely that the escape hatches will remain closed. For this reason, we see contracts to close the escape hatches as 'holding' the client while they work through their thoughts of suicide, harm to others or 'going crazy' on the way to making new decisions (see specifically Chapters 7 and 10) to live, to be non-harmful and to be sane.

A Final Word About Contracts

In order to make contracts as useful and effective as possible, they need to be stated in clear, precise language understood by both counsellor and client. A contract to 'perambulate diurnally in a recreational outdoor amenity while inhaling and exhaling diaphragmatically' is less likely to be achieved than a contract to 'take a daily walk in the park and breathe deeply'.

The counsellor should also be alert for contracts which contain hidden loopholes. Often these take the form of a qualifier — words such as 'more', 'less' and 'better'. These obscure the real meaning. For example, what does it mean to 'make more and better contact with others'? How much is more? What constitutes better contact? Who are these others and how many are there? These unquantified aspects need to be avoided by careful questioning on the part of the counsellor to elicit more precise and specific goals. Similarly, there are phrases like 'try to', which implies a lot of effort and no success, or 'be able to', which contains possibility but no action. Either the client is going to do something or they are not. This needs to be clear within the contract.

Note that TA counsellors do not encourage their clients to make what are called Parent contracts — those which please our parents (or others we may see in a parental role). TA is interested in helping people to truly discover themselves and what they want, not parenting models from their childhood. This encapsulates the difference between a promise and a contract. Though the content may be similar, the process in making a contract is different in that a contract is a commitment primarily to oneself (and in counselling witnessed and supported by the counsellor) whereas a promise comprises a commitment to or for another.

Most of all, avoid contracts which involve 'getting rid of' some part of the self. For example, "I'll stop being vulnerable" or "I'll cut out my angry feelings." These contain a belief that there is something wrong with the client as they are and invite the counsellor to collude with this belief.

Our Contract with You, the Reader

Though we are not meeting face to face, we can in a sense make a contract with you now about this book. We undertake to present some of the major concepts in TA and show how they can be used by a counsellor. For each theoretical concept, we will include a section on its application and a section of exercises to be used by readers for themselves and for their clients. We do not undertake to cover every aspect of TA theory but we will include a comprehensive reading list at the end for those readers who would like to learn more. Where, for clarity, we use our own terms instead of the more commonly used TA terms we will indicate this with reference to the original terminology.

Your side of the contract, as the reader, is that you have acquired this book, from a shop, library, the publisher, friend or colleague. This means that, at some point, payment has been made for our services and those of the publisher. This is the extent of your side of the contract. You have not contracted to read it. You may even have bought the book because it's just the right thickness to prop up that wobbly table in the kitchen. However, if you do decide to read it, we hope you will find it interesting and helpful to you. We would be happy to hear your comments on it.

Exercises

Self

1 Make a list of five things you want to do today. Choose one. Do it. This may sound simple but you have just made a contract with yourself and kept it. How do you feel? Do you have a sense of satisfaction in having made a plan for yourself and fulfilled it? Perhaps you are someone who does this regularly. If so, you already know the benefits of making a plan and then relying on yourself to keep to it. If it is new for you, allow yourself to think and feel about the experience.

2 This time, make a list of five things you want to do or ought to do but have been putting off. Choose one. Why have you been putting it off? Do you still want to do it? What could you do to make it easier? Are you willing to do it? If so, how will you reward yourself for having done it? Now do it. How do you feel? You can do the same with the other things on the list if you want to.

3 Choose one of the contracting methods we have introduced in this chapter and answer the questions for yourself. You may choose to do this with your own counsellor.

4 Experiment with a friend, colleague or counsellor (someone with whom you feel free to be open) in having two separate conversations. In one, start by saying what you want to talk about and what you want to get out of having the talk. In the other, just talk about whatever is on your mind at the time without making a plan and ask your partner to listen empathetically to what you are saying. Notice the difference in the two experiences and assess for yourself the advantages and disadvantages of each.

Working with Clients

1 While you are listening to and talking to your client, stay aware of your own experience and notice when you need clarification of what the client wants. Gently, find out what your client wants either by asking directly, as in, "What would you like from me about this?" or "How would you like to be different?" or by checking assumptions, as in, "Do you want to do something about that?" or "It sounds as if you need to let off steam about that right now, is that right?"

2 Invite your clients to picture themselves as they want to be. Pay attention to how they will be different from the way they are now. How will they feel, think, walk, sit, talk, eat, dress and so on?

3 Use one of the contracting methods or one of your own and invite your clients to be specific about what changes they are going to make in their lives.

Chapter 3

EGO STATES

As mentioned in the introduction to this book, ego states are the building-blocks of TA theory.

Definition and Description

In his last book, *What Do You Say After You Say Hello?*, Berne defined ego states as 'coherent systems of thought and feeling manifested by corresponding patterns of behaviour'. Simplified further, structurally, an ego state is a state of being or experience which involves our thinking, feeling and behaving. You may already be asking yourself if there are any states of experience which do not involve thinking, feeling and behaving. The answer is no. At any moment in time an experience will, in some way, involve all three. As you are reading these words you will be thinking about what you are reading, having a feeling response to the words and concepts and simultaneously exhibiting a behaviour called reading, involving looking, seeing, body posture, manner of holding the book, facial expression, and so on. Inevitably, then, at any given moment we can be said to be in an ego state.

Now that you have read a further sentence or two you are in another ego state with the thinking, feeling and behaviour belonging to the new moment. Looking back in time, you can now see that by this definition your life has been made up of millions upon millions of ego states, one after the other. But how can this possibly be of any use to us in our quest for some understanding of ourselves and other people? To answer this question, we need to look yet more closely at ego states. On closer inspection, we observe that some of these ego states are not new. They are not fresh, 'of the moment' states of experience but repeats of past ego states. In other words they involve thinking, feeling and behaving in exactly the same way we once did in our near, mid, or distant past. A further question arises: does this matter? It matters only insofar as how much the re-experiencing of a past ego state interferes with our current functioning in life. For example, you may be reading this book right now, yet at the same time reliving a negative experience you had when struggling to understand a book on, say, geometry when you were nine years old. Your thinking is confused and has a nine-year-old's capacity, you feel sad and despondent and your behaviour is agitated (you put the book down, you pick it up, you clean your fingernails with the cover, and so on). We hope this is not the case, as clearly this will be interfering with your enjoyment and learning.

Conversely, you may be reading this book and reliving a positive experience of learning a new subject as a student. You are thinking clearly, you feel excited by the ideas being presented, you read with concentration and do not even notice your fingernails. We definitely hope this is more the case. The latter experience, of course, may not be an old ego state at all. It could be a purely current experience. In which case, all well and good. The point of the examples, however, is to show that, even if we are reliving an old ego state, it is not necessarily dysfunctional for us. What we are looking at, then, in our own lives as well as those of our clients, are those ego states which are interfering negatively with the way we are functioning or want to function in the present.

Already we can see that there are distinctions we can make between ego states. Firstly, we can say that some ego states are current — our set of feeling, thinking and behaving is in relation to the here and now reality — while others are historic — our thinking, feeling and behaving belong to the past. Secondly, we can make another distinction by applying some assessment and judgment as to whether an ego state is functional or dysfunctional, whether it enhances or interferes with our experience.

The Adult Ego State

The term used to describe an ego state that is in direct relation to here-and-now, consensual reality is an Adult ego state. We talk of being 'in' an Adult ego state or 'in Adult' where there is no historic interference. We are thinking, feeling and behaving in the moment. The words that might be used to describe a person in an Adult ego state could include responsive, alive, vibrant, in good contact, spontaneous and autonomous. This is not synonymous with being happy or persistently 'full of the joys of spring'. We are talking about reality here and reality involves being appropriate to whatever is the situation. For example, in response to the death of a friend, people feel sad and despairing, they question their own existence and the point of life, they cry and get angry. All of these are Adult ego state responses to the here-and-now reality of bereavement.

Experientially, we see the Adult ego state as an empty ego state that is filled in each moment as we respond to a new situation from the wealth of our experience and potential. It is in this sense, each instant, filled with a succession of ego states through time. Moment by moment, the reality changes, as does our response to that reality. Once past, each Adult ego state becomes one of the many historic ego states from which it was distinguished only by its current nature, its here-and-now relation to the situation.

Clearly, in an Adult ego state we are not totally 'new'. What is new is our unique response to a particular situation. However, we can draw upon our past experiences (historic ego states) constructively and creatively. Indeed, if we are to grow and change, it is vital that we do just that. Our whole learning process is dependent upon our ability to use the past in this way and benefit from our experience. This capacity for drawing upon other ego states or integrating them is suggested in the fuller labelling of the Adult as the Integrated Adult ego state. The historic becomes integrated into the here and now.

Further Distinctions

Unfortunately, we do not always use our past experiences constructively or creatively, nor do we necessarily use them consciously. As stated earlier, sometimes the past impinges upon the present without being consciously integrated and interferes with our current functioning. We 'go into' historic ego states sometimes partially, sometimes totally.

The concept of 'going into' historic ego states implies that these ego states are stored within us. Where and how we store such experiences remains a scientific mystery. Berne posited the concept of 'psychic organs' but these remain merely as conceptual constructs. Suffice it to say that there are reservoirs of past experience and that they can be re-experienced. Such re-experiencing involves more than thoughts about our past experience. It is not an act of remembering. It is a 'reliving' of a past experience in the present involving all three of our criteria of an ego state, namely, thoughts, feelings and behaviours in a coherent system. Let us take a look at these reservoirs of past experience, known in TA structurally as the Child ego state and the Parent ego state.

The Child Ego State

In order to emphasize its historic nature, the Child ego state is more fully referred to as the Archaic Child ego state. This label, though the singular form is commonly used, describes the multitude of historic ego states which constitute the person's own past experiences. They are called 'Child' ego states to emphasize that these ego states often have their origins in childhood. Most of the work that we do in counselling is likely to focus on childhood experience. However, we conceptualize all past experience as being stored in the Child or Parent ego states, including the moment just past. Thus Adult ego states form in the present but, once past, are stored within one of the two types of ego state reservoirs.

When a person thinks, feels and behaves in ways which are a repetition of past, often childhood experiences, we say they are in a Child ego state. For example, John, on arriving home from work, realizes he has forgotten to pick up the groceries. As his wife moves to greet him, John's first thought is that she will be angry with him, he feels very scared and hurriedly leaves the room. Outside of his awareness, he has responded to a current situation in the way he responded when, as a six-year-old, he forgot to run an errand for his mother. In the past situation his mother was, in fact, violently angry and he fled the room in fear of her wrath. Thus the past experience is relived in the present. In the Child ego state John thinks, feels and behaves in ways inappropriate to the current reality. Had he remained in an Adult ego state, he could have greeted his wife, told her he had forgotten the groceries, apologized, offered to return for the groceries and so on, even if his wife did get angry.

The Parent Ego State

The second store or reservoir of historic experience is called the Parent ego state. This singular label again describes a multitude of past ego states. These are distinct from Child ego states in that they are not our own direct experiences but the ego states of our parents or parent-figures which we have taken in (introjected) as our own. This ego state reservoir is consequently often more fully referred to as the Introjected Parent.

Again, though the emphasis is upon introjection that occurred in childhood, we conceptualize the Parent ego state as also accommodating introjections of later important figures in our adult lives, which may include friends, colleagues, counsellors, teachers and others. When a person thinks, feels and behaves in ways borrowed from parents or parent-figures, we say they are in a Parent ego state.

Many actual parents, though determined *never* to treat their offspring in the way their own parents treated them, nonetheless 'find themselves' (often to their dismay) admonishing their children with the same words and phrases, intonation, gestures and feelings to which they were exposed by their own parents. In other words, they 'go into' a Parent ego state. But responding to others in this way is not the prerogative of actual parents. Each of us, at times, transacts from a Parent ego state. Observers and teachers of even small children will often observe how children 'become' their parents at times.

Let us go back to John who, in the previous example of the Child ego state, forgot the groceries. As much as he has access to a Child ego state wherein he is scared and runs away from his angry mother, equally, he has access to a Parent ego state which contains the introjection of his angry and chastizing mother. It would not be suprising, therefore if, had the situation been reversed and his wife had forgotten the groceries, John thought, felt and behaved towards her from his Parent ego state in the violently, angry manner in which his mother had once dealt with him, by responding, for example, with, "You stupid fool, how could you forget such a simple thing!" This is why we often come to the uncomfortable realization that our fear of the way others may think about us, feel about us and behave towards us arises precisely because it is the way we could easily think, feel and behave towards them.

The PAC Model

You now have the basic structural model (known in shorthand as the PAC model) of ego states. When referring to these ego states, the initial letter is always capitalized to differentiate the ego states, Parent, Adult and Child, from actual parents, adults and children. The basic PAC structural model of ego states is shown in Figure 1.

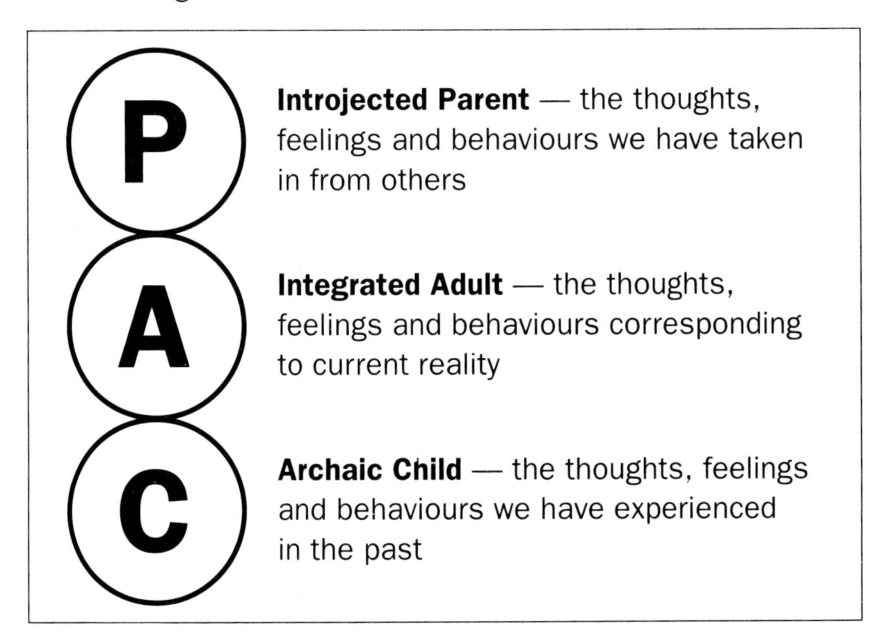

Figure 1 *The PAC structural model of ego states*

The Identification of Ego States

In his book, *Transactional Analysis in Psychotherapy* (New York: Grove Press, 1961, 1966), Berne suggests four ways of identifying from which type of ego state a person is transacting.

Identification by Behavioural Diagnosis

By observing the demeanour, gestures, body posture, voice tone, vocabulary and facial expression of a person we may find some clue as to which ego state a person is in. For example, a man waving a fist while issuing words of command with an angry facial expression may be in a Parent ego state, reproducing the thoughts, feelings and behaviour of his father. Equally, it could be a person in an Adult ego state rehearsing his part in Shakespeare's *Henry V.*

As another example, a woman observed to curl up into a ball on the floor, suck her thumb and cry may be seen to be in a Child ego state. Equally, she may be behaving as her mother did when under stress, in which case, though her mother may have been in a Child ego state at the time (or behaving as her mother did), this woman would be said to be in a Parent ego state, having introjected her mother's thinking, feeling and behaviour. Clearly, a behavioural diagnosis, though perhaps giving some clues, is not enough.

Identification by Social Diagnosis

Social diagnosis concerns the reactions of others to the person being diagnosed. In our first example above it may be that, in response to the fist-waving man, others feel little and scared, think they are about to be dominated and, therefore, avoid confrontation with him. If such is the case, it is possible that our man is in a Parent ego state eliciting a complementary Child ego state response in others. If, however, this is a Shakespearean actor rehearsing his role, the social response of others is likely to be Adult and indicate the complementary Adult ego state of our actor.

In our second example, if others respond to the thumb-sucking, curled-up woman from Parent ego states ranging from over-protective urges to nurture her to equally strong urges to shake her and tell her to 'Grow up!', it is likely that she is in a Child ego state. But what if, as suggested earlier, she is in a Parent ego state, behaving as her mother once did under stress? The others might still respond from Parent ego states as if to a child because this is the Child in her Parent ego state (mother's Child) though, technically, this is her Parent ego state. Clearly, even with the behavioural diagnosis, a social diagnosis is not enough.

Identification by Historical Diagnosis

This simply means checking the origins of the observed behaviour, feelings and thinking with the person in question. For example, we could ask the fist-waving man to be aware of how he is behaving, thinking and feeling and ask him if this is how others in his past behaved. If he says his father used to behave in this way, use the same gestures, express the same thoughts and feelings, it is a pretty good indication that he is in a Parent ego state — unless, of course, he tells us that he is consciously copying his father's behaviour for his role of Henry V, in which case he is in Adult.

In the example of the curled-up woman whose behaviour, along with our social response, has led us tentatively to identify a Child ego state, we may ask if she remembers being like this as a child. She may even remember how old she was at the time and fully corroborate the identification of a Child ego state. Conversely, she may remember her mother being like this and identify a Parent ego state. Or she may even be entertaining her grandchild with an enacted story, in which case she could identify being in Adult. By now, being corroborated by the person in question, the diagnosis may be getting much clearer. There is one more mode of identification.

Identification by Phenomenological Diagnosis

Here the identification is encapsulated within the subjective experience of the person re-experiencing the past. The person experientially relives the original event. The fist-waving man in our example may verify being in a Parent ego state as he currently 'feels' himself to be his father waving an angry fist and giving commands, just as his father had done 30 years ago when our subject was a child. Our hypothesis that the woman is in a Child ego state may be verified as she continues to suck her thumb, sobs deeply and, feeling sad and abandoned, cries out, "Mummy, don't leave me!" just as she had done as a child when her mother left her alone in the house at a very early age.

We hope we have here emphasized enough the importance of including all four means of diagnosis when identifying ego states. It is fine to have hunches when working with your clients; this is a helpful starting-point. It is even better to check them sensitively before acting on them. If you do not, at best you may be unhelpful, at worst you may be insulting or even abusive.

Application

How is the identification of ego states useful? In our introduction we wrote that TA is a way of looking at what goes on between people and inside people in order to help them make changes. The identification of structural ego states is an important step in this direction. If we learn to identify our own ego state responses, we provide ourselves with important information and widen our choice of response options. For example, Susan, a successful and competent lecturer, faced hundreds of students in lecture halls all over the country but avoided social situations. This was because, when entering a room where others were informally gathered, she would feel acutely embarrassed and would run from the room. She turned down invitations to parties, dinners and drinks with the neighbours and was becoming more and more socially isolated. This was the problem she brought to counselling. The counsellor asked her to talk about the differences between the two situations. She made the following distinctions:

- lecture hall as opposed to people's front rooms;
- formal as opposed to informal;
- presenting ideas as opposed to presenting myself;
- seats in rows as opposed to casual seating;
- feeling confident as opposed to feeling nervous and embarrassed.

The counsellor shared with Susan the concept of ego states and his hunch that when lecturing she was in an Adult ego state and in the social situation in a Child ego state. She agreed that in the social situation she did feel extremely little. The counsellor suggested that she close her eyes and imagine herself as a child and to 'take herself' into a situation where she was in someone's front room, at an informal gathering where people are casually sitting around and where she is presenting herself in some way. Almost immediately Susan said she felt scared and embarrassed. She experienced wanting to run away. She thought, "They think I'm silly. They're laughing at me." The counsellor encouraged her to stay with these thoughts, feelings and behaviours even though they were uncomfortable. He asked her where she was and she told the counsellor, "I'm at my aunt's house. I'm six years old. I'm very excited to be here at a grown-up party. I'm dressed as a fairy . . . [Susan here is looking very frightened, wringing her hands in her lap and trembling slightly] Yes, of course!" At this point, Susan 'came back' to the present. She did not need to stay in her six-year-old Child ego state any longer. She reported that she had run into the room where the grown-ups were casually seated. Wanting to present herself as a 'real fairy', she'd leapt into the air as an entrance. Unfortunately, she fell awkwardly, snapped her wand and tore the paper wings which fell about her as she lay on the floor. All she could hear was the laughter of the grown-ups as she ran from the room in great distress, feeling acutely embarrassed.

Susan could see that, outside of her awareness, she had been repeating the feelings, thoughts and behaviours of this archaic event each time she had presented herself at an informal gathering. Making the conscious connection, in other words identifying the Child ego state, helped Susan recognize that she had options in such situations. With this recognition and some work on her original embarrassment, she began to attend social gatherings and would stay in her Adult ego state. If she felt nervous or embarrassed, she would remind herself that she was not six years old, she was not about to leap awkwardly into the room and that others were not going to laugh at her; they would be seeing the attractive, confident and competent woman that she was.

In this example, Susan's Child ego state had been interfering with her Adult functioning. By identifying that ego state, Susan could choose to respond to current reality in an appropriate way.

Exercises

Self

Now you are familiar with the three types of ego states of the structural model, you can practise being aware of whether you are in Parent, Adult or Child ego states. Being aware at the time you move into a particular ego state (even better, predicting which one and when you might move into it) will enhance your options in any particular situation. However, it may take some time to reach this level of self-awareness. To begin with, observe which ego state you have been in after the event. Think back over the many different situations in which you were engaged. Isolate certain events and for each situation ask yourself the following questions:

1 Did I think, feel and behave in ways that my parents used to (or other grown-ups used to when I was little)?
2 Did I think, feel and behave in ways that were appropriate and a direct here-and-now response to what was going on?
3 Did I think, feel and behave as I did at some time in my recent, mid or distant past?

Work through several events until you come up with an example for all three ego states and, having found at least one of each, write them down as follows:

PARENT: I felt..
I thought...
I behaved by...

ADULT: I felt..
I thought...
I behaved by...

CHILD: I felt..
I thought...
I behaved by...

In the case of the Child ego state, see if you can identify the origins: what was happening for you in your life; how old were you; who else was involved?

In the case of the Parent ego state, see if you can identify the person whose feelings, thoughts and behaviours you re-enacted today. Why do you think you were influenced by this person? Why do you think in this particular situation you went into Parent?

Given that you could have been in any of the three ego states in the situations in which you have chosen to self-observe, let us experiment with alternatives:

1 Imagine what would have happened if, in your example of a Child ego state, you had been in a Parent ego state.
2 Imagine what would have happened if, in your example of a Parent ego state, you had been in an Adult ego state.
3 Imagine what would have happened if, in your example of an Adult ego state, you had been in a Child ego state.

Note: The exercises above may also be useful to give to your clients if you are thinking of introducing TA into your counselling practice. Though the following exercises are to help your clients to become aware of their own ego states, clearly, in the counselling situation, *your* ego states will play an important role. You will need to aim to be in an Adult ego state at all times if you are to be effective in your counselling, even if you choose to draw upon historic ego states for the benefit of your clients. You cannot be helpful if you are unknowingly in a Parent ego state, subtly controlling your client in the way your father subtly controlled you, for example, or in a Child ego state, responding to your client with the thoughts, feelings and behaviours of the eight-year-old you once were. The aim should be for all your transactions to be Adult-monitored. This will mean constant self-supervision, supervision by others and counselling or psychotherapy for yourself to work through your unresolved past experiences and parental influences. Becoming an Integrated Adult is clearly an ongoing process, and by 'ongoing' we mean lifelong.

Working with Clients

Choose a client with whom you will go through the exercises in this book. You may decide upon a new client or one with whom you have already established a counselling relationship. One of the best ways to learn to use TA concepts and skills effectively is by recording the sessions on audio or video tape. Many TA counsellors record sessions as a matter of course for self-supervision or supervision by others. Do inform your client that you will be recording the sessions and clarify the extended confidentiality contract involved.

1 *Using your intuition*
When working with your client (and when listening to or watching a recorded session) use your intuition to assess which ego state your client is in at any particular moment. Watch and listen for behavioural clues as your client moves in and out of ego states. Remember that each client's ego states will be unique to that individual. Observation will need to take place over several sessions before you begin to notice certain patterns. Remember, the pattern should include thoughts, feelings and behaviour.

2 *Behavioural clues*
Use your intuition to make tentative hypotheses as to the type of ego state to which these patterns belong. Make a note of these under Parent, Adult and Child headings (leaving space for further notes and further diagnosis). Remember that these behaviours will belong to one of the three types of ego state particular to the individual client — one person's Child behaviour may be another person's Parent behaviour, and so on. For example:

PARENT: This particular client folds arms across chest, clenches fists, jaw rigid; voice sharper, staccato, higher pitched; uses words like 'should', 'have to', 'never'; short of breath, angry and frustrated; speaks contemptuously of self and others. (Like father?)

ADULT: This same client sits with feet well-grounded, relaxed; makes good eye-contact; breathes fairly deeply and regularly; thinks clearly and talks of self and others in a lively and interested manner; expresses feelings clearly and directly.

CHILD: This same client sits with shoulders dropped, head bowed; speaks softly (often inaudibly); avoids eye-contact; agitates fingers, expresses anxiety, thinks others (including me) are angry with her; fears she has done something wrong; looks about five years old.

3 *Social clues*

The social clues are your experience in response to these behavioural clues. What are your feelings, thoughts and behaviours at these times? Check them against the intuitive identification of your client's ego states so far. Do you experience yourself in Child when your client is in Parent? In Parent when your client is in Child? In Adult when your client is in Adult? Check the consistency of your responses and add these under each of the headings.

4 *Historical clues*

By asking appropriate questions, you can check further on your ego state identification so far. When you think your client is in a Child ego state, the following types of questions may be useful:

- Do you remember feeling/thinking/behaving like this in your childhood?
- How old do you feel right now?
- What was happening in your life then?
- What are the similarities between your past experience and your current one?

When you think your client is in a Parent ego state, the following types of questions may be useful:

- Who in your past used to say what you're now saying?
- Who in your past behaved like this?
- Are you expressing your feelings or are you expressing familiar feelings expressed by someone from your childhood?
- Who was this? What was the situation?

Familiarity on your and your client's part with the historic ego states will help identify the Adult ego state by a process of elimination. You can directly ask your client if they experience themselves in Parent or Child right now, or if they feel in the present.

5 *Phenomenological clues*

In Parent or Child ego states your client may be aware of re-experiencing the past. If you think your client is in a Child ego state it may be useful to ask directly what is happening right now, what is the client's experience, what the client is feeling and thinking, what is the time and place of the client's experience, who else is there, and so on. Similarly, with the Parent ego state, ask your client to express their experience right now: who is it that is grimacing in such a way, who is it that is saying these dismissive words, who is it that feels so despondent at such times? And so on. For the Adult ego state again, asking your client to express what they are experiencing at the moment will help to confirm your identification of an Adult ego state according to the response.

Chapter 4

TRANSACTIONS

When we wrote earlier of TA showing what goes on between people and inside people, we were referring to transactions. We define a transaction as a two-way communication. This can either be internal (intrapsychic) or external (interpersonal). In this chapter we will deal with interpersonal transactions: I speak to you and you speak to me; Sam waves to Bill, Bill waves back; Jenny smiles at Jim, Jim frowns at Jenny. A communication is made from one person to another and a communication is returned. In more behavioural terms, a *stimulus* is given to which a *response* is made.

When analysing transactions (which is sometimes called transactional analysis proper), we can use the PAC structural model of ego states introduced earlier to help understand what is going on between two or more people. When two people meet, they have three types of ego states each and we can analyse the various ways in which these two sets of three ego states constellate. For example, what is going on when Sam waves to Bill and Bill waves back? Obviously, we would need to talk to Sam and Bill about this and identify each person's ego state from the various diagnostic clues. If we did, we might discover that Sam sees Bill, who is an old friend, is pleased to see him and waves in greeting. Likewise, in response, Bill is pleased to see Sam and waves back in greeting. We would probably diagnose such a transaction as an Adult to Adult stimulus (S) with an Adult to Adult response (R). This is known as a *complementary* transaction: the ego state to which the transaction is directed is the one which responds back to the original ego state. This transaction is shown in Figure 2.

Alternatively, we may discover that Bill is Sam's boss and reminds him of his authoritarian father. Thus when Sam waves to him it is a placatory wave from a Child ego state addressed to Bill's Parent ego state. In response, we may discover that Bill comes from a Parent ego state, waving as his mother used to

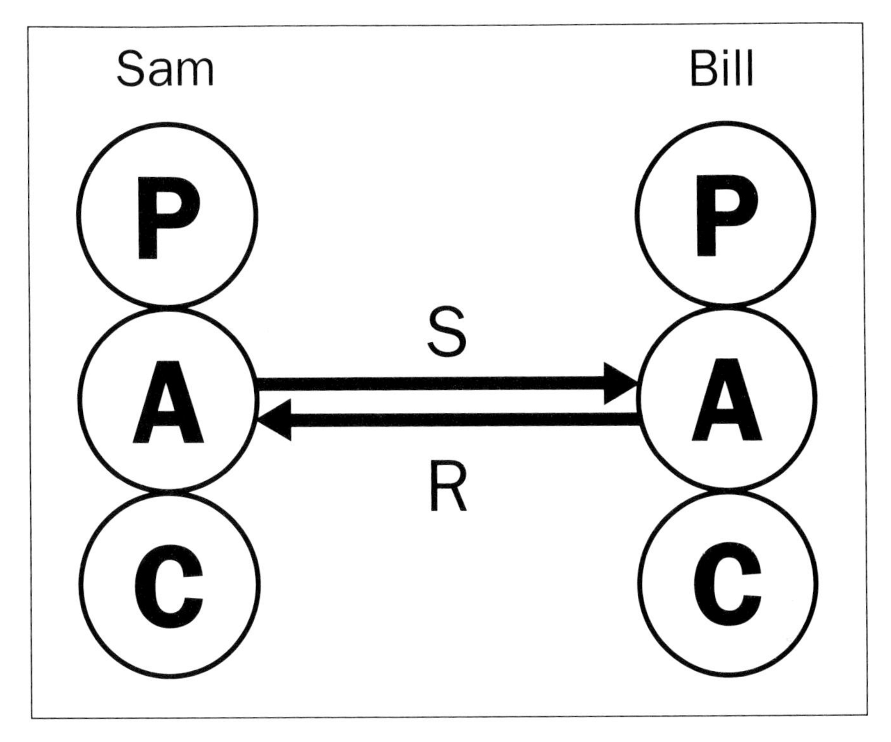

Figure 2 *An Adult–Adult complementary transaction*

wave to the neighbours of whom she felt contemptuous and whom she considered beneath her. This is a complementary transaction between Child and Parent ego states. Sam's Child ego state addresses Bill's Parent ego state. Bill's Parent ego state responds to Sam's Child ego state. This transaction is shown in Figure 3.

This is the first rule of communication: *as long as transactions are complementary, communication can proceed indefinitely*. Complementary transactions are not necessarily negative or positive. This can only be ascertained from the context. For instance, a long and boring discussion could be complementary all the way through. In the first example, the Adult–Adult transaction of Sam and Bill could have continued with:

SAM: Hi, I'm really pleased to see you.
BILL: Same here, do you have time for a coffee?
SAM: Yes, of course. How's your new job?
BILL: Well, difficult but I'm getting the hang of it.
SAM: I admire you for changing jobs like you did.

And so on.

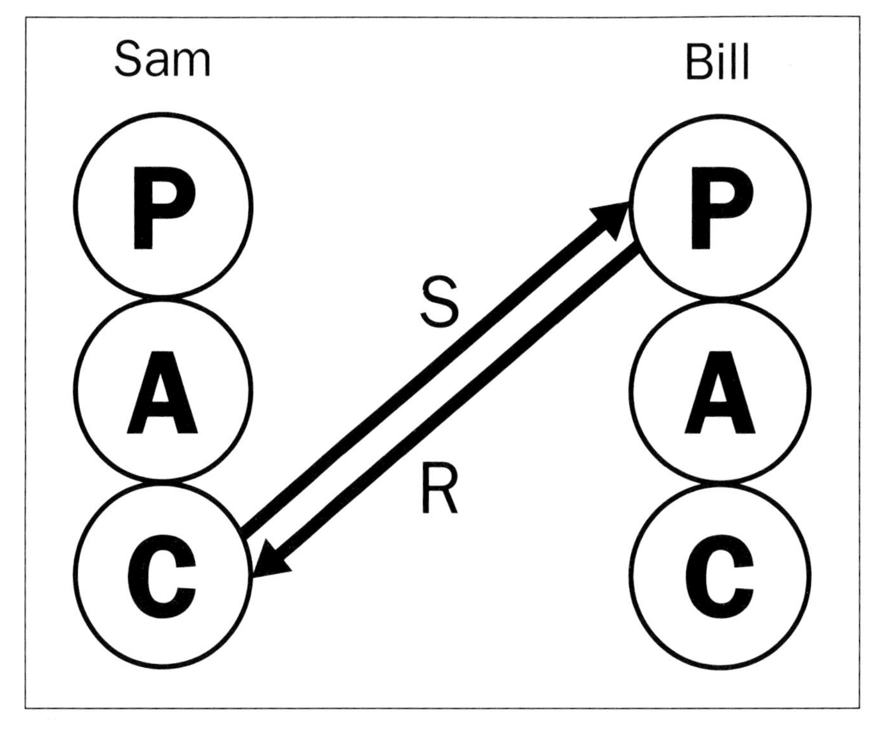

Figure 3 *Child–Parent/Parent–Child complementary transaction*

Equally, Sam and Bill could have continued with:

SAM: I'm glad I've bumped into you, I'm so angry with you!
BILL: Why?
SAM: You said you'd fix my car today and I need it to get to Oxford.
BILL: Oh no, I thought you didn't need it till the week-end.
SAM: No, I told you! Now, how am I to get to Oxford?
BILL: Look, stop shouting. It won't help. I'll think of something ...

And so on.

This is still a sequence of Adult to Adult complementary transactions, despite the fact that they are arguing.

In the second example, the Child–Parent/Parent–Child complementary transactions of Sam and Bill might have continued with:

SAM: Hello, Mr Thomson.
BILL: Hello, Sam. Are you keeping busy?

SAM: Oh, I was just going over to the workshop now, honestly.
BILL: Step to it then, it'll soon be lunch-time.
SAM: OK, Mr Thomson. I'll run on ahead.
BILL: Don't run! Don't you know about 'more haste less speed', as my dear mother used to say?
SAM: Sorry, Mr Thomson.

And so on.

Let us move on to Jim and Jenny. Jenny smiles at Jim. Jim frowns in return. This could be a complementary transaction similar to the last example of Parent–Child/Child–Parent transactions between Bill and Sam. In other words, Jenny is giving a placatory smile to an authority figure who, in response provides a disapproving frown from his Parent ego state. Again, in order to be more certain, we would need to use the four diagnostic criteria for identifying ego states (see pages 27–9). We may discover that something completely different is going on. It may be that, when Jenny smiles at Jim in a friendly way, it is because she thinks he looks interesting and she would like to get to know him. This would be described as an Adult–Adult stimulus. However, when Jenny smiles at Jim he sees, not Jenny's smile, but his mother's: the one she adopted when she wanted him to look after her when he was a child. He therefore frowns in response, just as he did as a child in expectation of being manipulated by his mother. This would be described as a Child–Parent response. Jenny is probably completely puzzled by Jim's childish behaviour. If you look at Figure 4 you will see why this is called a *crossed transaction*.

Sometimes the vectors do not actually cross, for example where an Adult to Child transaction is responded to by an Adult to Parent transaction, but as, by and large, they do, they are still referred to as crossed transactions because the sender expects a certain type of response but their expectation is crossed. This is the second rule of communication: *if the vectors of a transaction are crossed (which means the responding ego state is different from the one addressed or the addressed ego state responds back to a different ego state than the initiating one), communication is broken off and something different will happen.* As with complementary transactions, crossed transactions may be positive or negative according to the context.

In our example, when Jim crosses the transaction, he interrupts

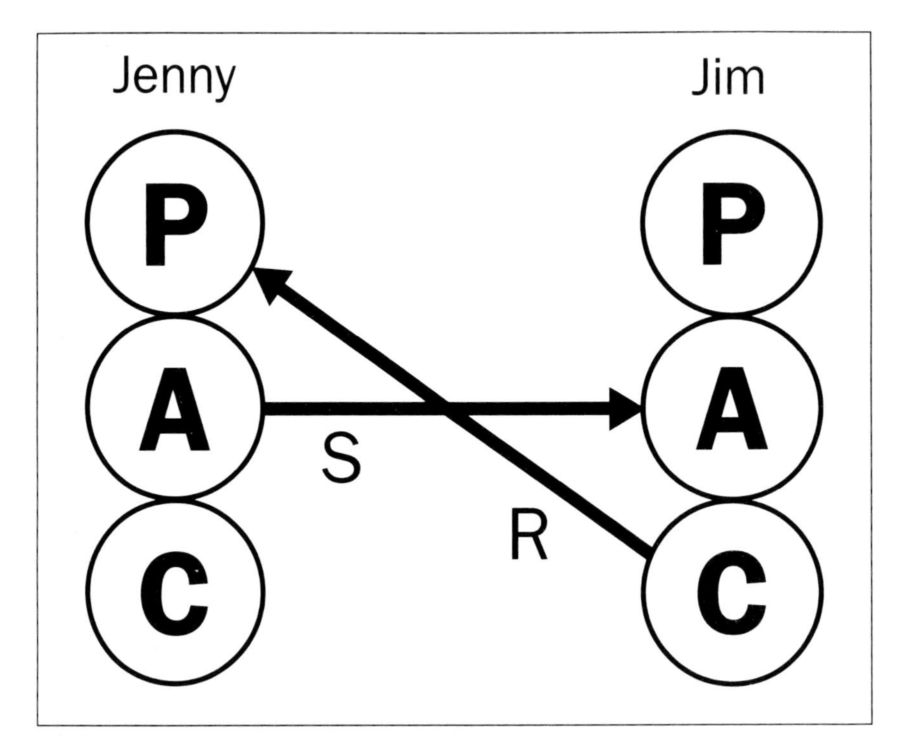

Figure 4 *A crossed transaction*

the possibility of smooth-flowing, complementary transactions and Jenny is left puzzled. Communication probably stops at this point. If not, it is likely that Jenny will now respond (notice that one person's response is another person's stimulus and vice versa) from an ego state other than Adult. She may go into a Child ego state and feel hurt, thinking, "Nobody likes me!" and run off crying, just as she had as a child in the face of rejection. Or she may move into a Parent ego state and get angry with Jim, shouting at him, "How dare you look at me like that, you creep!" just as her mother used to shout at her father.

So far we have dealt with transactions at the social level, overt messages between two people. But there are often (some would say, always) covert communications beneath the social level transactions. These are called *ulterior* transactions. Let us move to a new couple, Peter and Pamela. Peter meets Pamela outside the cinema (where, let us imagine, we are also waiting in the queue). We hear the following simple exchange:

PETER: What time is it?
PAMELA: It's half-past seven.

On the social level, we would probably represent this as an Adult–Adult complementary transaction: information was asked for and information was given in return. But if we look closer (an action replay), we notice that, as Peter asks what time it is, he raises his eyebrows and furrows his brow, his hands are clasped together in a supplicatory manner and he avoids any eye-contact with Pamela by looking at the ground. We might justifiably suspect that Peter is not in an Adult ego state. We would need to mobilize our four diagnostic modes to identify a Parent or a Child ego state. We might then discover that this is how Peter behaved as a child towards his parents (a Child ego state) and that the communication beneath his simple, "What time is it?" is "I know I'm late but please don't be cross with me."

If we look more closely at Pamela as she is telling Peter the time, we notice that her mouth is tight and her jaw clenched, she avoids eye-contact by looking over his head at the sky, her arms folded across her chest, her foot tapping. We may discover, if we questioned her, that this is how Pamela's mother behaved towards her husband whenever he was late. The communication beneath the simple, "It's half-past seven" is "Yes, you are very late and I'm extremely cross with you!"

The complete set of social level and ulterior transactions can be represented as in Figure 5. (Ulterior transactions in TA are always drawn as a broken line.) Neither Peter nor Pamela enjoy the film, but clearly, it was not the verbal content of the transaction that led to this outcome. This brings us to the third rule of communication: *the behavioural outcome of a transaction is determined by the ulterior, psychological level communication rather than the social level communication.*

Application

Using the structural model of ego states to analyse transactions, we can clarify and better understand what is going on in the process of communication. We can see how historic ego states may be interfering with our relationships and causing dysfunction within those relationships. By being aware of our transactional

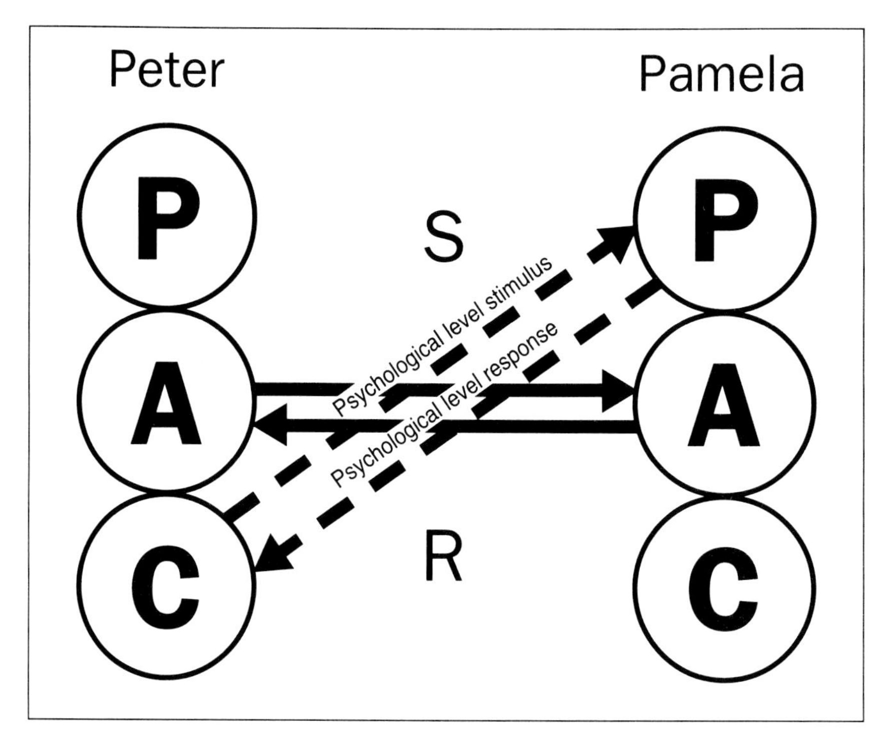

Figure 5 *The ulterior transaction*

patterns, we open up options, realize our choices and move towards greater autonomy.

For example, in a counselling group, John, in the process of learning to nurture himself, is wanting to find ways of structuring his time in the evenings in more enjoyable ways than hitherto. He is in an Adult ego state asking for information. Other members of the group provide him with some suggestions and to each of these he responds with thoughtful consideration. This procedure continues smoothly with Adult–Adult complementary transactions (Figure 6 (a)). Pat, however, says, "You should be grateful to have time to yourself in the evenings!", at which point there is a silence (Figure 6 (b)). John eventually says, "I'm sorry, I think I've taken too much time on this" (Figure 6 (c)). The counsellor suggests looking at what has just happened in the group by drawing a diagram of the transactions and the group works out the sequence referred to above.

Pat now quite clearly sees how she had crossed the transaction by coming from her Parent ego state (containing the feeling, thinking and behaviour of her mother, who allowed Pat no leisure time as a child) and invited John into a Child ego state

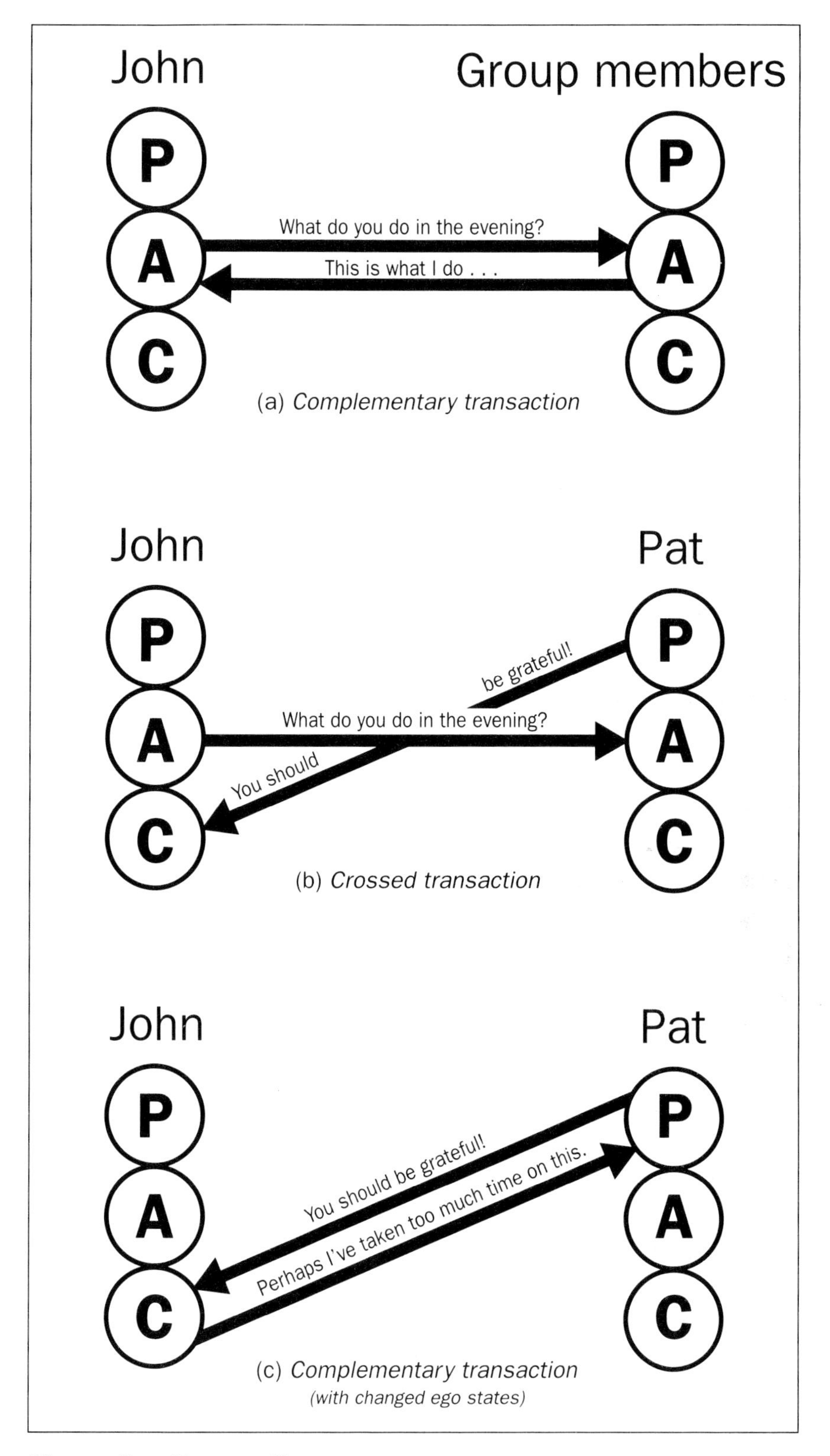

Figure 6 *Transactions sequence*

(easily complied with by John, whose childhood experience is almost identical, hence his current focus of work in the counselling group). John later realizes that he had a choice in the situation: he could have stayed in Adult and either persisted in asking Pat for the specific information he wanted or simply continued round the group.

When the counsellor asks Pat what she might have been experiencing in her Child ego state, Pat has no problem in identifying that her Child was saying, "I want some fun in the evenings too!" Having recognized this, she then spends her time in group more usefully in an Adult ego state, looking at ways of having fun.

Exercises

Self

Think back over the past week and choose several conversations you have had with different people in different situations. Write them down (as accurately as you can remember them) and analyse them transactionally, using the following guidelines:

1 Does the conversation have a flavour of continuity and interconnection from beginning to end (this may be boring or interesting)? If it does, mark the conversation as 'Complementary Transactions'.
2 In each of these complementary transactions, diagnose which ego state you were in and which ego state you think the other person was in and mark them Adult–Adult, Parent–Child or Child–Parent and so on.
3 If you were in a Parent ego state and the other in a Child ego state, think about whose borrowed feelings, thoughts and behaviours these were and why you might have used them at this time. Was this useful? What might have been a better option?
4 If you were in a Child ego state, think about where you originally experienced these feelings, thoughts and behaviours and why you might be using them at this time. Again, was this useful? What might have been a better option?
5 In the Adult–Adult complementary transactions, what was

qualitatively different about them compared to the others?

6 In the conversations that do not seem continuous or interconnected, identify the point at which something different happened. In other words, identify where the crossed transaction occurred.

7 Go back a few transactions and identify the ego states up to this point.

8 Now identify the ego states involved in the crossed transaction.

9 If you crossed the transaction at this point, why do you think this was and why did you move into this particular ego state?

10 If the other person crossed the transaction, why do you think this was and why do you think you accepted the invitation to go into the particular ego state that you did?

11 In these instances of crossed transactions, what would have happened if the conversations had remained complementary? Would this have been more constructive/appropriate/useful?

12 Choose one of your conversations which includes a crossed transaction. Go through each social level transaction and see if you can find an ulterior message. Rewrite the conversation using the ulterior transactions only.

Working with Clients

Clients will often bring communication problems to the counselling session and provide verbatim accounts of problematic conversations, rows, arguments and frustrations they have experienced. When this next happens, ask your client — who by now is familiar with the ego state model — to do some 'transactional analysis proper' with you by working through the conversation transaction by transaction, using the transactional model of two sets of stacked circles, as in Figure 5. In this way, using the guidelines you have used for yourself in the above exercises, identify the complementary, crossed and ulterior transactions to show where the 'stuck points' may have been occurring and how the situation could have been handled differently.

Similarly, you may do transactional analysis proper on transactions between you and your client. This is often very helpful in unravelling the parallel process of an outside issue being enacted in the consulting room. For example:

CLIENT: Good morning, Jean.
COUNSELLOR: Good morning.
CLIENT: Why are you cross with me?
COUNSELLOR: Cross with you?
CLIENT: Yes, I know you are but I've not come to argue with you. I'm having enough trouble at home with my wife.
COUNSELLOR: Before we move on to her, let's look at what's just happened between us.

Chapter 5

FUNCTIONAL AND TRANSACTIONAL OPTIONS

We have mentioned options several times in previous chapters. We have indicated that, by becoming aware of our ego states, particularly the ones which are interfering with our current functioning, we can become more aware of our options in any given situation. Awareness means having both responsibility and choice. Once aware that we are responding to a situation from a Child ego state, for example, we are then responsible for exercising choice as to whether we continue in this ego state or look for other options. Awareness implies that we have already moved into an Adult ego state. At the moment we recognize we are in a Child ego state we must already have moved, however partially or momentarily, into an Adult ego state in order to assess what is currently happening. In that moment we have the choice of monitoring and choosing how we are functioning from this Adult position.

Notice that we have said choosing *how we are functioning*. This includes the thinking patterns (attitudes) that are often linked with functional behaviour. Though the idea of choosing another ego state may be useful, it may also be difficult to shift totally and simultaneously from one set of feelings, thoughts and behaviours to a whole new set. Our awareness may be in an Adult ego state but our feelings may remain in a Child ego state. Changing our behaviour and the attitudes that reinforce that behaviour is one of the best ways of also changing our thoughts and feelings. Hussain, for example, is often in a Child ego state when he goes for a job interview: he is scared, he thinks he will be rejected and he stoops, just as he did when facing his cruel and rejecting father as a child. By deciding to adopt a more open body posture, regulating his breathing to relax himself, talking to himself encouragingly and smiling in a friendly way, Hussain discovers that he begins to *feel* more at ease and that he is *thinking* less negatively about the outcome of the interview. Thus, by changing his behaviour and attitude, he has changed his feelings and thoughts and moved out of a dysfunctional Child ego state.

To help look at our functional and transactional options, TA provides a further model which describes a wide range of behaviours. This model is often confused with the structural ego state model. This is because, perhaps unfortunately, the model is represented by the same three stacked circles using the same Parent, Adult and Child labels and is further confounded by the adoption of the title 'The Functional Ego State Model'. We consider the term 'ego state' for this second model to be a misnomer, as what the model deals with is behavioural options rather than ego states proper. We therefore suggest 'functional modes' as a preferable and less confusing term.

As the label 'functional ego states' is so much a part of the terminology used in other TA literature, let us explain our two main objections in more detail before presenting the whole model. Let us take one example: one of the terms used in the functional model to describe a certain type of behaviour is the 'Nurturing Parent ego state'. Firstly, according to the definition of an ego state, this implies that we are dealing with a set of feelings, thoughts and behaviours, but, as will be seen, we are often dealing in this model only with behaviour or with behaviour and reinforcing attitude. Secondly, this label implies that we are dealing with a Parent ego state (ways of nurturing we have introjected from others) yet we know that we can also nurture from an Adult ego state (the nurturing appropriate to the here-and-now reality) and a Child ego state (the ways of nurturing others we used as a child). We suggest using the term 'mode' as a way of avoiding some of the confusion caused by the term 'ego state' when using the functional model. Thus a Parent ego state becomes in our version of the functional model a Parent Mode. Though we have kept the terms Parent, Adult and Child for these behaviours, we hope that the use of the term 'mode' in conjunction with them makes it clear that these are purely descriptions of types of behaviours that can be found in each of the three structural ego states (as we will describe later) and they are not themselves ego states.

The Functional Model

This model describes a range of functional modes — by which we mean the gestures, words, voice tones, body postures, facial expressions, attitudes and so on that we discussed in Chapter 3 when dealing with behavioural diagnosis — from which we can choose how to respond in a given situation. They can also be used to describe how a person is behaving whether they have chosen to or not; in other words, they can describe the behaviour in any structural ego state, current or historic. This is useful shorthand when shared with clients but, like most types of shorthand, needs to be used with a full explanation.

Figure 7 shows the five basic functional modes.

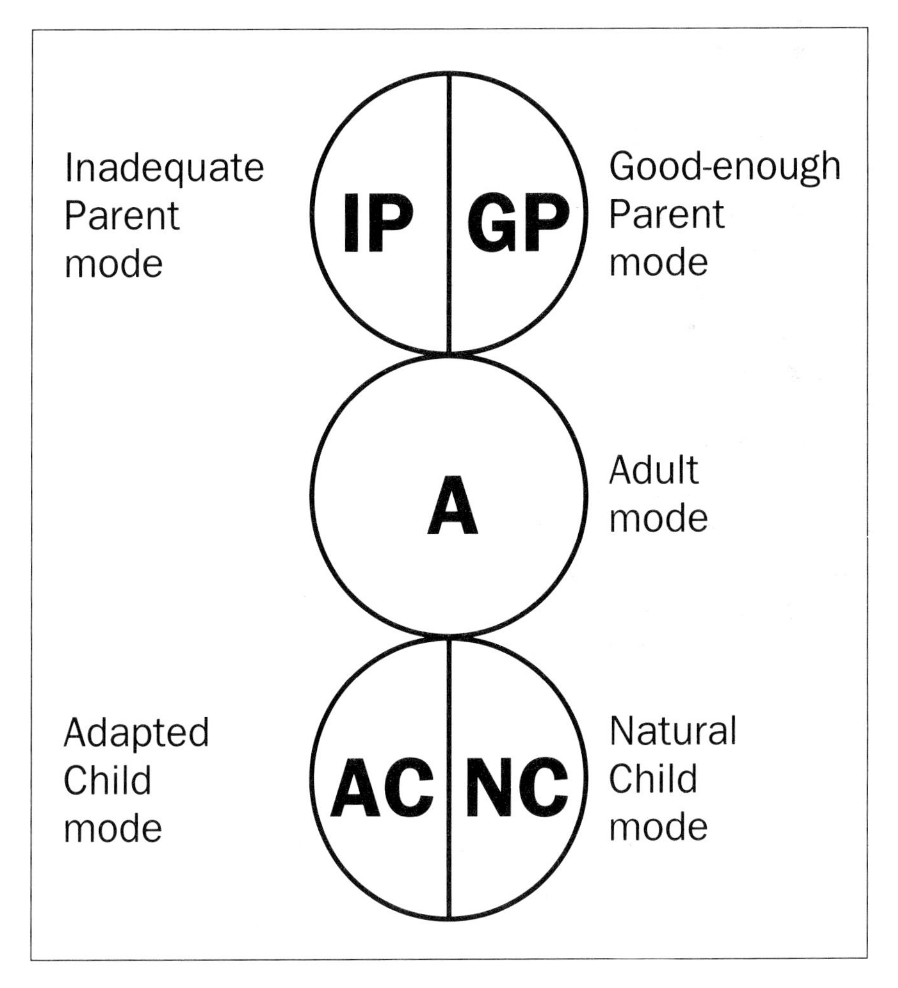

Figure 7 *The functional model*

We have chosen the terms Good-enough Parent (GP) and Inadequate Parent (IP) in preference to the more usual Positive or Negative Nurturing Parent and Positive or Negative Controlling Parent (terms found in the TA literature) as we consider these latter terms exclude other parent-type behaviours and attitudes such as indifference, carelessness, passivity and ignorance.

The Good-enough Parent Mode (GP)

In this mode we include those parental behaviours and attitudes which promote the well-being of ourselves and others (an I'm OK — You're OK position). This mode would include those behaviours and attitudes which are encouraging, concerned, caring, loving, giving, accepting, comforting, understanding, constructively critical, usefully advising, caringly controlling, appropriately nurturing, protective and permission-giving. Here are some ways we might recognize someone in a GP mode:

- the person leans caringly towards another and keeps good eye-contact as they speak;
- the person speaks with a tender tone;
- the person smiles at another's success;
- the person greets another with open arms at seeing their distress;
- the person shouts assertively to prevent some danger to the other;
- the person takes enough holidays for themselves to stay fit and healthy;
- the person sets suitable boundaries.

The Inadequate Parent Mode (IP)

In this mode we include those parental behaviours and attitudes which disempower the other person or another part of ourselves in an attempt to dispel our inadequacy. This mode would include those behaviours and attitudes which are destructively critical, belittling, prejudicial, controlling for power, dismissive, indifferent, ignorant, over-protective, careless, cruel, persecutory, condescending, judgmental, authoritarian and moralistic. Here are some ways we might recognize someone in an IP mode:

- the person menacingly towers over another;
- the person, with hands on hips, talks *at* rather than *to* the other;
- the person, unrequested, supports the arm of an elderly but physically able person;
- the person points a finger accusingly while shouting;
- the person shows lack of interest in another's distress by making no eye-contact and yawning;
- the person 'fusses' over another as they prepare for some event;
- the person uses judgmental words like 'ridiculous', 'stupid', 'disgusting' and so on to describe their own or others' behaviour;
- the person gives advice to another about something they themselves know nothing about.

The Adult Mode (A)

In this mode we include those behaviours and attitudes which are objective, informative, interested, evaluative, precise, observant, practical, clarifying, rational, goal-setting, analytic, creatively resourceful and constructively questioning. Here are some ways we might recognize someone in an A mode:

- the person clarifies the situation by careful questioning;
- the person talks in an even voice and is precise in choice of vocabulary;
- the person hypothesizes and processes information;
- the person sits upright with an open body posture;
- the person is alert and thoughtful about a problem they are facing.

The Natural Child Mode (NC)

In the Natural Child mode a person has access to expression of any of the ramifications of the four basic feelings: fear, sorrow, joy and anger. In this mode we also include those behaviours and attitudes which are spontaneous, energetic, creative, fun-loving, exuberant, free, open, emotionally responsive, uninhibited, curious and noisy. There is a carefree quality to the actions and attitudes of someone in a Natural Child mode. For the most part this is a positive and creative mode in which to be. There are, however, occasions when such Natural Child responses may be inappropriate. For example, enjoying an exhilarating game of rough and tumble with a friend on a spacious beach would be fine. Playing the same game close to the edge of a cliff would be folly. Here are some ways we might recognize someone in an NC mode:

- the person hugs another in the excitement of succeeding in some task;
- the person cries at the news of the death of a friend;
- the person runs and leaps into the air while out for a walk;
- the person rolls on the floor, doubled up with laughter at a joke;
- the person says, "I really love you" or "I really love myself";
- the person looks startled at a loud noise;
- the person expresses anger in response to an insult;
- the person, in their excitement, takes an unnecessary risk.

The Adapted Child Mode (AC)

In this last mode we include those behaviours and attitudes which are, as the mode suggests, in adaptation to others or other parts of ourselves. This includes the expression of feelings which are substitutes for those of the Natural Child; for example, where the Natural Child would be angry, the Adapted Child expresses sadness (*see the discussion of rackets, Chapter 9*). This mode can include not only behaviours which are compliant but also those which are rebellious, rebellion of this type being an adaptation to others, albeit in opposition. Thus we include behaviours and attitudes which are defiant, disobedient, rude, displeasing, stubborn, disrespectful and demanding, as well as those which are yielding, obliging, placating, obedient, polite, censored, pleasing and dutiful.

Compliance or rebellion in the Adapted Child Mode may be

appropriate or inappropriate according to the situation. Compliance with someone's demand for us to stop as we are about to step carelessly out into a busy road is clearly appropriate. Unquestioningly obeying the same demand when we are safely having fun may not be. In the same way, to rebel against tyranny and oppression may be appropriate, while rebellion against the goodwill of others may not be. Here are ways in which we might recognize someone in an AC mode:

- the person physically and verbally 'digs their heels in';
- the person questions and challenges the authority of another;
- the person shouts defiantly, "I won't!" in response to a request;
- the person arrives drunk at a counselling session;
- the person drives recklessly, endangering themselves and others;
- the person expresses anger where sadness would be more appropriate.

Or:

- the person cowers, with head down, as they ask for something from another;
- the person says, "please" and "sorry" repeatedly in a conversation;
- the person complies with another's wishes;
- the person's voice tone is whining and placatory;
- the person does not ask for things for themselves;
- the person expresses fear where anger would be more appropriate.

Or (more positively):

- the person negotiates a compromised agreement with another;
- the person shares their last piece of chocolate with another;
- the person gives up their bus seat at the request of an elderly passenger.

In order to see how these modes may operate in a given situation, let us go back to the friends who are playing a game of rough and tumble on the beach and analyse the various modes they may be adopting. The tide is coming in while Sergio and Stella are playing. Both are in Natural Child mode, oblivious to the incoming tide. Suddenly, Sergio notices.

"Hey, Stella," he says, "the tide's almost to the rocks." (Adult mode)

"How long do you think we can stay on the beach?" asks Stella. (Adult mode)

"It's too risky to stay any longer," says Sergio, holding out a hand to her. "We'd better go." (Good-enough Parent mode)

"Oh, we were having so much fun!" laughs Stella as she hugs him. (Natural Child mode)

"Well, we'll be trapped if we don't go now," says Sergio. (Adult mode)

"It's too soon. I'm not going!" says Stella, pulling away from him and stamping her feet. (Adapted Child mode)

"Come on, now!" shouts Sergio. "We really must go." (Good-enough Parent mode)

"Look at you, you're just like a scared kid! Pull yourself together!" replies Stella, pointing at him. (Adapted Child mode moving to Inadequate Parent mode)

"Don't you talk to me like that, my girl!" shouts Sergio, with hands on hips. (Inadequate Parent mode)

"I'll talk how I want!" pouts Stella. (Adapted Child mode)

"Look, we have about five minutes before we're trapped," says Sergio, indicating the tide level. (Adult mode)

"Oh, all right!" says Stella, taking his hand. (Adapted Child mode)

"Let's run!" laughs Sergio. (Natural Child mode)

"OK. Race you to the rocks!" cries Stella, getting a head start. (Natural Child mode)

Remember, what we have been analysing here is their functional modes, *what it is they are doing and saying*, their process of communication, *not* their structural ego states, which would give us further information as to the *origin and reasons* for their behaviour. We will return to this later when we look at how the two models may be combined.

Application 1: A Microscopic View

In the above example of Sergio and Stella on the beach, we have in effect taken a microscope to what is going on between two people and analysed their transactions according to their functional modes. By doing so, we open up the possibility of choice and options. The functional model provides us with a ready source of alternatives. At any moment in their communication, there was the possibility of one or more alternative modes. Let us take just one set of verbal transactions:

SERGIO: It's too risky to stay any longer. We'd better go.
STELLA: Oh, we were having so much fun!

In response to Sergio's Good-enough Parent mode, Stella had a choice of options. Here she answers from a Natural Child mode. She could also have echoed Sergio's Good-enough Parent by responding from her own Good-enough Parent:

Yes, I don't want us to get trapped.

She could also have come from an Adapted Child position:

OK, if you say so.

Or

I won't! You're always so bossy!

Or an Inadequate Parent mode:

Don't make such a fuss. It really doesn't matter.

Or an Adult mode:

Yes, I think so too. It's coming in quickly.

The choice of some of these alternatives would have altered (however slightly) what followed. We know already that the outcome of their total communications was a positive and healthy one but if Sergio had stayed in an Adult mode continually, merely providing accurate observations, the outcome may not have been as effective. Likewise if Stella had stayed in a rebellious Adapted Child mode. The fact that they move between different modes quite fluently and achieve a positive outcome is, perhaps, some indication of their psychological health.

But sometimes people are not so fluent. They get stuck in the same functional mode, with results ranging from the tedious and entrenched to the despairing and disastrous. By developing awareness of their functional options and making more conscious choices, people can avoid such outcomes and ensure more fun, joy, satisfaction and creativity.

Drawing the functional diagram as a transactional diagram when working with clients provides a useful tool for looking at behavioural options (Figure 8). Here the three rules of communication

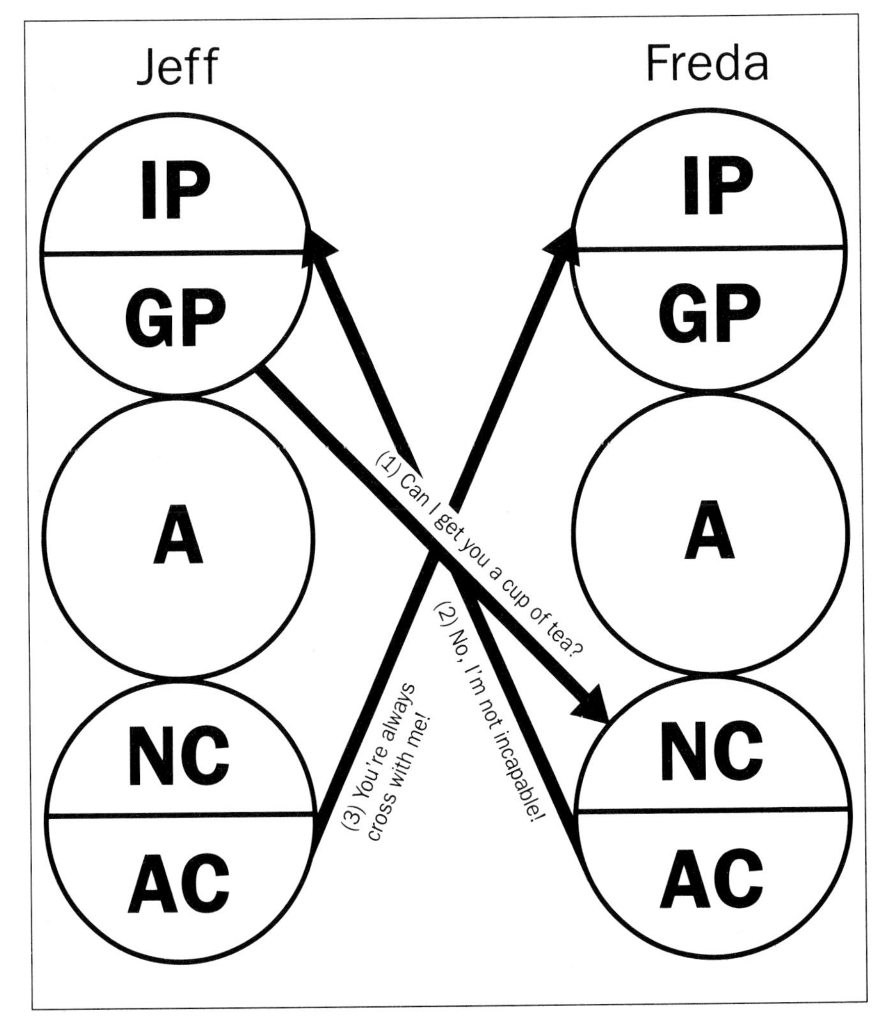

Figure 8 *A functional transactional diagram*

introduced earlier in relation to the structural model may be usefully applied. Using the model transactionally, it is clearer if the Parent and Child modes are split horizontally rather than vertically.

In this example, Freda is developing yet another row with her husband Jeff. The stimulus is from Jeff's Good-enough Parent Mode intended for Freda's Natural Child: "Can I get you a cup of tea?" But Freda responds from her Adapted Child intended for Jeff's Inadequate Parent: "No, I'm not incapable!" In other words, there is a crossed transaction. Jeff responds with another crossed transaction, this time from his Adapted Child to Freda's Inadequate Parent, "You're always cross with me!" And the row ensues.

Now, it may be that Jeff was sending an ulterior transaction from his Inadequate Parent to Freda's Adapted Child with the message: "You are incapable" and that this is what Freda is responding to. It may be that, if we did a structural analysis of Freda's ego states, we might discover she is operating from an Introjected Parent ego state and that is the way her mother always responded to her father when Freda was a child. This may usefully be worked on in the counselling situation. However, if Freda wants to stop rowing with Jeff right now, she can do so by choosing to respond from different functional modes. So what could she choose?

1 She could keep the transaction complementary by saying: "Yes, I'd love a cup of tea!" or "No thanks, not right now" from her Natural Child back to his Good-enough Parent.
2 She could usefully cross the transaction and invite something different to happen by saying: "I know you mean well, but sometimes I think you do too much for me" from her Adult to his Adult.
3 She could cross the transaction another way and affect the outcome differently by saying, "Oh no, really, I'll get the tea this time" from her Good-enough Parent to his Natural Child.

When transactions are analysed according to their functional modes and alternatives experimented with, many stuck patterns of behaviour in relationships can be overcome. For this reason, the functional model is one of the most useful TA models to use when working with couples.

Exercises

Self

1 Write down a recent conversation you have had with someone and label each transaction according to the functional mode adopted. You may need to recall the body posture, gestures, voice tone and so on to assist in your analysis.
2 Choose one of your transactions at any point in the conversation and supply a response from as many alternative functional modes as you can find.
3 Experiment in this way at various points in the conversation. Would any of your alternatives have considerably altered the course of the conversation? Would these have been preferable options to have chosen? Which in particular? Why would they have been more useful?

Working with clients

1 Introduce your client to the functional model and explore your client's functional modes.
2 As and when your client presents an incident concerning their communication with others, invite them to write down the transactions and analyse them according to the functional modes adopted.
3 Draw a diagram of the transactions that seem to be important turning-points in the conversation. What was going on transactionally? Were the transactions complementary or crossed? What were the possible ulterior transactions?
4 For each of the transactions in the diagram, explore the alternative functional modes that could have been used.

Application 2: An X-ray View

The functional model of behavioural and transactional modes may also be used to look at what goes on inside people, the internal (intrapsychic) transactions we have between various parts of ourselves. You may recall the person we mentioned right at the beginning of this book (page 2) who is stuck in a lift between floors. If you turn back to it, you will most likely now be able to analyse those internal transactions in the same way we have analysed transactions between two people using the functional model.

Often these internal conversations are outside our awareness, but by observing ourselves in various situations we can become more attuned to them. We may discover that a lot of our internal transactions are from our own Inadequate Parent mode and are complied with or rebelled against within our Adapted Child mode; or that we are using a Good-enough Parent mode to encourage our Natural Child mode; or that much of our time is spent in observing and objectively clarifying what we are experiencing from a functional Adult perspective.

As with the options we have in our transactions with others, so too we have internal options. The exercises we have used in Application 1 may also be used to explore and change our internal transactions. There is, however, yet another way of using these internal transactions and that is in the service of problem-solving and decision-making. This technique was devised by Stuntz and is known as the 'five chair technique' (Stuntz, 'Multiple Chairs Technique', *TAJ*, 3,2, 1973).

The Five Chair Technique in Operation

In her counselling session, Sonja informs the counsellor that she has been offered a better paid job which will entail moving to another part of town as the job requires her to be 'on call' on certain days. Since receiving the news she has been in a state of confusion. The counsellor suggests she may achieve some clarification of the situation if she brings into awareness her internal transactions and explores her options by using the five chair technique. They set out five chairs, arranging them like the five on a dice to represent the five functional modes as they appear in the functional model diagram (see page 49). The counsellor suggests Sonja begins by sitting on the Adult chair to outline the problem objectively. A shortened version of this part of the session continues as follows:

SONJA (*Adult*): I've been offered a job which is a promotion for me. The pay is much better than my current job but it means I will have to move to another part of town. I'm really excited by —

COUNSELLOR: It sounds like you've moved into a Natural Child mode now. See what you have to say from that chair.

SONJA (*Natural Child*): Yes, I am excited by the offer. I think the work will be much more fun and it will be good to meet new people and make new friends. But I don't want to move because I'll see less of my old friends.

COUNSELLOR: OK, see what you say in Adapted Child mode.

SONJA (*Adapted Child*): I don't think I'm good enough really. I think I'll probably be a bit of a failure. Then they won't like me and I won't make any friends and I'll be lonely living in a strange part of town. (Pauses) I think I know where this is coming from.

COUNSELLOR: OK, move to that chair.

SONJA (*Inadequate Parent talking to her Adapted Child*): Yes, you really should stay where you are. You know you aren't really up to the job. You may have fooled them at the interview but they'll find out soon enough and then you'll regret it.

SONJA (*switching to Good-enough Parent*): That is not true. You did a good interview because you knew you had the right skills and experience. You're quite capable of doing this job well. Furthermore, people like you and you can make friends easily. I understand you're a bit scared. It's natural to be scared when making such a change but you can still go ahead and take this opportunity. Don't scare yourself even more with these negative thoughts. As you say, it's exciting too.

SONJA (*switching to Natural Child*): Right. It is exciting and I am scared but I don't have to let that stop me by telling myself negative things. That's a relief. But I'm still concerned about my old friends.

COUNSELLOR: Move back to Adult and see what solutions you can think of to this problem of friends.

SONJA (*Adult*): Well, let's see. If I want to keep in touch with my old friends once I've moved, I need to organize it. I could make sure that I arrange to go to friends or for them to visit me. This is possible at weekends or holidays or even when I'm doing a late shift the next day and don't have to be 'on call'.

COUNSELLOR: It seems you could see your old friends quite regularly.

SONJA (*Adult*): Yes, I think I was allowing my Inadequate Parent to use this as yet another reason for staying put without even looking for solutions. If I listened to that part of me, I'd never do anything.

COUNSELLOR: Do you want to finish on the Natural Child chair and express your feelings about this?

SONJA (*Natural Child*): Sure. What a relief. I feel like a whole weight's been removed — I hate that Inadequate Parent that squashes everything. I will accept the job. I'm glad I've dealt with it so well. In fact, I'm really pleased with myself!

Use of the five chair technique will not always result in such a clear resolution. It will, however, help bring to light the various attitudes being adopted in response to the situation or problem. Bringing these into awareness and clarifying in which mode these attitudes are being adopted can greatly assist in the problem-solving process. Using five chairs and moving from one to another is not essential — your room may not be big enough! — but the physical changing of position does assist in identifying our attitude in a particular mode and helps to differentiate more clearly between each mode. If it is not possible to move from chair to chair, it would be useful to adopt a different posture for each functional mode, a posture that your client associates with each particular one. Making a diagram of this, or the client sketching it out, are other ways of proceeding. As with all the suggested exercises in this book, your experimenting with and adjusting exercises to suit the counsellor you are is essential if you are going to operate from an integrated Adult ego state and not in response to newly introjected material.

Exercises

Self

1 Think of a current decision you need to make and use the five chair technique to help in your decision-making process.

2 What do you notice about the responses from your different functional modes? Are some more helpful than others? Between which modes do you experience the most disagreement? How might you use other modes to resolve this?

Working with Clients

When your client presents a decision-making problem or some confusion in their response to a situation, explore their functional modes by using the five-chair technique. Encourage the client to move into all five functional modes to get a total picture. Facilitate your client in moving from one mode to another as and when you or they think it appropriate. Opening up the dialogue between two modes may be constructive and lead to resolution or it may reach a sticking point. If there are certain points when you think moving to another particular mode may be useful, invite your client to move to that chair. You might invite your client onto the Adult chair to provide a commentary on what they see happening between the other modes. Providing an objective overview often indicates which next move might be helpful.

Application 3: A Macroscopic View

Another of the ways in which this model may be used for oneself or when working with others is as a descriptive overview of how a person is functioning in their lives in order to assess where changes may usefully be made. It can be used to answer such questions as:

- Does this person use the whole range of functional modes?
- If not, which are lacking? Which might be more usefully developed?
- Which mode does the person adopt most? Is this useful?
- Does the person use the same modes towards self as well as to others?

We have adapted Jack Dusay's original concept of the egogram (*TAJ*, 2,3, 1972) to produce a pie chart of functional modes (Figure 9): a diagrammatic representation of the spread and adoption of functional modes. The five functional modes are allocated 'slices of the pie' according to the comparative amount of time and energy a person spends in each functional mode. Clearly this is more an intuitive assessment than a scientific one. The best way to draw such a chart for yourself is to assess intuitively which functional mode you adopt the most and draw an equivalent section of the pie chart to represent this. Then assess which functional mode you use the least and draw its representative slice adjacent to the first. The next three sections can then be added by assessing them in relation to these two. You could check this with people who know you well. Technically, if you analysed all your transactions in a given day, you could get a very accurate picture.

The Constancy Hypothesis

Jack Dusay suggested in his article that: 'When one ego state [*mode in our model*] increases in intensity, another or others must decrease in order to compensate. The shift in psychic energy occurs so that the total amount of energy may remain constant.' Thus it may be that a person, by increasing their time spent in Natural Child mode — by arranging more free time to be with

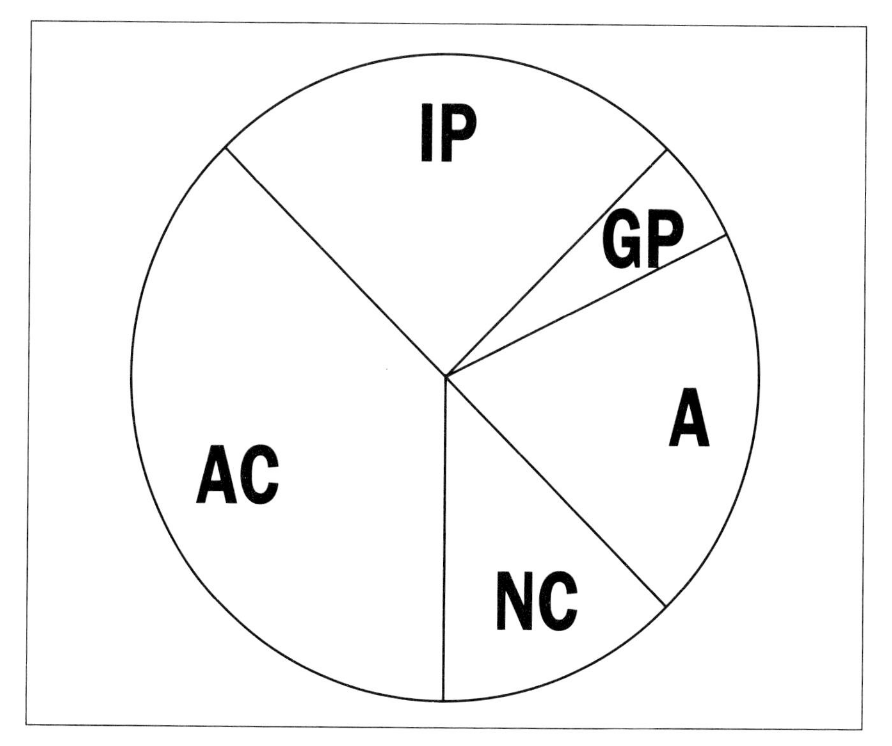

Figure 9 *A pie chart of functional modes*

friends, organizing more fun and recreation and so on — concomitantly reduces both their Inadequate Parent mode and their Adapted Child mode. The use of a pie chart shows clearly this redistribution of energy as any change in one section inevitably means a change in another or others.

Let us look at the pie chart above (Figure 9) as an example. This person, James, by drawing this pie chart, realized that he spent a large amount of his energy in both an Adapted Child mode and in Inadequate Parent mode. These two modes were clearly interrelated and mutually reinforcing. In the Adapted Child mode he would obediently respond to others' demands without question. In the Inadequate Parent mode he would fuss around others, offering to do things for them. This, in turn, set a precedent for them to make demands on him which resulted in his return to the Adapted Child mode and so on. The pie chart graphically emphasized for him the lack of Natural Child and Good-enough Parent modes, as well as a much-depleted Adult mode.

In his counselling James decided to focus on expanding his Good-enough Parent mode to others and to himself. To others, he became more appropriate in what he offered to do, waited for others to ask (not demand), let them use their own problem-solving skills and contributed his own skills when they were really needed. He realized that a Good-enough Parent allows independence and personal power in others. Towards himself, he adopted a more nurturing attitude, stopped to think what his own needs might be and encouraged himself to ask for those needs to be met when appropriate. In this process, he concomitantly increased the energy in his Natural Child mode and in his Adult mode, as shown in the second pie chart (Figure 10).

Exercises

Self

1 Using the five functional mode headings, list the types of behaviours you have adopted during the day. It would be useful to repeat this exercise over a number of days to get a more general

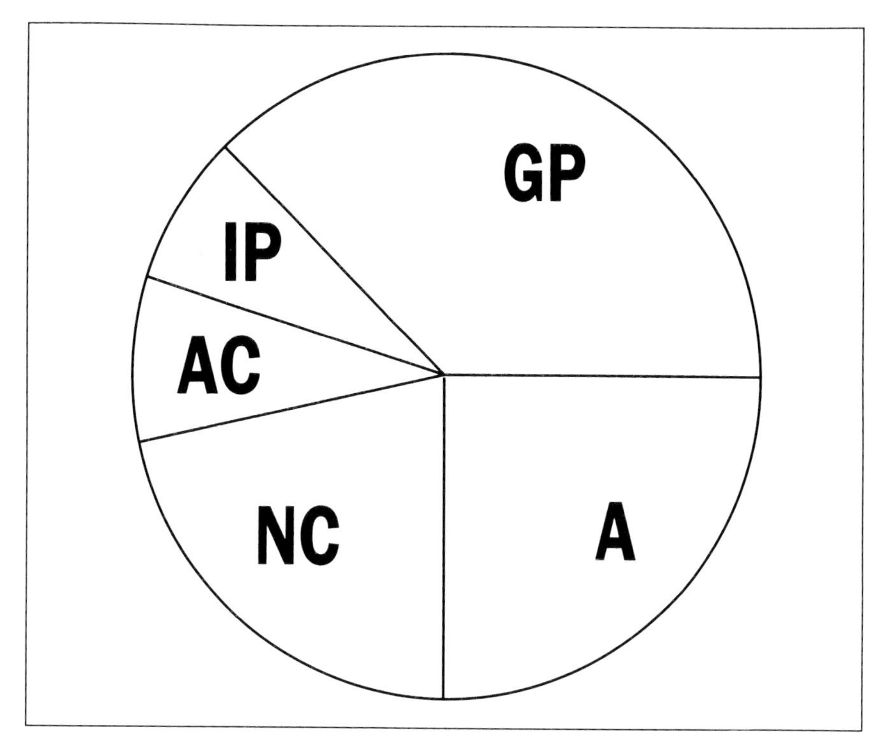

Figure 10 *James' later pie chart of functional modes*

view of how you function and assist in recognizing your functional modes more easily.

2 Draw your own pie chart of functional modes, using the method outlined earlier. It may be interesting to draw a pie chart for different situations in your life. Some people discover a very different pie chart with regard to work from a chart for when they are at home or in other social situations. Explore these varying functional modes by comparing your pie charts.

In a group, it can be illuminating to ask others to draw a pie chart of how they see you and compare it to the way you see yourself. If there are discrepancies between the two, see if you can work out why this might be.

Having drawn your pie chart, are there things about it that you want to change? If so, focus on the functional mode that would most usefully be increased. Refer back to some of the behaviours you have listed and those which we suggested as examples under each heading. It may be that you need to increase the frequency of behaviours you already adopt or it may be that you need to adopt some new behaviours. Choose a set of behaviours and make a contract to practise each of these behaviours a specified number of times each day. Remember, the more specific you are, the easier this will be.

Use the pie chart as a measure of change in your distribution of functional modes by drawing another at the end of a two-week period. If you asked others to draw a chart of you initially, ask them to redraw how they observe you now. Having focused on increasing one functional mode, what do you notice about the others? How does this fit the constancy hypothesis? It may be that you have concomitantly decreased a mode inadvertently which you do not wish to decrease (for example, by focusing on increasing your Good-enough Parent, you may have caused your Natural Child mode to suffer). Are there further changes you wish to make? If so, repeat the steps above.

Working with Clients

1 Use the first exercise above to help your clients familiarize themselves with their functional modes.
2 Together with each client, draw a pie chart to represent a general overview of your clients' functional modes.
3 Discuss with your clients what it is they want to change in their chart and make a behavioural contract for change. For example, your client may choose to increase Natural Child mode and make a contract to arrange at least one hour of recreational time with others each day. Encourage your client to list the ways in which this time will be spent – playing tennis, going for walks, talking and expressing feelings openly with another, and so on.
4 Within a specified period, redraw your client's pie chart as a measure of change.

Combining the Structural and Functional Models

We have already pointed out that sometimes people confuse the structural and functional models. As both models are represented by three stacked circles, it is often assumed that one diagram can simply be superimposed upon the other. This is not so. If we do this we are in effect implying that the Introjected Parent ego state solely functions in an Inadequate Parent mode or a Good-enough Parent mode, that the Integrated Adult ego state functions solely in Adult mode and that the Archaic Child ego state functions solely in an Adapted or Natural Child mode. This view is not only restrictive, it is inaccurate. The fact is, we can function from each of the structural ego states in each of the five functional modes. We can represent this by locating a functional diagram within each ego state of the structural diagram, as shown in Figure 11.

Let us explore this combination using Ramya as an example. Starting with her Introjected Parent, we might identify an ego state that is made up of the feelings, thoughts and behaviours borrowed from, for example, Ramya's mother. In order to further illuminate how she might function in this introjected ego state we can use the functional modes. In other words, we can use

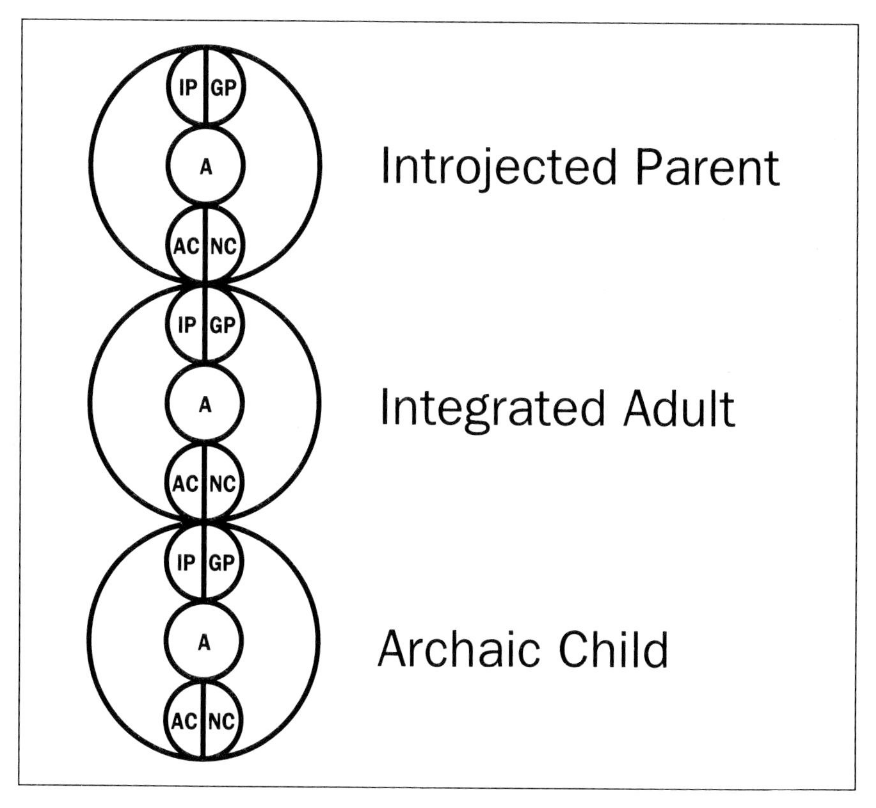

Figure 11 *The combined structural and functional models*

these five modes to describe how Ramya may function from this structure. Drawing a functional mode pie chart of Ramya's mother's functional modes would provide further information as to the general levels of these modes.

We might discover that her mother has a high Inadequate Parent mode whereby she is very dismissive of Ramya and of her own Natural Child mode. This may be further substantiated by a low Good-enough Parent mode lacking in nurturing skills. Her functional Adult mode may be very poor at problem-solving, which may be reflected in a high Adapted Child mode showing her dependence on others to tell her what to do. Her Natural Child mode may be almost non-existent. All of these functional modes will be a part of Ramya's structural Parent ego state.

If we turn to Ramya's Archaic Child ego state and explore the functional modes adopted here we may discover something very different. For example, we may find that in this ego state Ramya has a high Good-enough Parent mode in that she used to look after her inadequate mother much of the time as a child. In this case, her Inadequate Parent mode may be fairly low. She may have a high functional Adult mode, again because, from an early age, owing to her mother's inadequacy, she had to be independent and self-sufficient and do much of the problem-solving for herself. It is likely that her Natural Child mode will be quite low, as clearly she had to take a 'grown-up' role within her family and her Adapted Child will be high as a result of being compliant to her mother's needs.

In her Integrated Adult state, when there is no interference from either her Introjected Parent or her Archaic Child, we may find that Ramya is flexible and fluent in her choice of functional modes. She may from this ego state consciously 'draw upon' the more constructive functional modes of her Child ego state, there being little to 'draw upon' from her Introjected Parent ego state unless she introjected more positive aspects from her father or from later important figures. It may be that she recognizes a deficiency in her Natural Child mode and, like many clients, is wanting to make changes in this respect. In the Integrated Adult ego state she can usefully model herself on others in her current life and consciously practise new options.

Application

By presenting the above example of Ramya, the application of the combined structural and functional models may be made quite self-explanatory. Basically this combination can be used to explore simultaneously both the content of ego states (structure) and the process (function) by which a person may transact in each ego state. It may also be used to further illustrate the multiplicity of functional options a person has to choose from in any given situation. However, we do not suggest you use a fifteen (or more) chair technique unless you have a lot of time and a lot of space and are the sort of person who can regularly remember the football scores of a whole division!

Exercises

Self

1 Choose one of the parents or parent-figures that are now part of your Introjected Parent ego state. Use the five functional mode headings and under each describe the behaviours and attitudes of this person towards themselves, yourself and others.
2 Do the same for one of your Archaic Child ego states. Describe how you function in each of these modes.
3 Repeat this exercise to explore your Integrated Adult ego state. Are there functional modes here which are unique to this ego state? Which ones? Which functional modes do you integrate from your Parent and Child ego states? Are there any functional modes you may need to develop?

Working with Clients

1 Use the exercises you have just done for yourself when working with your clients to explore further the contents of their ego states and the process by which these may be manifested.
2 Use this combination of the two models creatively to widen the range of possibilities when exploring options in a given situation.

Discover, for example, what resources they have in their Introjected Parent by asking, "What would your mother/father/teacher/neighbour have done in this situation?" or, "As a child, how did you use to handle such a problem?" Invite your client to be that person, or the child they once were, and use the five chair technique to discover these resources.

Chapter 6

STROKES

People need other people. Developed and nourished inside a mother for nine months, we are born needing and seeking contact. All through our lives, in one way or another, this need and this search continues. Even a hermit had need of parents and probably still seeks regular contact with them (or others) albeit inside his or her head.

In our vcry early life, if we were left to fend for ourselves we would quickly die. Our obvious need is for food and warmth and protection. Yet, even if we were well provided with these things, without contact with another, though we might not die, our emotional, psychological and physical development would suffer. It has been recognized that those babies who by necessity are kept in incubators for the early weeks of their lives — and thus provided with food, warmth and protection — survive well, make better recovery and show healthier development when they have physical contact with others, even though this may be through gloved apertures in the incubator. At the other end of the developmental spectrum, many hospitals have introduced animals onto the wards of elderly patients, having recognized that the stroking involved (both ways) has a healing and beneficial effect.

Eric Berne used the terms *recognition-hunger* and *stimulus-hunger* (see also Chapter 8) to describe our need for such contact. He used the term 'stroke' to describe the contact itself, defining it as 'a unit of recognition' or 'any act implying recognition of another's presence'. All transactions are therefore, by definition, exchanges of strokes. As we grow up, though physical stroking may still be important to us and to the quality of our lives, the frequency of our need for such strokes may decrease (though social and cultural conditioning may account for the extent of the decrease). We learn instead to replace our need of physical strokes with verbal strokes and stroking gestures which will satisfy our stimulus and recognition hunger. A simple "Hello", a smile or even a frown from a stranger is a stroke and can, however minimally, satisfy our need. At the very least, it indicates that we exist and we can take comfort from the recognition of that fact.

Types of Strokes

Physical, Verbal and Non-verbal Strokes

We have mentioned already the importance of physical strokes. These are any strokes where physical contact is made: a hug, a pat on the back, shaking hands, a massage, a grip on the arm, even a punch in the mouth are all physical strokes. Verbal strokes are those transactions which involve speaking to one another, whether it be a single word, an exciting conversation or a torrent of verbal abuse. Non-verbal strokes are the stroking gestures we use, sometimes independent of words but most often accompanying our verbal communications: a smile, a frown, a toss of the head, a hug (physical strokes being included here too), a dismissive wave, would all be included here. It is the discrepancy between the verbal and non-verbal communication that may sometimes lead us to question the genuineness of the verbal stroke. Non-verbal strokes are also the common vehicle of ulterior transactions.

Positive and Negative Strokes

Any stroke which is intended as pleasant is a positive stroke. Likewise, any stroke which is intended as unpleasant is a negative stroke. It is the intention of the stroke which defines it as positive or negative, whether it is received in this way or not. "I'm so pleased to see you," is a positive stroke. The person receiving this stroke may respond with a similarly positive stroke, "I'm pleased to see you too." Or they may respond with a negative stroke, "Well, you could have come to see me sooner!" and invite negative strokes from the other. You may now recognize this as a crossed transaction. But why should someone do this? When positive strokes are so much more likely to make a person feel good, why should they invite negative strokes at all? Why is it that sometimes people seem to prefer to hear a negative stroke when a positive stroke was intended?

To answer these questions we would need to look back to the person's childhood environment. We may discover that in a particular family there were few strokes given at all. In preference to stroke-deprivation, a child may devise ways of attracting negative strokes. Negative strokes are better than no strokes at all. Being insulted may be preferable to 'being sent to Coventry'. Being punished physically may be preferable to the stroke-deprivation of solitary confinement. Or it may be that we discover that in a particular family negative strokes were the only currency of stroke-giving. Thus the child grows up in the belief that negative strokes are the only strokes and seems not even to hear the positive strokes; they have become desensitized to them through lack of familiarity. Those of you who are teachers in schools are probably well aware of pupils from these stroke-deprived or negative-stroking environments. You may start out with the best of intentions to give positive strokes to them — you know this is what they need — but in the end, your energy depleted by their disruptive behaviour, you give them the negative strokes with which they are so familiar. Changing these stroke patterns can be a tough job. With such pupils it can take a long time and your success will often depend on the supply of positive strokes in your life. If you are positive stroke-deprived it is hard to give positive strokes to others, especially if they seem to be demanding negative ones. This goes for working with clients in counselling too.

Conditional or Unconditional Strokes

Conditional strokes are those strokes which depend upon our doing something. In response to our behaviour we may receive a positive or negative stroke. "That was a wonderful meal you cooked" is a positive conditional stroke. "I really don't like your hair-style" is a negative conditional stroke. Unconditional strokes are those strokes which require no action; they are for our being. They are for existing as we are without having to perform in any way. The most obvious and desirable positive unconditional stroke is, "I love you!" with its negative unconditional counterpart, "I hate you!" "You're so good to be with" is a positive unconditional stroke. "I don't like your being so tall!" is a negative unconditional stroke.

Of these four types of stroke, three are important to the continued well-being of the human organism, but the fourth, the negative unconditional stroke, causes only harm. It is important to find ways of dealing with the negative unconditional strokes which we are almost inevitably going to meet with in life. We do not have to accept or 'take on' these types of strokes. We may, for example, ignore the stroke or we may explore what seems to be the underlying cause of the negativity.

Reinforcement Through Strokes

Our natural hunger for strokes plays an important part in the development of our life script (see Chapter 7) and the way we live as adults. Because of our need, as children we adapt our behaviours to receive as much stroking as possible. If a child attracts strokes for a particular behaviour, that behaviour is reinforced. The child repeats the behaviour, gets the same stroke and the behaviour is further reinforced. It is likely that in adulthood such behaviour will be perpetuated, so long as it is reinforced with strokes from others — or internal strokes from their Introjected Parent — of similar frequency and intensity.

Imagine a child in a low-stroking family sitting hungry for food and recognition while her parents watch the television. She says she is hungry but receives no response. She feels abandoned and begins to cry. She is ignored. She cries louder but is still neglected. Eventually, she screams. This time one of her parents goes to her, furiously picks her up and shakes her, shouting at her to be quiet. Her physical hunger may still be ignored but her hunger for strokes is satisfied, albeit painfully. The next time she feels hungry or neglected, the child omits to ask for what she wants, skips the crying and sobbing and goes straight for the screaming. Again, one of her parents goes to her and shakes her. Negative reinforcement is in progress. The quality of the stroke is physical and negative, the intensity of the stroke is high, the frequency is becoming regular. This child now knows that if she screams she will get some attention. It is likely that as an adult she will attract negative strokes from others of a similar quality and intensity by being loud and demanding *even when this is inappropriate to the current situation*. She will be perceiving the world through a Child ego state.

Take the same scenario but this time imagine that even the child's screams are ignored and that this situation is repeated several times. She eventually 'gives up' and sits quietly by herself. When her parents have finished watching the television, they perfunctorily feed her and put her to bed. If there is a consistent pattern of non-stroking in response to this child's needs, it is likely she will grow up passive and undemanding, not asking for her own needs to be met but waiting in the hope of others eventually stroking her for her passivity should they even notice her. This person may experience a scarcity of strokes in her adult life *even when this is not the current reality*. Again, we have a Child ego state perception of the world.

Supposing, though, this child's needs had been answered. Supposing she had been fed, or even told she had to wait a while but that she could come and be cuddled while waiting. Supposing she even cried because she had to wait but was still cuddled and told she is a lovable child. Such positive stroking would reinforce this child's asking for her needs to be met. As an adult she is likely to act in the world in such a way: to ask for what she wants, to express her feelings, to deal with delayed gratification at times and to experience herself as lovable.

From these examples, it can be seen that stroking patterns in childhood influence our adult behaviour and that we perceive and experience the world according to these patterns.

The Stroke Economy

In his book, *Scripts People Live* (New York: Grove Press, 1974), Claude Steiner recognized that these stroking patterns in stroke-depriving families have certain rules rather like a financial economic system. These rules control the stroke market by maintaining a scarcity myth. The price of a stroke in the market (family) is thus kept high and the consequent behavioural exchange is often extortionate. In this way, parents control the stroke economy and their children's behaviour: a control that has far-reaching effects into adulthood. Steiner referred to the stroke economy as 'basic training for lovelessness' (page 137).

A belief that human beings have only a limited capacity for stroke-giving is programmed in childhood. In reality humans have an infinite capacity for recognizing and appreciating the existence of others. The rules of the stroke economy are:

- Don't give strokes if you have them to give;
- Don't ask for strokes when you need them.
- Don't accept strokes if you want them.
- Don't reject strokes when you don't want them.
- Don't give yourself strokes.

Let us go through these rules one by one.

Don't give strokes: Based on the scarcity myth, if strokes are in such short supply, it is deemed better to hold on to them than to freely give them away. We withhold the strokes we could give even though we may be thinking positively about someone or feeling a positive response to someone.

Don't ask for strokes: This is probably the most familiar to us all. It is based on the belief that, if we have to ask for it, it is going to be worthless. It will be counterfeit in some way. But if we bear in mind the first rule about not giving strokes, we can see that often the stroke we want and could ask for is one which someone may genuinely be wanting or willing to give. By asking for a stroke we may be positively altering the other person's stroke economy as well as our own. If we are not convinced by the stroke, we can always check it in some way or ask for another.

Don't accept strokes: This rule again may involve a certain amount of distrust based on the scarcity myth. If someone is freely giving me a stroke can it be worth much? Why would they be giving it away if it was? Or, if they are giving me a stroke, they must be wanting something back from me in exchange. Or, they are just being kind. Or our reluctance to accept a stroke may be based on our perception of ourselves as worthless or undeserving.

A common example of non-acceptance of a stroke is illustrated in the following exchange:

"I really like your jersey."

"Oh, this old thing. I got it at a jumble sale."

Here the stroke is not accepted. It seems unheard. The information given by the second person is totally irrelevant to the first person's liking the jersey.

Don't reject strokes: This may seem to contradict the above but there are some strokes which we have been conditioned to accept which we might appropriately question, challenge or reject. Women may accept strokes about how they look when really they want to be treated as a whole person with a mind as well as a body. Or men may accept strokes about their physical strength when really they want to be acknowledged for their sensitivity. Rejection of such conditioned stereotypical strokes combined with asking for those strokes which are more valued is a simple way to change the stroke economy.

Don't give yourself strokes: The British seem to set a lot of store by this rule: modesty is a virtue, being positive about yourself is 'showing off', self-deprecation is almost applauded while masturbation is a sin. Changing this rule means challenging many of the messages we received as children and which we perpetuate by repetition from our Introjected Parent ego states.

Application

Whether or not we are aware of it, we are giving strokes to our clients and, in so doing, are positively or negatively reinforcing aspects of their behaviour. Instead of Carl Roger's phrase 'unconditional, positive regard', we could say we are often giving unconditional positive strokes. Accepting the person as they are without judgment is reinforcing the way they are. For every 'Mm hm' of the most non-directive counsellor we can assume that some reinforcement has occurred. If we take into account every 'yes', 'no', 'I see', every nod, smile, frown, body movement and every time we do *not* say something (which the client may experience as withholding strokes), we can begin to estimate just how much stroking and concomitant reinforcement is taking place. If we ask a client, "How do you feel?" we are stroking their existence, their feelings and their expression of feelings. We are making a judgment that feelings are OK in general and that it is OK for this person to express them. It is not so much a question then of do we or don't we stroke and reinforce our clients' behaviour but of awareness of when, how and why we are doing so. By observing our own and our clients' stroke patterns (see later exercises), we can increase our awareness of how and when we are stroking healthy or unhealthy behaviours. We can also increase our vigilance in being aware of when, how and why we may be using the client to get our own needs met and reduce such behaviours by making sure we get our own good-enough supply of strokes from others outside the counselling relationship.

The TA counsellor utilizes strokes creatively to help the client change. These may be physical, verbal or non-verbal strokes: a hug, a "that's great", a smile in response to some thinking, decision, behaviour or feeling that may be a step towards autonomy for the client. The TA counsellor will also be aware of the need not to stroke those thoughts, decisions, behaviours and feelings which may perpetuate the client's problems. Clients, outside their awareness, may attempt to induce the counsellor to enter their frame of reference and seek strokes for their conditioned and unhealthy behaviours. As examples, a client may say something negative about themselves while laughing and an unthinking counsellor may join in the joke (known as a *gallows transaction*); they may be passive and wait for the counsellor to ask what they want or arrive consistently late expecting sympathy, or negative strokes, from the counsellor.

In a counselling session, Robert tells of a recent job interview where he was not offered the job:

ROBERT (*laughing*): I was terrible! A two-year-old could have done better!

COUNSELLOR (*not accepting the invitation to laugh*): In what way do you think you were terrible?

ROBERT: Well, you know, I was just stupid.

COUNSELLOR: No, I don't know. I don't think you're stupid. I think you're very bright. So what happened?

ROBERT: I got scared. They asked questions I didn't know anything about.

COUNSELLOR: Not knowing something is not stupid. I'm sorry you got scared. What were you scared about?

ROBERT: I don't know. Yes I do! My father always expected me to know everything. I was terrified when he asked me questions I didn't know the answers to because I knew it meant a beating.

COUNSELLOR: That sounds terrible for you.

ROBERT: Yet, it was. He said I was stupid. And that's what I tell myself now.

COUNSELLOR: I think you've made a good connection there. I respect the way you think things through.

ROBERT: Yes, I know I'm not stupid really.

COUNSELLOR: That's true. So what do you need to do about the next interview?

ROBERT: Well, I know I don't need to know all the answers but I do need to do a bit more research.

COUNSELLOR: OK. That sounds like a good idea. Anything else?

ROBERT (*laughs*): Yes, I won't take my dad with me to the interview next time!

COUNSELLOR (*laughs too*): That's great!

Exercises

We stress the importance of making sure that your stroke needs are adequately met in order that (a) you do not feel depleted by the amount of attention and stroking your clients need and, therefore, run the risk of giving negative strokes (or inappropriate positive ones) through tiredness or frustration; and (b) you do not rely upon strokes from your clients and therefore seek to extort them for your own ends. This is not to say that it is wrong for your clients to give you strokes, but that you are not dependent upon your clients to meet your stroke needs. The following exercises are to help you to identify your own and your clients' separate stroke needs and plan for healthy ways to achieve them.

Self

1 Look back over your past week and under the following headings list those transactions or occasions where you *received* these strokes:

Positive physical strokes.
Negative physical strokes.
Positive verbal strokes.
Negative verbal strokes.
Positive non-verbal strokes.
Negative non-verbal strokes.

2 Identify those strokes which were conditional and those which were unconditional.
3 What do you notice about your stroke inventory? Are there more positives than negatives? More conditional than unconditional? Are there gaps in your inventory, or types of strokes which are very few? Which are these? Do you want to change this picture? Do you need to decrease the negatives in certain places and increase the positives?
4 Make a plan to change your stroke-receiving inventory to a more positive one. Think of how you can do this. You may need to ask for more strokes. You may need to be more specific in asking for the types of strokes that you want. You may need to be more active in acquiring positive strokes — get yourself a massage each week, allow others to be more physical with you, listen or look for positive strokes with the same energy you have probably used up to now when looking or listening for the negatives. Write down your specific plan of action. For example: I will ask for positive strokes for each meal that I cook. I will listen to and accept strokes from my boss without turning them into negatives. I will book myself a massage each week on a Friday after work. And so on.
5 Use the same headings to make an inventory of the strokes you have *given* over the past week.
6 Identify the conditional and unconditional strokes.
7 What do you notice here? Use the questions in **3** to survey your stroke-giving inventory.
8 Make a plan to change your stroke-giving in ways that will

be positive to you and your friends, acquaintances, colleagues, neighbours and strangers. Make a list of the specific stroking behaviours you will put into operation. For example: I will say hello to my neighbours each time they are in the garden. I will give my partner a ten-minute back rub each evening before supper. I will compliment my colleagues on the work they are doing at least once a day. And so on.

9 Repeat **1** to **3** for the strokes you have given yourself over the past week and make a self-stroking plan now. For example: I will luxuriate in a hot bubble-bath by candle-light while listening to Mozart on Sunday evening. I will treat myself to a meal in town every Tuesday. Each day I will read some of my favourite author before I go to bed. And so on. Make these unconditional.

10 If you are in a support group or counselling group take it in turns to 'brag' for three minutes each (or more). The listeners encourage the person bragging with a 'strokeful' commentary as they move from one self-stroke to the next. This could become a regular part of the group each week.

11 Make a list of the most important and significant affirmations for yourself. Pin them over the bathroom mirror or around the house and repeat them aloud to yourself each day. For example: I love me. I am really lovable. I am a clear thinker. I like my sense of humour. And so on.

Working with Clients

1 Introduce your client to the concept of strokes and the vital part they play in our lives.

2 Share the rules of the stroke economy with your client and discover which rules your client follows.

3 Encourage your clients to ask for strokes from you and to stroke themselves — you could include the bragging exercise in the counselling session.

4 To assist your client to accept strokes, ask them what stroke they would like from you. Encourage your client to keep eye-contact while you say the stroke — you will need to be genuinely willing to give the stroke and, if not, to explain why — to listen carefully and, as the stroke is given, to take a deep inward breath. This helps your client to focus and hear the stroke as well as 'take it in' on a psychological and physiological level.

5 Use the self exercises to make a plan of action to help change your clients' stroke inventory in ways they want.
6 Be aware of how you stroke your clients. Avoid colluding with self-deprecation on the part of your clients. Stroke those behaviours which are constructive and healthy changes.

Chapter 7

LIFE SCRIPT

Each of us has a life script. That is, early in our lives each of us makes decisions, in response to our perception and experience of life at the time, as to how our life will be in the future. We often generalize from our specific, current experiences and assume these will always be so. As we saw in Chapter 6, if a child experiences constant negative stroking in childhood, this may become an expectation of life: the world is then perceived as a negative-stroking place populated by negative-stroking people and this expectation for the most part is fulfilled.

The script is a personal life plan developed mainly before the age of seven under parental, familial, social, cultural and religious pressure. It determines the most important aspects of a person's life. The script is 'written' in early childhood, rehearsed and revised in later childhood and performed in adulthood. (We will explore the means by which the script is fulfilled and, therefore, further reinforced, in later chapters on games and the racket system. For now, let us stay with scripts.)

Because of small children's dependence on their caretakers and their overall lack of experience and knowledge of the world and of overall perspectives, they rely on others to define the world, themselves and others. Imagine a child learning to walk. Each time she falls over, as all children learning to walk must do, her parents laugh at her and call her clumsy. The child, hearing the laughter, stops herself crying and laughs too. Imagine this same child at various later ages and stages falling down the stairs, dropping a plate, cutting herself, tripping over the cat and each time being laughed at and told she is clumsy. Imagine this girl in her teens dressing rather gawkily and clowning about in her peer group to maintain some popularity. This girl is not only receiving verbal and non-verbal *strokes* each time she does these things, she is also receiving an *attribution* that she is clumsy. Further, the nature of the non-verbal stroke, laughter, also carries with it the suggestion that this girl's pain is not important.

In response to such experiences, this child may decide upon a script which involves some or all of the following: I am clumsy. Being clumsy gets attention. Being clumsy makes people laugh. Being clumsy pleases people. I'd better do clumsy things or I'll lose others' attention. No one in the world really cares. Even when I hurt I will laugh. My hurt feelings are not important. Being hurt gets attention. If I hurt myself I will get attention.

From her specific experience with her parents and later rehearsal with her peers, the girl has generalized such experience into a life script which involves beliefs about herself, how others will respond and how the world is. It is now likely that as an adult she will behave clumsily, find people who laugh at her even when she hurts and experience the world as an uncaring place.

Now it may be that, if we question the parents in this example, they will have a totally different perception. They may say they really cared about their daughter, that when they laughed it was out of sympathy with her, that they did not want her to hurt herself and so on. Their intentions, as far as they were aware of them, may have been well-meaning. What is important here is that it is the child's perception of her experience, however skewed, mistaken, misinterpreted or misinformed, and her response to that perception that form the basis of her script decisions. This is not to release the parents or caretakers from their responsibility to be aware of the possible impact of their behaviour on their child. It is the grown-up's responsibility to attend to their own behaviours and unresolved issues, not the child's responsibility.

Children begin developing a script instead of following their own autonomous nature as a result of their vulnerability and dependence, attributions, their developmental stage, their suggestibility, the modelling they receive from caretakers and older siblings, trauma, verbal and non-verbal messages, and in response to fantasies and dreams.

Script Messages

In the light of the above, when we write of 'script messages', we mean the messages received from parents or other figures in childhood *as perceived by* the child. Many of these messages, however they are delivered or received, will contain the parents' fears, ignorance, unresolved conflicts and unmet needs which give rise to these injunctions to the child. In other words, many of the child's received messages will be the script messages of the parents. Let us take a look at the way such messages may be conveyed.

Verbal and Non-verbal Messages

These will be familiar to you from Chapter 6, where we pointed out that verbal communication is often accompanied by non-verbal communication, the verbal message being corroborated or not by the non-verbal message. In transactional terms, the non-verbal communication carries the psychological message of the ulterior transaction beneath the social level transaction. It is the ulterior transaction which carries the significant message at the psychological level. For example, a busy mother picks up her crying child and holds him close to comfort him. She may even say soothing and loving words to him. But if she is tired and tense, it is likely that her face is tense, too, and her voice tone strained. She may hold him too tightly or rigidly or, conversely, hold him loosely, with little energy involved. The social level message may say, "I love you and I care about you. I like holding you. You are safe with me", but the psychological level message may be, "I don't want you. You're too much for me. I don't really care. You are not safe with me."

Modelling

The behaviour of parents and other authority figures in childhood is another vehicle for the communication of script messages. Telling children to 'do as I say, not as I do' is pointless. Modelled behaviour is much more influential than imploring words. This is particularly noticeable in the use of advertising. In a family setting, seeing father get what he wants from mother by shouting at her, Tom is likely to conclude that this is how to behave when he wants something, despite any lectures about the rudeness of shouting. Or seeing little brother get more attention from mother for being 'dyslexic', Christine may decide it is better to fail than succeed at something despite the verbal homage paid to success.

Another form of modelling is that found in story books, radio and television stories, films, songs, nursery rhymes and so on. For example, Monica is very impressed at the age of four by the story of Tarzan and begins to model herself and make decisions in line with becoming strong, wild and very involved with animals.

Commands

Direct instructions or commands to children may also be taken on as script messages, depending upon the frequency and intensity of them. If the verbal message is matched by an equivalent non-verbal message, clearly they will be doubly potent. "Just go away and don't pester me!", if repeated often enough, loudly enough or if accompanied by physical gestures of dismissal may be received as "Your needs are not important" or "You're not wanted." "Pull yourself together" or "Don't cry" may be received as "Your feelings are not important" or "You're weak if you show your sadness."

Attributions

In the earlier example, the child who was told she was clumsy grew up to be clumsy. Similarly, a child told he is stupid may decide this is true and grow up acting stupid in response. A child told, "You're just like your Uncle John" may connect this with their uncle's ineptitude in social situations and construe that they too must be socially inept in response to this message. Often in families different members are given different roles and proceed to live up to them. An example of this would be one child being deemed 'the clever one', another child 'the practical one' and yet another 'the musical one' and so on.

Even more potent are the attributions by a parent or parent-figure made to a third party about you in your hearing: "Oh, he's such a naughty boy" or "Julie's the quiet one in the family" or "It's no use asking Ann for a sensible answer" may carry more weight by 'going public' in this way.

Trauma

Although the repetition of certain negative experiences and their associated perceived messages could be taken on as part of the life script, one traumatic event may be enough for a child to make momentous script decisions about themselves, others and the world unless these traumatic experiences are treated sensitively and respectfully. Death of a parent, loss of a sibling, physical and sexual abuse, accidents, illness and surgical operations are but a few of the shocking and terrifying experiences a child may suffer. As a consequence, the child may make far-reaching decisions about themselves being worthless, shameful, sick, non-sexual, crazy, unlovable or undeserving of life; about others being malevolent, untrustworthy, unloving, sadistic, violent or rightfully abusive; about life being pointless, dangerous, desolate, chaotic, cruel or not worth living. These are just some of the possible messages a child might perceive and decide upon in response to trauma. Sadly, for many of our clients, even these shocking experiences were repeated and the subsequent decisions further reinforced.

Positive Messages

So far we have given examples of negative script messages when discussing how these messages may be conveyed, but positive script messages can be given and conveyed in the same ways — excluding trauma, for which there seems to be no exact positive equivalent other than its absence, the nearest being, perhaps, an unexpected, exciting event such as winning a national lottery.

A child attributed with being "like Aunt Florence", who happens to be a very successful career woman, may take this on as a message to be successful too. A child who overhears a parent proudly singing the praises of their achievements may similarly take this as a permission to achieve. A child genuinely and consistently hugged warmly by a parent and told "You're so lovable" is likely to believe and grow up believing they are lovable. A child whose parents listen to and respect each other's needs and wants is likely to model their own behaviour on such attentive respect. Again, the intensity and frequency of such messages will determine their potency.

Just as a single, traumatic experience may influence a child to develop a negative lifescript, so too an isolated, positively dramatic incident or intensely satisfying peak experience may promote a positive life script. For example, Susie wins the final race of the day which wins her house the school trophy. She is treated like a heroine. From this incident, part of her script is devoted to winning the day on behalf of others. As mentioned earlier, even positive scripts may be limiting to the person's individual potential, being based as they are on the premise that the individual is *only* OK if they are achieving X, Y or Z. It may be, therefore, that Susie has to win for others in order to feel OK.

Depending on their perception of the message, children receiving positive messages are likely to develop positive life scripts. In the same way, children receiving (or perceiving) negative messages are likely to develop negative life scripts. Most of us have quite a mixture of messages and develop equally mixed scripts. However, whether positive, negative or a mixture, they are all scripts; they are life plans based upon our response to our experiences as children and, as such, may be interfering with our autonomy as adults. Receiving the attribution that you are like your successful Aunt Clarissa, the actress, is all very well and positive, but if, at the end of drama school training and ten years 'treading the boards', you realize you have never really wanted to be an actress at all then this could be a problem. Similarly, modelling yourself on your father's lifelong dedication to his work may be fine, but if you would be happier living cheaply and working less, there doesn't seem much point in being like him. Clearly, many people may never even realize they have lived their script rather than their life. If it is a happy, exciting, creative and fulfilling script, which does no harm to others, maybe this does not matter. If awareness of their script would enhance life further, maybe it does.

Autonomy

In the present context, the opposite of script is autonomy, which Eric Berne described as our capacity for awareness, spontaneity and intimacy: three qualities which, in response to perceived messages and subsequent script decisions, we may lose touch with, if indeed we had a chance to touch them. Autonomy means living our life in Integrated Adult. Any moment lived in a Child or Parent ego state is inevitably script, unless it is Adult-monitored or Adult-integrated. Put another way, our script is expressed through the contents of our Child and Parent ego states. If we automatically replay the contents, we are in script. The way out of script, then, is through our Integrated Adult awareness which, as we stated earlier, involves choice and, with choice, responsibility.

Given this, perhaps it will not surprise you to learn that we have yet to meet a human being who is totally autonomous. Living a script-free, autonomous life is an ideal towards which we can only aspire. As counsellors, our task is to help others in this process of increasing autonomy. Whether this is in one particular area of their lives or in many will depend upon the goal and timescale of the agreed contract, but, whatever these may be, we will find it useful to the process to explore and work through those perceived messages and subsequent decisions which detrimentally affect our clients' lives.

Exploring Script Messages and Decisions

Script messages start out in childhood as external transactions. The resultant decisions are perpetuated by internal transactions between Parent and Child ego states and will most likely be reinforced by 'projecting' one or other of these ego states onto someone else, returning to an external transaction. Here is a much simplified example.

External Transactions

Sarah's mother, as the result of her own script, is a very dependent, clinging woman who is scared of responsibility. She has a lot of support from her husband when Sarah is born but, even so, struggles to cope with the newborn baby, finding her needs almost unbearable. Sarah is regularly left to cry alone. When she is attended to by mother, the attention is perfunctory and tense. The perceived messages here — the external transactions transmitted non-verbally at this early stage — could include, "My needs are more important than yours", "You are too much for me", "I don't care about you" and "Don't be a baby, grow up quickly."

When father dies some years later, mother becomes even more helpless, but by this time Sarah is able to take on the nurturing role father had played. The external transactions, now transmitted verbally as well as non-verbally, could include such messages as, "You are so good to take care of me", "What a big girl you are", "I'm so pleased when you stay at home", "You were such a demanding baby but look at you now", as well as the repetition of the earlier, non-verbal messages. Sarah responds by looking after mother.

Decisions

Sarah makes her script decisions in response to these messages. She decides that her acceptability (OKness) is conditional upon her looking after others, that others' needs are more important than her own, that if she looks after others they may care but that really she is too demanding. She also decides that children are too demanding. Though we are focusing here for simplicity on the decisions in response to mother, Sarah is also making decisions in response to father. This may include the decision, based on father's early death, that the only way to cease looking after others is to die.

Internal Transactions

The original external transactions are now internalized within her Parent and Child ego states. In her Parent ego state she has introjected a helpless and demanding mother who shows pleasure when Sarah neglects her own needs to look after others. In her Child ego state are her experiences and responses to such a mother and her consequent decisions. Now, whenever she feels needy, Sarah replays the internal dialogue (the script) whereby her Parent admonishes her for being needy and exhorts her to look after others if she wants to feel OK, and thus reinforces the script decisions. It is most likely that the script decisions are so fixed that the internal dialogue is somewhat redundant and totally unnoticed. However, it is important to remember that behind each decision lies an internal dialogue which once was an external dialogue containing the kernel of the script message and consequent decision. Sarah will most probably need to bring these dialogues and messages into her awareness if she is to challenge and change them.

Externalizing the Internal

The process now comes full circle as Sarah, in her grown-up life, projects her needy and demanding Parent onto others. It may be that she subconsciously 'selects' people who, like mother, appear helpless and demanding but, even if they are not, she will perceive and respond to them *as if they are* in order to fulfil her script decisions involving looking after others and keep herself OK. She may further externalize the internal by repeating similar transactions with her own children from her Parent ego state. Thus she experiences them as too demanding and gives them messages that invite similar script decisions to her own. So the script may be passed on to the next generation, just as it was probably passed on to Sarah's mother.

A Script Diagram

Using the structural model of ego states we can illustrate Sarah's external to internal script process as in Figure 12. Here we can see that the messages originate in the three ego states of mother and are sent to Sarah's Child ego state. Sarah experiences these messages in her own individual way, responds to them and makes her script decisions. Simultaneously, Sarah introjects mother's messages into her Parent ego state. Her responses and decisions are later further reinforced by the same messages being sent internally from her Introjected Parent ego state to her Child ego state.

You will notice that the messages from mother's Child ego state are drawn with the broken line of psychological level or ulterior transactions. This is because, for the most part, these are the type of messages a parent would not consciously give to

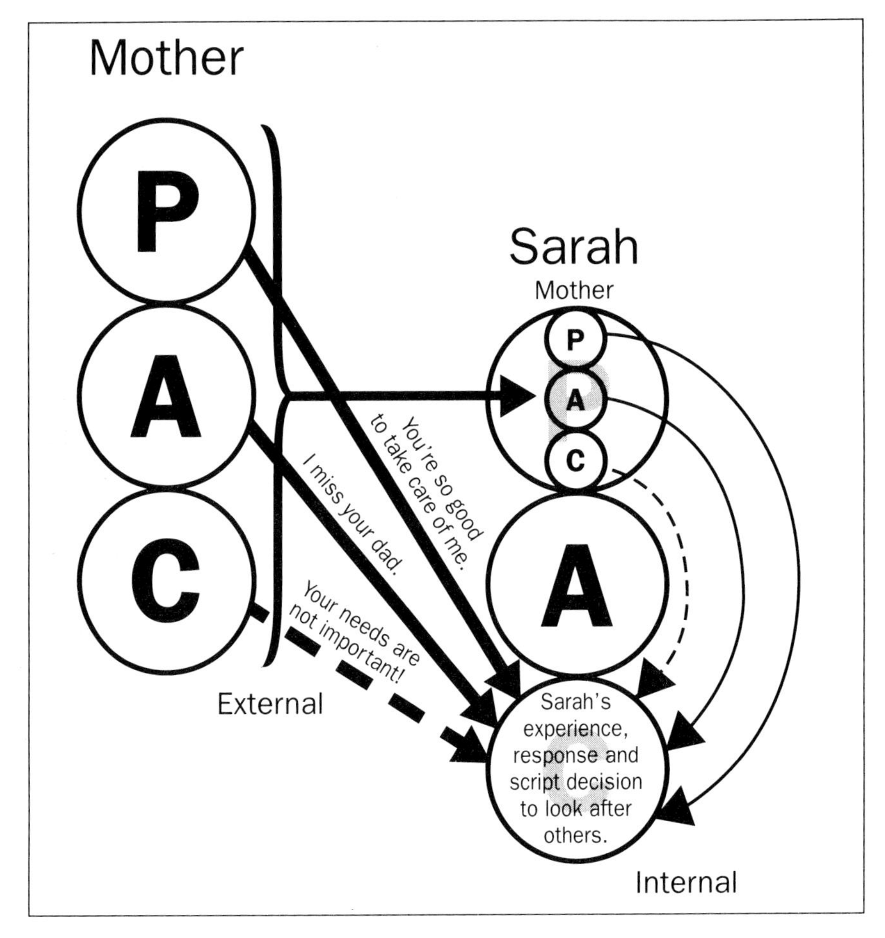

Figure 12 *Sarah's script process*

a child. They are the covert expression of the unmet needs, adaptive responses or restrictive script decisions of the parent's Child. We will refer to these as *psychological level messages*.

The messages from the mother's Parent ego state are drawn with an unbroken line. This is to show that, for the most part, these are the type of overt messages a parent probably would not think twice about giving to a child. In fact, they may be quite proud in saying, for example, "I always told my kids that honesty is the best policy." Such messages are the identical messages they received from their parents and their parents before them. We will refer to these as *social level messages*.

Some TA writers refer to the messages from the parent's Adult ego state as the 'programme', the 'here's how to' messages which often support the script, but we believe that these messages, if they directly support the script, will not come from an Integrated

Adult ego state but from the Introjected Parent or Archaic Child of the parent. If we had shown Sarah's father's messages in diagram form, the 'here's how to look after mother' would have been drawn from either his Parent or Child ego state, not his Adult. We see the Adult messages as more those Integrated Adult messages which, though appropriate to the here-and-now reality of the parent, may be interpreted differently by the child. In our example, from her Integrated Adult, Sarah's mother sends the message, "I miss your dad." Sarah may (and most likely will, in the light of the other messages) interpret this to mean she must take the place of her father in looking after mother. Often these Adult messages, by their definition as appropriate responses to the here-and-now reality, will be the more positive and constructive messages of the script and provide a buffer or alternative to the more restrictive aspects. We will refer to these messages simply as *Adult-intended messages*. If they are not Adult-intended, they belong in either the Parent or Child ego states.

The Script Matrix

There are several versions of the script matrix in TA literature based upon the original matrix devised by Claude Steiner (*TAB*, 5, 18, 1966). Basically, the matrix opens out the structural diagram of ego states, usually showing both parents but sometimes other figures from the past, to illustrate the origins of the contents of ego states. Figure 13 is our amended version using the labels we have described above and showing the introjection of the message-giving ego states of the parents into the Parent ego state of the offspring from whence the script may be replayed and reinforced. We also include Berne's aspiration arrow, to which we will refer later.

Social Level Messages

These messages which parents give to their children in an overt manner are probably familiar to all of us. They will have been given often and in many and various situations in our childhoods and further reinforced by other grown-ups. Getting in touch with

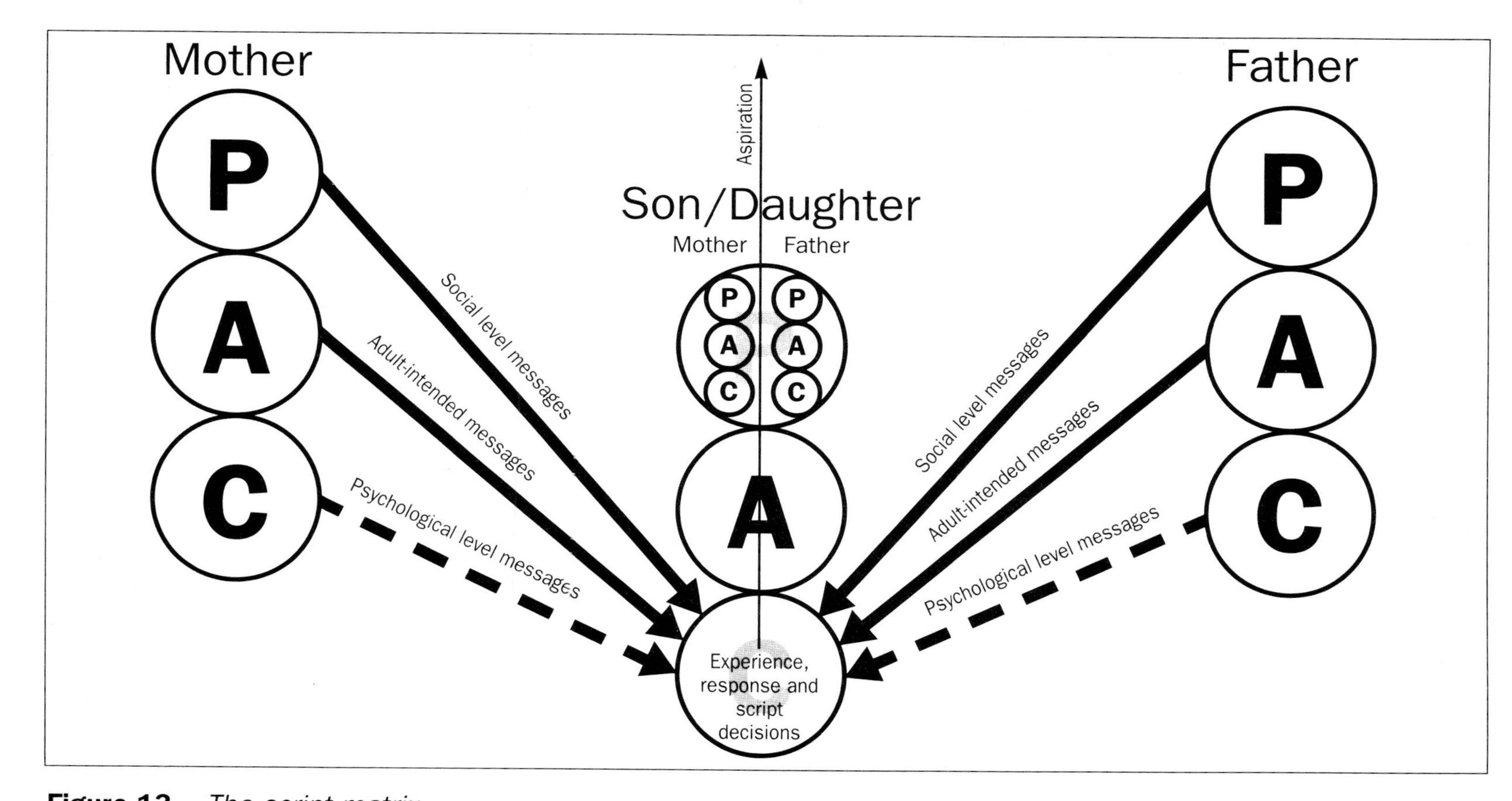

Figure 13 *The script matrix*

social level messages from the past is often easy: we 'hear them' internally even now. Such messages include, "Be a good girl", "Now do your best", "It's rude to grab", "Use a handkerchief!", "Boys don't cry", "Always look smart" and "It's dirty to lick your fingers", many of which may prove socially useful as we grow up and as adults in certain situations. However, not only may some of these messages not be useful but their automatic and unquestioning use may be restrictive and dysfunctional. For example, a child told to "Always look smart" may take this in as an all-pervasive rule of life and consequently spend much time and energy on achieving a smart appearance. They may go to great lengths to avoid entertaining or creative activities which involve looking anything less than smart. They may miss out on the fun and relaxation of such activities and, as a result, appear cold and aloof and thus find difficulty in making friends and good relationships. 'Smart but lonely' may be the outcome of such a response to the original message.

There is a driven quality to the way people respond to these social level messages. This is because, implicit within the message, there is some positive but conditional stroking. The message often becomes, "If you are like this, only then are you acceptable" or "You're OK only if you . . .". As children wanting strokes to satisfy our recognition-hunger we readily adapt to such conditions. As adults we continue the adaptation, believing that our being OK is conditional on behaving in certain ways. We feel 'driven' in search of recognition and acceptance. Taibi Kahler (*TAJ*, 4, 1, 1974) recognized that these driving, social level messages could be categorized under five headings. For obvious reasons, they are called *drivers*:

- Please People
- Be Strong
- Be Perfect
- Hurry Up
- Try Hard

We all carry these five drivers around in our Parent ego state in one form or another and respond to them in our Child ego state. However, because of our different family environments where a different emphasis was placed on what are important ways to behave, we prioritize them differently. Recognizing someone's most-used driver behaviour will give some clue as to the script messages they were given. There is nothing intrinsically wrong in the five types of driver behaviours. Striving to be perfect while doing a graphic design may be fine, as may hurrying up to deal with the situation at the scene of an accident. It is, clearly, the more persistent and driven aspects that may be dysfunctional, the belief that we are only OK if we are achieving one or more of these behaviours.

Psychological Level Messages

These covert messages are communicated for the most part non-verbally at the psychological level. While social level messages from the past are easily available because of their verbal content and the words still playing inside our heads, the psychological level messages are experienced more physiologically and thus may take more time to acknowledge. That churning of the stomach each time we are close to someone, the banging heart and racing pulse when we are expecting criticism or the blushing that occurs when we are given attention: all may be signs of response to a psychological level message.

These messages originate in the Child ego state of the parent. As we know from the discussion in Chapter 3, Child ego states may be positive and constructive; in which case, these psychological level messages may be experienced by the receiver as encouraging and life-enhancing. For example, a mother playing with her child may transmit the joyful and carefree experiences of her childhood to her own child in the manner in which she plays, the tone of her voice, the laughter she shows, the open look on her face, and so on. The psychological messages perceived by her child could include "Life is fun!", "It's OK to be close", "You're fun to be with", "You can express yourself openly" and the subsequent decisions be positive and life-enhancing. Such messages are referred to as *permissions*.

On the other hand, we know that Child ego states may also be negative and destructive. They may contain the restrictive experiences and decisions, the unresolved issues and unmet needs of the caretaker's childhood. For example, a mother who was not allowed to play as a child may go through the motions of fun and laughter with her own child, yet, at the psychological level, be transmitting negative messages from a jealous and resentful Child ego state. The third rule of communication applies here: the child perceives the psychological level communication rather than the social level. The perceived messages may be experienced by the child as "Life's a struggle", "You aren't really wanted", "You shouldn't take up my time like this", "Don't be close to me" and the subsequent decisions be negative and life-restricting. Such messages are referred to as *injunctions*.

Bob and Mary Goulding (*TAJ*, 6, 1, 1976) categorized these negative, inhibiting messages into twelve injunctions, as follows:

- Don't exist
- Don't be you
- Don't be a child
- Don't grow up
- Don't make it
- Don't (do anything)
- Don't be important
- Don't belong
- Don't be close
- Don't be well (Don't be sane)
- Don't think
- Don't feel (Don't express what you feel)

Clearly, this list of injunctions can be turned into a list of permissions by deleting the 'don't' and substituting 'You can'.

As with drivers, this categorization of messages into a list of injunctions (or permissions) can be a useful shorthand for further exploration. It is important, however, to work with the client's own experience and the particular messages — and wording of those messages — which are unique to each client.

Adult-intended Messages

These are the messages that originate in the parents' Integrated Adult ego state. If a parent is responding to their child with feelings, thoughts and behaviours appropriate to the here-and-now reality, it is likely that they will be perceived in this way by the child and taken in as constructive and positive. These may provide a counterbalance to the Parent and Child ego state messages and, depending upon the intensity, frequency and potency of these messages, be taken in rather than the more negative script messages. However, as in our example of Sarah, the child may perceive even Adult messages in a way that fits the restrictive Parent and Child ego state messages where these are more potent and pervasive.

Decisions

In response to the perceived messages from parents, the child makes decisions about themselves, others and the world. Again, the categorizations could be used as shorthand descriptions of these decisions: "I will try hard", "I will please others", "I won't show my feelings", "I won't be important" and so on. These can be very useful and clarifying when working with clients. However, it is important to use these as a starting-point in the process of discovering a client's individual and specific decisions, as often these are more complex than may at first appear. Sonny, for example, in exploring his script, discovers that he spends a lot of time in a 'Please People' driver. He decides he wants to change this and begins to say "No" to people, to look after his own needs and to let others do things for him, all appropriately and consciously. Contrary to his expectations of feeling better about himself and enjoying his life and his friends more, Sonny feels depressed, out of touch with others and has suicidal thoughts. He reverts to 'Please People' behaviour and feels better and close to his friends again.

In counselling, he further explores his script and discovers that the most potent psychological level messages he perceived were 'Don't exist' and 'Don't be a child with needs.' An unplanned pregnancy and a difficult birth, he arrived in an already large family, an unwanted child among much older siblings, and his needs were very much marginalized. In order to survive as best he could in this family, Sonny made a script decision which could be expressed as, "I can stay alive here if I grow up quickly. Then I can get some attention if I please others in my family by putting aside my own needs to look after theirs." Thus it was that, when Sonny attempted to change his driver behaviour of pleasing others, he ran up against the other components of his script. If he did not please others, his own needs came to the fore. If his own needs came to the fore, he was a child with needs and as a child with needs he found it difficult to exist. Hence his subsequent depression, distance from others and thoughts of suicide. In counselling, Sonny needed to address first his issues about staying alive, then those of being a child with needs and finally his driver behaviour.

In this example, Sonny 'does a deal' in response to the perceived messages, one component being conditional on the next. It will always be the case that, where decisions contain more than one component, the psychological level message will be defended by the social level. Put another way, driver behaviour will be used to defend against injunctions. In this case, Sonny used a 'Please People' driver to defend against a 'Don't be a child with needs.' This part of the decision was, "I can get some attention if I please others in my family by putting aside my own needs to look after theirs." Another deal was made at the psychological level, one injunction being used to defend against another. In this case, Sonny defended against the more severe 'Don't exist' injunction by agreeing to the less severe 'Don't be a Child with needs' injunction. This part of the decision became, "I can stay alive here if I grow up quickly." When we consider injunctions, they will need to be addressed in the order of their severity.

If we draw a script matrix for Sonny we may discover that the perceived 'Don't exist' message came from mother and the 'Don't be a child' from father. The decisional 'deal' may then be in playing off one parent's message against the other. In this case, "If I grow up for dad, I don't have to die for mum." As long as Sonny obeys his father's injunction, he is protected from his mother's more destructive injunction. In each of these examples, Sonny complied with the directives of his script messages. He could equally, however, have rebelled against them — if this could have ensured his survival — and stayed a child, stayed needy, refused to do anything that might please others, and so on. But he would still be in script. He may have a sense of autonomy but it is false. His defiant decisions have still been made in adaptation to the parental messages. His life plan is dependent upon his disobedience of these messages. This type of script response is called an *antiscript*. It is often experienced during adolescence in an attempt to break free of the script.

As we have already mentioned, a child may be given positive messages and permissions and make positive script decisions in response to such messages. These are still part of the script and may be usefully explored in counselling in order that the client may now assess, amend, keep or discard these decisions from their Integrated Adult ego state. They may also be explored and utilized creatively in the service of undoing the more negative script decisions. Bringing a client's strengths and positive decisions into awareness may sometimes be forgotten in the script exploration. Such an over-emphasis on negative aspects of the script and an ignoring of the positives is disadvantageous to the client in its neglect of important resources.

Whether our script decisions are compliant, defiant, seemingly positive or negative, creative or restrictive, we need to respect them. Though they may now be inappropriate to our grown-up lives, they were made by us in order to survive as best we could in the circumstances of our childhood. Whatever changes we may now undergo, whatever new decisions we may now make, the Child within us deserves to be given acknowledgement, understanding and gratitude for bringing us thus far.

Aspiration

There is one arrow of the script matrix diagram (Figure 13) that we have not yet discussed. This is the arrow which begins in the heart of the Child ego state, forges up through the Adult and Parent ego states and continues upwards beyond the ego states to infinity. Berne includes this arrow in the script matrix shown in his book, *What Do You Say After You Say Hello?* (1972). It is the arrow of aspiration.

Whatever our script messages, we each have our own autonomous aspirations, the creative yearnings and dreams of what we may be, of what we may do and the ways in which we may achieve such longings. Berne referred to these aspirations as our secret gardens. To continue the analogy: the garden of our aspiration may be weathered by the downward elements of the script, the storms, the drought, the sun, wind and rain of our parental messages yet survive, grow, thrive and blossom nonetheless. Berne sees that the object of script analysis is to free our clients 'so that they can open the garden of their aspirations to the world' (page 131). As counsellors, our task is to help release our clients from the restrictive and sometimes destructive elements of their script, to release their potential and achieve their aspirations.

In his first book, *The Mind in Action* (1949) and many of his later writings, Berne reintroduced the pre-Socratic concept of *Physis* — 'the force of nature, which eternally strives to make things grow and to make growing things more perfect' — to describe the natural tendency of human beings towards health and growth. This creative force for change may be seen as the energy or power that is drawn upon by counsellors and their clients in the quest for the fulfilment of their aspirations. Our colleague, Petruska Clarkson, has written more extensively about the concept of Physis in many of her writings, in particular in her book, *Transactional Analysis Psychotherapy: an integrated approach* (London & New York: Tavistock/Routledge, 1992).

Application

In this chapter we are dealing with the exploration of the life script and its formation. The emphasis is upon covering and exploring the life plans that our clients have made as an aid to making changes. This is known as *script analysis*. In analysing the script many clients make changes. By bringing into awareness the underlying messages, responses and decisions that are now inappropriate and restrictive in their lives, clients make new responses and new decisions while in the process of exploration. Thus, in itself, script analysis opens up the opportunity for choice and the possibility of change.

George, for example, came to counselling at a time when David, his lover, was threatening to leave the relationship after they had spent two years together. George, like his father, was a successful architect. At 32, after several short-term relationships, he had met David, bought a house with him and thought that all was well until David threatened to leave. George was shocked by this sudden announcement. He wanted to save the relationship. David's complaint against George was the lack of time they spent together. George worked in his office in town each day, often until late in the evenings, and brought work home at weekends. The solution seemed apparent: work less, spend more time with David, save and enjoy the relationship. In practice, however, it was not so simple. Like many 'solutions', it was really a goal. In fact, the solution became the counselling contract. Using it as a solution before entering into counselling, each time George determined to spend a weekend relaxing with David he would somehow pick an argument, and in response to David's angry retaliation would storm off to do some work. George told his counsellor that he really loved David and wanted their relationship to work, but that, "Sometimes, I seem to pick a fight in spite of myself. I know I don't want to fight but I still do it! I seem to be sabotaging the relationship even though it's the last thing I want to do." The counsellor suggested they do a script analysis. She asked George to tell her what it was like to be a child in his family, what his parents were like, what their relationship was like, what expectations they had of him, what the family sayings were, what the family values were, and so on.

The life story that emerged was as follows: George's father had become a successful architect when George, an only child, was quite young, setting up his own firm by working long hours at the office and at home. George had many recollections of sitting quietly, watching his father working meticulously at his drawing-board, tearing plans up and starting again at the slightest error. Sometimes his father would teach George the skills of drawing and design and was supportive and encouraging of his efforts, for which he certainly seemed to have a natural aptitude. But these times were rare owing to the pressure of work. His mother supported her husband's career and seemed quite happy to play a background role. George thought she was never happier than when his father was working in his study and he was doing his homework in his bedroom and she busied herself in the kitchen. At times when he wanted attention, he remembered that his mother would get very angry and tell him that he could not have what he wanted until all his work was finished. If he cried, she would tell him to pull himself together, that boys don't cry and that if he wanted to get anywhere in life, he should be like his father. He could not recall seeing his parents spend time together except at meal-times and these were often very tense, usually ending up with his mother getting angry with father over some trivial matter and his father storming off back to his work. Thus George's early experience of life and how it is lived involved his parents' modelling of relationship and work, the command to be like father, positive messages about his drawing skills and many experiences of neglect of his need for closeness and attention.

George and the counsellor drew a script matrix (Figure 14) to summarize some of the perceived messages relevant to his current problem. In response to these social level, psychological level and Adult-intended messages perceived by George as a child, he made the following script decisions: "To survive in this life, I must be strong and work hard like my dad who says I'm good at this anyway. If I have any needs, others will get angry. I can hide my needs by staying away from others and I can do this by working. Others will love me if I'm out of the way."

Through analysing these aspects of his script in this way, George could see the interconnectedness of these compound decisions. It was not just a case of cutting down on his work. If he simply did this, as he had attempted to do, he was not just going against the decision in response to the social level message to be like dad and work hard, he was also coming up against the decision in response to the psychological level messages not to get his needs met and not to be close, which he had covered by going away and working hard. Thus, with David, simply organizing more time to be with him was not enough. Out of Adult awareness, he would sabotage the attempt by inviting David to be angry with him. This way, he obeyed his decisions not to be close and not to get his needs met, which at the same time, paradoxically, he believed would mean David would love him. The counsellor gave encouragement to George by pointing out to him that he was already moving out of script in coming to her to have his needs met and be close to her in so doing. She also gave permission for him to have his needs met and be close to David. David, too, was only too pleased to give him this permission. This did not mean that David would never be angry with George again but that George would not hide his needs (especially his need for closeness) from David by running away to work. His awareness of how he might 'set things up' to get David angry with him was all that was needed for him to avoid doing this.

You can see from the above example that full script analysis

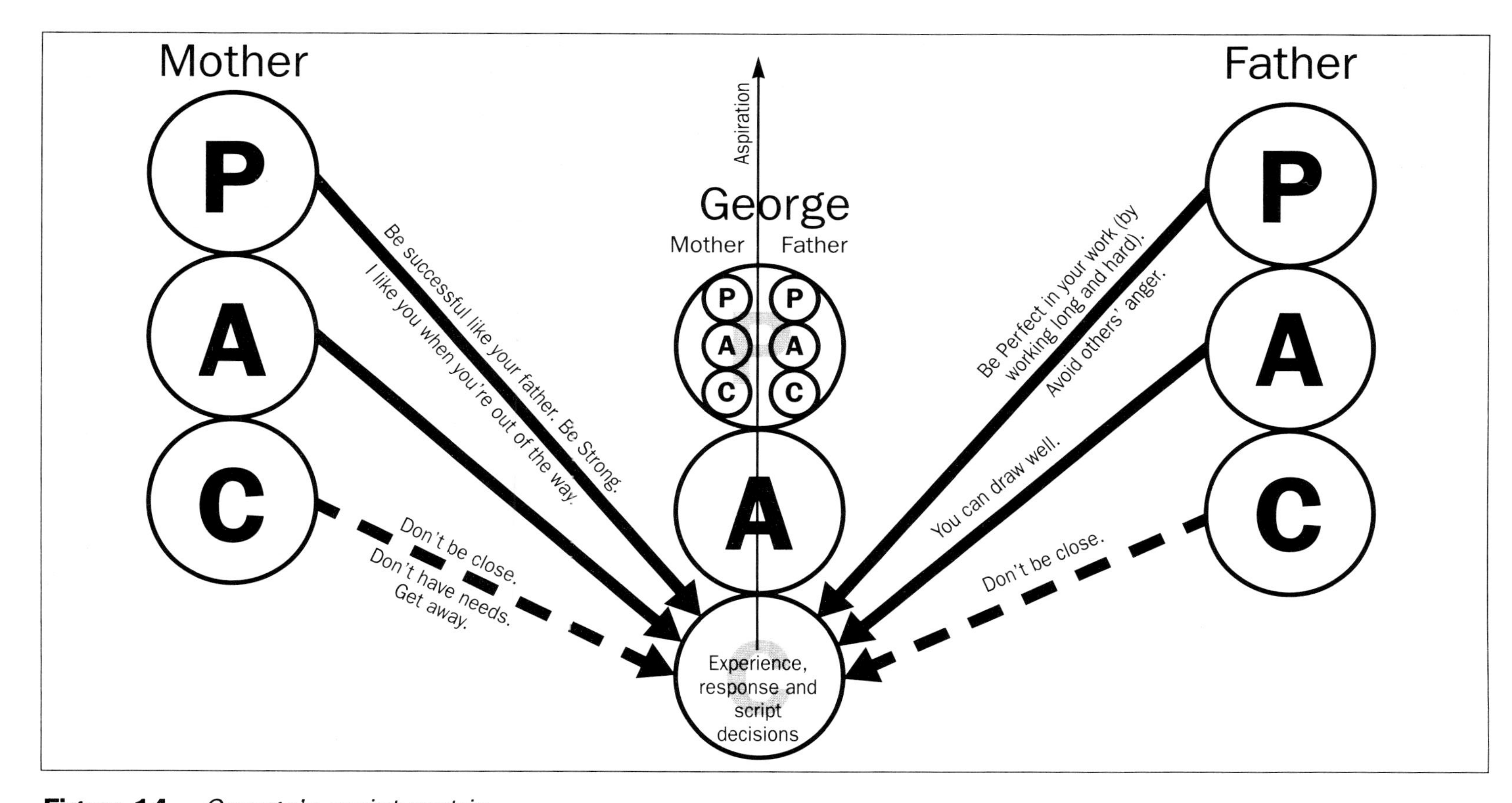

Figure 14 *George's script matrix*

entails the conceptualization and amalgamation of many variables extrapolated from the client's history. However, just as it is possible to use a précis, a trailer or a fractal to understand the essence of a book, film or a whole picture, so too the basic essence of a person's script may be seen in the mini-versions of it that are played out, for example, in the counselling situation.

Exercises

Self

1 SCRIPT THEMES

Fairy tales, legends and myths are stories of universal life scripts. Their themes of quests, love, relationships, tasks, hopes and fears, success and failure, and the conditions and environments in which they are set reflect the themes of human life. In particular, they often reflect a child's-eye view of the world: a world populated on the one hand by giants, ogres, witches, monsters, dragons, kings and queens, gods and goddesses (for all of which read parents or other authority figures) and on the other hand by seemingly powerless beings, poverty-stricken offspring, ragged and downtrodden stepsons and stepdaughters, defenceless and ill-treated animals (for all of which read children). The two ingredients that so often bring about a change of fortune in these stories are magic and royalty! Through magic, Cinderella goes to the ball, through royalty she leaves the family and lives happily ever after. How wonderful for us, as children reading these stories, to feel our powerlessness change to power. How sad, however, that we often go on believing them and, as adults, spend our lives waiting for the magic or the rescuing prince or princess and keeping ourselves powerless.

One way of exploring our own scripts and their general themes is via the route of these universal scripts. It is likely that those stories which attracted us most as children are those which contain the major general themes of our own particular script. It is also likely that the films, plays, novels or stories we are attracted to today are connected in some way with the script that we are still playing out. To help you begin to identify aspects of your own script, first choose a favourite early childhood fairy story, song, nursery rhyme, myth or legend and write down the story as you remember it. Now choose an influential story, play, poem, or song from your primary school years, another from your teenage years (this may be from a pop song or film) and a current one. Write these down as you remember them and then ask yourself the following questions for each story. (We suggest you write the stories now before looking at these questions, which otherwise might influence your natural response.)

What themes does your story express? With which of the characters do you identify? How does this character play their part in the story? What do they do and how do they do it? How does the story begin and how does it end? What part do the other characters play in the unfolding of the story and its development? How would you describe the story: is it hopeful or pessimistic, constructive or destructive, magical or pragmatic, funny or serious (and so on)?

Look for the themes of the story that may in some way reflect your own life script. Having written notes on the themes and aspects of each story, what do you notice? Do they remain the same in each case? If not, how do they differ? Is there some general development from one to the other? Are they totally different? How do these stories reflect the themes of your own script that you identified from the first story? How do you account for the similarities or differences at different ages of your life? How do they reflect the decisions you have made? How do they reflect the aspirations you have fulfilled or would like to fulfil? What are the negative and positive aspects of your script that are reflected in the stories?

2 SCRIPT MESSAGES

Draw a script matrix for yourself and use the following as a guide to complete it. For the social level messages: ask yourself how you most often behave towards others, and in accomplishing tasks, in a way in which you feel driven by the belief that, if you did not, you would not be an acceptable person. You may find it helpful to refer to the later exercise for identifying driver behaviours when working with clients. From the five drivers, Please People, Be Strong, Be Perfect, Hurry Up, Try Hard, choose the one under which these types of behaviour would come. Which of these would come second? Is there a third or fourth driver behaviour which you persistently adopt in your life?

Enter these on your script matrix on the social level arrow according to which of your parents or caretakers you think sent such messages. These might be from both or one of your parents. Remembering that these are useful shorthand phrases, see if you can identify the more specific messages that they are describing. Think of the modelling, the commands and attributions of your parents or caretakers. How did they, for example, encourage you to please people? What are the words you still hear in your own head? Add these to your script matrix.

Injunctions

At the psychological level, because these messages were received much earlier and are mostly pre-verbal or non-verbal, some of the injunctions may be more difficult to identify for yourself. They may be usefully explored in your own counselling or psychotherapy. Others may be more apparent to you immediately or, looking down the list provided on page 97, you may identify them from your physiological response as you read them.

One way of exploring what these psychological level messages may be is to deduce them from the messages at the social level. If you have a 'Please People' driver and messages which support this — "Put others before yourself", "What a good child to do that for me", "Always mind your manners" — it is likely that one or more of the following injunctions would apply: Don't be you, Don't be a child, Don't be important or Don't Feel (Don't express what you feel). Conversely, Don't grow up, Don't be well and Don't make it, may be pleasing to a parent who wants their child to remain dependent. Similarly, if you have a 'Try Hard' driver, Don't make it, Don't (do anything) or Don't think may apply; with 'Be Strong': Don't be a child, Don't belong, Don't be close or Don't feel; with 'Be Perfect': Don't be you, Don't be a child, Don't make it, Don't belong or Don't be close; and with 'Hurry Up': Don't be you, Don't be a child, Don't make it, Don't belong or Don't think may apply. The Don't exist injunction may well apply whatever the driver. These are only guidelines to help in your exploration. They are by no means the only possibilities. Add these messages to your script matrix on the psychological level arrow and, as with the social level messages, write more specific messages in your own words.

Adult intended messages

It is to be hoped that you received many Adult messages from your parents and made many positive decisions in response. These messages could be listed separately as a recognition of the strengths you have as a resource in your life. For the script matrix, however, we are looking at those Adult-intended messages which you perceived as being a further reinforcement of the Parent and Child messages. They may have shared feelings, thoughts and behaviours which were appropriate to the here-and-now reality, such as shouting, "Stop!" and grabbing your hand as you were about to push a knife into an electric socket. Without subsequent explanation, you may have perceived this as going with other prohibitive injunctions like, "Don't explore" or simply "Don't". Look at the other messages of your script matrix and see which Adult-intended messages you may have perceived as fitting these. Add them to your matrix.

Decisions

Now you have completed your script matrix, express in your own words what decisions you made in response to these messages. Remember that these are likely to be compound decisions which often contain 'deals' or 'trade-offs' between injunctions and drivers or sets of injunctions. At this stage, the four script 'stories' you have already identified in the exercise on pages 105–6 may help to highlight some of these decisions.

3 YOUR SCRIPT

Having explored your script themes, script messages and decisions, how do they fit each other? For example, how are your drivers reflected in your favourite stories? Where do the injunctions fit? How do your decisions relate to the themes? Use this analysis to clarify your script for yourself.

4 CHANGES

What changes do you want to make in your script? What are the new decisions you may need to make in order to make these changes? Write these down along with what you will need to do to make these changes. Remember, if they are compound decisions, you will need to work from the more severe injunctions to the less severe and from injunctions to drivers. What will you need to change first? What were the aspirations you identified for yourself and what are the aspects of your real self that need freeing? Who and what will you need to help you to make these changes? If you are having counselling or psychotherapy (and if working with clients, we believe this is imperative), discuss these changes first with your counsellor or psychotherapist. In Chapter 10 we will be looking at the process of change in TA which will help you to achieve these changes.

Working with Clients

1 Explain the idea of a life script to your client and use the first exercise on pages 105–6 to explore the general themes of their life script.
2 Driver spotting (using the clues in the Table on page 110). Driver behaviour often occurs very briefly for a few seconds as the person experiences stress and feels driven to obey the message. First of all practise identifying them by observing television characters.
3 Explore the more specific messages of your client's script by drawing a script matrix and using the second exercise on pages 106–8.
4 Work through the script matrix with your client to discover how it relates to their presenting problems and issues brought to counselling. Use the script matrix to discover what changes your client is wanting to make and help them to uncover and encourage their autonomous aspirations.

PLEASE PEOPLE

WORDS Would you . . .? Could you . . .? Is that OK? Sort of . . . May I? If you don't mind . . .

GESTURES Lots of head nodding, reaching out with hands towards the other, placatory movements.

FACIAL Raised eyebrow, horizontally wrinkled brow, a tense and persistent smile.

BE STRONG

WORDS Few, if any, feeling words. Separates self from feelings or thoughts by using generalizations: One should always . . . It's best to . . . People are . . . Rarely uses 'I' statements, preferring the above. Talks of people and objects doing things to him and takes little responsibility.

GESTURES Rigid, stiff, hardly moving. The posture is tight and closed: arms or legs crossed and close to the body.

FACIAL Flat, hard, cold, immobile.

BE PERFECT

WORDS Of course . . . possibly . . . most probably . . . one might even say . . . Tends to list the points in a conversation by numbers or by saying firstly, secondly and so on.

GESTURES Sits upright, counts off points made on fingers, scratches head, strokes chin to indicate thinking, puts fingertips together.

FACIAL Looks upwards and sideways as if scanning a prompt screen for the right (perfectly right) words. Stern and serious.

HURRY UP

WORDS Interrupts others with words like quick . . . move it . . . let's go . . . hurry up . . .

GESTURES Taps fingers, agitates foot, looks repeatedly at watch.

FACIAL Darting eyes, frowns.

TRY HARD

WORDS Uses the word try a great deal. Goes off on tangents. It's hard to . . . I can't . . . I don't understand . . . What did you say? What I'm trying to explain is . . .

GESTURES Leans forward, elbows on legs, hands to cheek or ear, straining.

FACIAL Looks perplexed, confused, screws up face as if it is an effort to understand.

Table 1 *Driver spotting*

Chapter 8

HUMAN HUNGERS AND GAMES

Hungers

Eric Berne identified six human 'hungers' which we need to meet in order to maintain physical, mental and emotional well-being. We have already addressed stimulus-hunger and recognition-hunger in Chapter 6. We return to them here and expand and elaborate upon them, along with the four additional hungers.

Stimulus-hunger

This comprises our biological need for sensory stimulation. Our five senses need contact and stimulation from the environment: in other words, we need to see, touch, hear, smell and taste the world in which we exist in order to adjust to that world with the best degree of accommodation possible. Furthermore, 'the arousal system' of the brain needs excitation for the health and continued functioning of the organism. When this sensory stimulus is lacking, adjustment and balance is difficult. Usually, within 48 hours of full sensory deprivation, people begin to have delusions and hallucinations, demonstrating that they are unable to retain their mental and emotional stability without stimulation.

Contact-hunger

In some respects this is a subset of stimulus hunger, in that it comprises our need for touch. However, it is different in that this is our hunger for contact with another being's skin (physical strokes). In the act of contact between one human being and another (this could include animals with a temperature of 98.6 degrees), an exchange of infra-red rays takes place and the reception of these rays from another person is both energizing and pleasurable to the recipient. The contact of mother and baby during feeding, for example, will provide such energy and pleasure as well as food. However, feeding babies when both parties are clothed and there is no bare skin contact between caretaker and child is the equivalent of shaking hands with gloves on. The same applies to grown-ups. People who seldom or never have skin contact with another, sometimes have this need met by developing symptoms such as ulcers or arthritis requiring medical attention which may partly fulfil their bodily-contact needs.

Recognition-hunger

The nervous system of the human being is so designed that verbal recognition and body language can, to some extent, substitute for physical contact and assist in the development of our self-image. This need for acknowledgement of our existence and our sense of self may be met in a simple "Hello" or a long discussion of political views. Each person needs a different quotient of recognition and has a personal preference as to the type of strokes they require. A pop star may hunger for applause from thousands while the person who delivers the post may be satisfied with one householder's smile of appreciation as they receive their letters.

Sexual-hunger

Like our hunger for contact, sexual hunger may be seen as a subset of stimulus-hunger but specifically involves stimulation and contact of our sexual organs (skin, breasts, genitals and so on) by self or others. Healthy human beings have these needs met by sexual contact with other consenting adults, or with themselves, in a way that causes neither hurt nor harm. People who do not manage to have their sexual needs met in healthy ways may have recourse to inappropriate means of gratification, for example with minors or unwilling partners.

Some theorists, particularly Freudians, suggest that it is possible to sublimate or divert our sexual hunger towards creativity or spirituality (through celibacy) while others would posit separate and distinct hungers for creativity and spirituality. Berne seems implicitly to include these within the other five hungers.

Structure-hunger

How to fill the 24 hours in a day, the weeks and years ahead of us and, similarly, how to organize our personal environment (homes, offices, gardens and so on) preoccupies all of us much of the time. In short, we are concerned with how to provide sufficient certainty and security in our lives for us to feel safe enough to encounter all those things in life over which we have no control. As the previous hungers have shown, our healthy survival depends upon our relationships with other human beings. There is, therefore, in every human encounter the potential for the fulfilment of healthy needs, but there is also anxiety: will we be accepted and what will transpire?

Eric Berne suggests that we manage some of this anxiety at the same time as attempting to get what we want by structuring our relationships and our life's time with six possible forms of behaviour. The first form of time-structuring is *withdrawal*, where we are alone or lose contact while with other people and, figuratively speaking, withdraw into ourselves. The second type is *rituals*, whereby we exchange fairly 'ritualized' strokes with people in a familiar way. The obvious example of this would be "Hello, how are you?" — "I'm fine thanks, how are you?" — "I'm fine too, thanks. In fact, I'm very well." — "Good, but it's ages since we met." — "Yes, what have you been doing all this time?" And so on. The third type of time-structuring is called *pastimes*. These are conversations which are less ritualized but still remain within familiar parameters in terms of both content and style. They are the sorts of exchanges we have about our jobs, our hobbies, our children, the way the road we are driving along gets totally snarled up as it approaches an important intersection and so on. This may sound as if pastimes are rather a trivial way of passing the time, but they are actually a vital part of human encounter. They are the way we can signal our interest in each other and our goodwill towards each other. They are an important part of our 'warming into' greater closeness with others. They are our means of finding out who has things in common with us. They are a means of exchanging positive strokes in a safe way, thereby fulfilling at least two others of our hungers, stimulus and recognition. The fourth way of structuring time, *activities*, refers to people engaging together in joint endeavours, be it at the workplace, on the sportsfield, at home or in the garden. In activity, those involved interact to complete a task. Their common purpose is a source of both strokes and satisfaction. The fifth type of time-structuring time is *games and rackets*. These are the repetitive patterns of negative behaviour that we engage in with others — in other words, those situations where we end up saying, "Oh no, how come it's turned out like this again?", usually closely followed by some comment like "I should have known . . ." or "I *knew* . . ."; people who have been playing games part feeling familiarly uncomfortable and unsatisfied. Games and rackets will be explored in greater detail later in this chapter and in the next. The sixth and final way of structuring time is *intimacy*. Intimacy occurs when two or more people exchange their thoughts and feelings, without defence and generously. They behave towards each other in an open manner, fully sensitized to the here-and-now experience. They part feeling enriched by the interchange.

The way in which the three of us interacted while we wrote this chapter illustrates how time-structuring works. The shared task of writing this book was the activity. At times, one of us would go into a daydream or prepare tea (withdrawal) whilst the other two continued writing together (activity). At other times, all three would stop to recognize the arrival of a colleague and exchange pleasantries (ritual) which would often extend into conversations ranging from the weather to the type of pizzas preferred (pastime). There were times when we shared our thoughts and feelings for and with each other, including both funny and poignant moments as we resonated to the material with personal memories of our own (intimacy). At the present moment, we have just had a discussion as to which games we might have been playing and have decided that so far we have been game-free in our interchanges with each other. If this changes we will let you know later in this chapter.

Healthy individuals structure their time across the above range of options in such a way as to meet their particular needs and proclivities. Different temperaments will require different blends and quantities of the six ways of structuring time. An unbalanced mixture can lead to an unhealthy life-style, for example that of the workaholic's over-devotion to work-activities.

Incident-hunger

This last hunger is connected with the previous one, but where in structure-hunger we look for stability, in incident-hunger we seek to be destabilized. It is the need for excitement, the unexpected and the new. When there is too much predictable structure or not enough stimulus in a person's life, boredom sets in. The hunger for incident may then drive that person to create some excitement in life. This can be constructive, as in choosing to make a successful parachute jump, going to the fair or interrupting proceedings to tell a joke, or destructive, as in reckless driving leading to a crash or a speed ticket, a violent argument or experimentation with dangerous drugs. People have different incident needs. For some, the celebration of Christmas is more than enough incident in the year. For others, a party every weekend may seem absolutely necessary.

The fulfilment of these six hungers is essential for people's health and survival. It is important for counsellors to recognize the significance and impact of these hungers in their clients' lives and in the counselling session itself. *If these hungers are not met directly, attempts will be made to meet them indirectly by the use of games — the fifth of the methods mentioned under the hunger for time-structuring.*

Games

The adoption of the word 'games' by Berne, with its implication of playfulness and creativity, is, perhaps, unfortunate and misleading. It is, however, so intrinsic to the accepted language of TA that the substitution of a preferable word would merely confuse the issue. When working with clients, we often use the phrase 'psychological games' to emphasize their distinction from the more positive and creative games which are a constructive part of human activities.

In his *Games People Play* (New York: Grove Press, 1964), Eric Berne called a game 'a series of moves with a snare'. The use of the word 'snare' is to suggest that, though a particular situation might at first seem ordinary, even pleasurable, it turns out to have a hidden, though predictable, catch in it. He also defines a game more formally as '*an ongoing series of complementary ulterior transactions progressing to a well-defined predictable outcome*'. We would add that this progression to a predictable outcome develops via a negative crossed transaction at the social level.

At the social level, transactions are being exchanged on a particular topic while at the ulterior (psychological) level, *and out of Adult awareness*, another series of transactions is going on; a series which is dictated by our script beliefs and which will lead to a script reinforcing 'pay-off' as the ulteriors are acted upon and become overt. Remember the third rule of communication, that the outcome of communication is determined at the psychological level. Here is an example: Tim, as the result of his experiences with his mother as a child, has a script belief that he is useless and, however hard he tries to please people, he cannot succeed. His wife, Alice, owing to her childhood experiences of her complaining mother, has an Introjected Parent belief that her needs will never really be met. When Tim says, "I'll make lunch today", Alice replies, "Thanks, that's great" and all seems well. The social level transactions are complementary (Adult to Adult) and pleasant. Meanwhile, however, a different set of transactions is going on at the psychological level. Here, Tim is saying, "I'm trying really hard to please you" (ulterior Child to Parent), while Alice is saying, "You just try because no one has pleased me so far" (ulterior Parent to Child). And sure enough, Tim somehow 'forgets' that Alice hates scrambled eggs, which is precisely what he places on the plate in front of her. He is shocked when the eggs come flying across the room at him with the retort, "You're bloody useless! You never do anything right for me" (overt Parent to Child) from Alice. In this way, at the end of the game, they both have a 'pay-off': the script beliefs of both of them are confirmed and reinforced. Tim, familiarly, feels hurt, rejected and useless, while Alice feels outraged that her needs, yet again, are unmet. Indirectly, their hungers for stimulus, recognition, structure and, as it turns out, incident have been met. The game can be represented transactionally as in Figure 15.

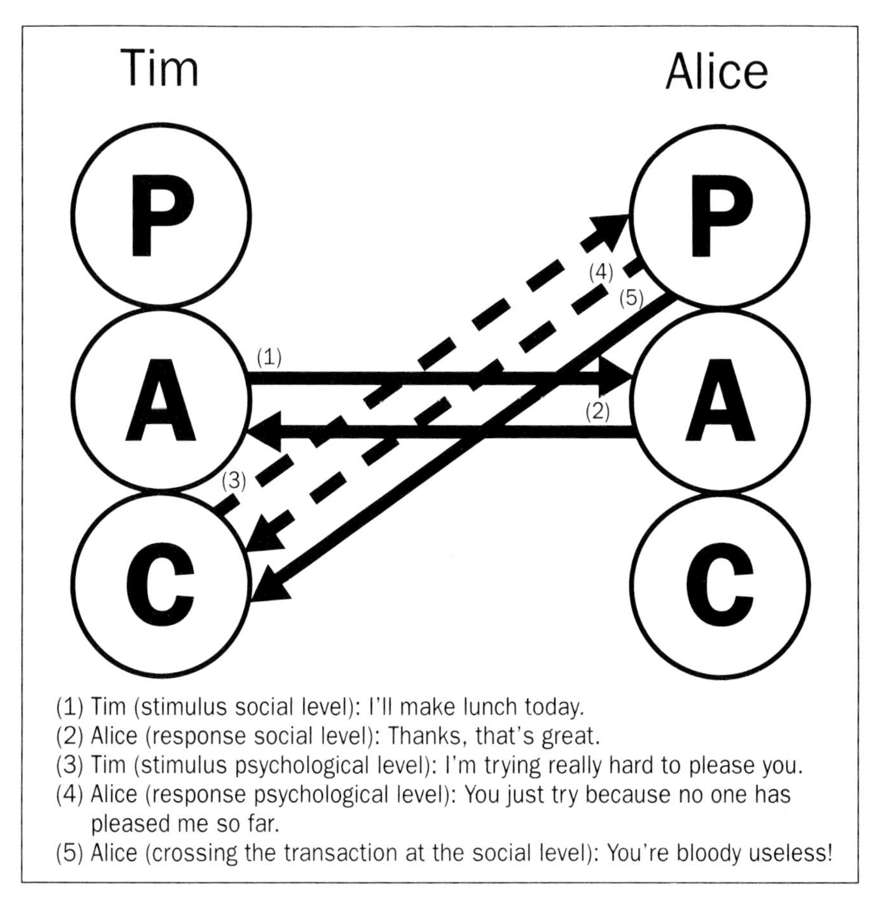

Figure 15 *A transactional game diagram*

Eric Berne might have put those psychological level messages in a much starker version such as:

TIM: Kick me.
ALICE: I'll get you.

These messages serve to illustrate the idea that games contain our script beliefs and expectations in their purest form. Every time we play a game, we reinforce some limiting belief about ourselves, others and the world. In other words, we fulfil our scripts. This is painful but has the advantage of being familiar and true to our earliest solutions to the problem of making sense of our lives. Through games we are also indirectly attempting to satisfy some or all of our six hungers. Further, games involve a high degree of stroke exchange. We have mentioned already that even negative strokes are better than no strokes at all: negative game strokes are sought in the face of some script belief that positive, pleasurable patterns cannot be evolved to promote positive stroking.

But how could this have been any different in the case of Tim and Alice? What are they doing that leads to this familiar outcome? One answer, and a very important factor implicit in all games, is that they are *discounting*: they are, out of their Adult awareness, ignoring information that could lead to the solution of the problem. At the simplest level, Alice could have told Tim what she wanted for lunch. Similarly, Tim could have asked what she would like. The fact that he 'forgot' that she hated scrambled eggs illustrates another form of discounting. Forgetting, not thinking, acting impulsively, exaggerating, over-generalizing and ignoring our feelings are just some of the ways in which we might discount information that could be used to solve problems. Discounting is an attempt to force someone else to take responsibility for some aspect of our lives without an overt contract so to do. In discounting, we ignore our hungers and appropriate ways to satisfy them and are likely to play psychological games instead. If Tim had recognized his hunger for recognition, stimulus and incident at that moment, he could have found positive ways of satisfying those hungers. Likewise with Alice and likewise with ourselves and our clients. The essence of games is that the players are operating 'on automatic' and do not let themselves notice their real needs, which consequently remain unfulfilled.

One of the simplest and most useful ways of looking at games is to look at the three possible roles we adopt when game-playing, the discounts inherent within these roles and the switch in roles that signals that a game has been played — that often dramatic moment when the covert becomes overt. These roles form the three corners of the drama triangle.

The Drama Triangle

The drama triangle was devised by Steve Karpman in an article entitled 'Fairy Tales and Script Drama Analysis' (*TAB*, 7, 26, 1968) as a means of analysing games. Figure 16 shows the three possible roles adopted by two or more players.

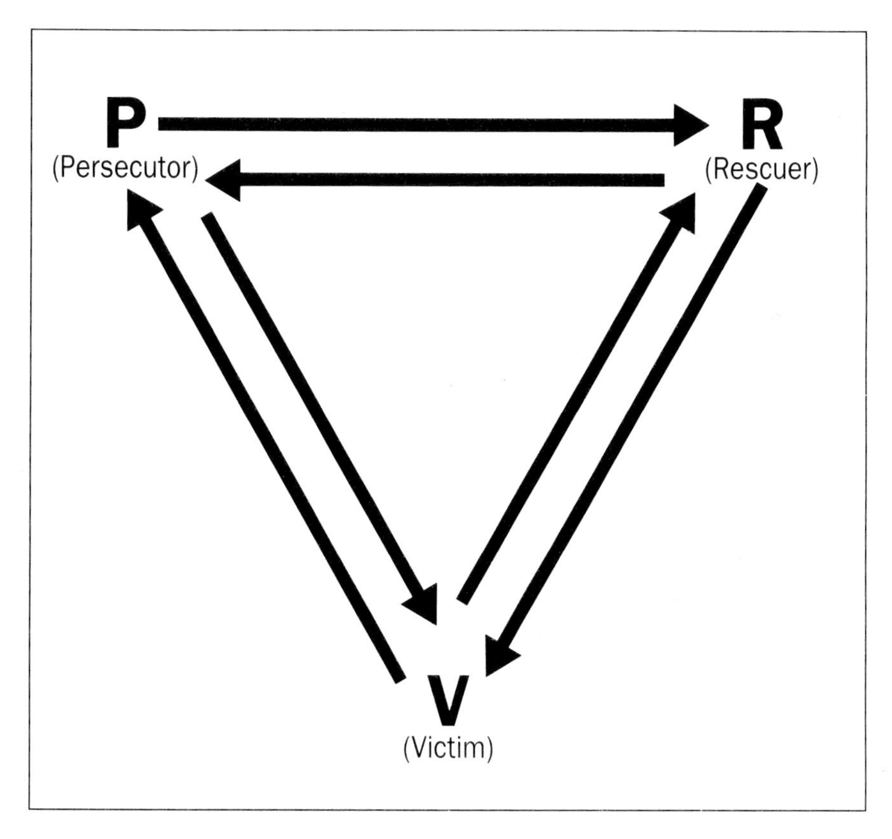

Figure 16 *The drama triangle*
(Karpman, 1968. Reproduced with kind permission.)

Victim

The Victim role is the most psychologically powerful of the three roles. Note the use of an initial capital for the game-role Victim. A game-role Victim discounts their own power and perceives themselves to be powerless in situations where this really is not so. An actual victim is powerless in the face of existential circumstances. For example, someone moaning about their lack of space because of their children's untidiness may be adopting the role of a psychological Victim. They are discounting their ability and power to take charge and control the situation. On the other hand, someone whose house has just been destroyed by an earthquake would be an actual victim of circumstance. They cannot control an earthquake. The distinguishing feature between these two examples is the level of power they have to change the situation. Even in the wake of an existential crisis such as an earthquake, real victims have the choice of adjusting creatively to the situation by solving the problem of their immediate needs of evacuation or responding in a Victim role by waiting for others to do all the problem-solving. It is the psychological Victim's belief that others are more powerful than them (a 'one-down' position) that keeps them in this powerless role. This is an I'm not OK — You're OK position. They somehow see themselves as deserving of others taking control of their situation.

Rescuer

Here again, we can make a distinction between an actual rescuer and a game-role Rescuer. An actual rescuer may witness someone being mugged and intervene successfully to save the intended victim. A game-role Rescuer is one who, in order to gain recognition, uses their perceived superiority (a 'one-up' position) ostensibly to benefit others but simultaneously keeps them powerless. They see people they want to rescue as not OK. They do more than 50 per cent of the work in any situation or take more than their fair share of responsibility. For example, the archetypal Rescuer insists on escorting a blind person across a busy road, oblivious to the fact that the person never intended crossing in the first place. The blind person is left stranded on the wrong side of the road while the Rescuer walks off feeling smug and superior. Just as circumstance brings forth real victims, society designates people as real rescuers in the form of social workers, fire-fighters, lifeguards, doctors, counsellors and so on. Of course, these people may be effective rescuers or ineffective Rescuers.

Persecutor

The Persecutor, like the Rescuer, comes from a 'one-up' position, seeing themselves as OK and others as not OK. However, in order to maintain their 'superior' position, instead of 'saving' others, they need to control and belittle them. For example, a white person may make racist remarks about a black colleague in order to secure a 'superior' position and feel OK about themselves. Or one person may order another about, treat them more like an object than a person and criticize them in order to avoid facing their own feelings of inadequacy.

Of course, as we have seen when discussing the Good-enough Parent mode, there is sometimes a legitimate need for one person to control another for that person's well-being or for the safety and well-being of others. Parents, magistrates, members of the police force, traffic wardens and so on should exercise control of a person's negative behaviour to such ends. It may be, however, that some people in such roles have a psychological need to persecute from a game role in pursuit of their own need to control, not just the behaviour, but the whole person.

Describing the Victim role as the most psychologically powerful may seem a contradiction in terms but, as can be seen, both the Rescuer and the Persecutor are dependent upon a Victim in order to maintain their roles and Victims are very good at finding and manipulating them.

Now we have described the three roles involved in the drama triangle, let us see how these are mobilized in the playing of games. We are all capable of playing each role but we will probably have a favourite and predictable role and a pattern in which we move from one particular role to another. We may feel compelled to start a game from one role while feeling equally compelled to finish the game in another. This final role will be the one which produces the pay-off which in turn will confirm our script. From the complementary transactions which pass between two people (or more), each maintaining their position in one corner of the triangle, an unexpected switch in role by one or both players (a crossed transaction) exposes a dramatic conflict of interests or confusion of communication. This may happen within a single set of transactions within a few moments or involve many sets of transactions over a much longer period of time, sometimes years.

The originator of this concept, Steve Karpman, saw how these roles and dramatic switches can be seen not only throughout ordinary human communication but in all forms of dramatization of the human condition, such as fairy tales, plays, myths, legends and so on. In the fairy tale of Little Red Riding Hood, for example, LRRH's mother could be seen as a Rescuer sending food to LRRH's grandmother. She does not go herself — as is often the case with Rescuers — but sends her daughter, LRRH, to do the deed. In the forest, LRRH meets the wolf who asks where she is going with the food, at which point, LRRH discounts all she ever knew about wolves — as is the case with Victims — and tells all. It is no surprise to us, therefore, that on arriving at grandmother's house, we find that grandmother (Victim) has been eaten by the wolf (Persecutor) who has taken granny's place in bed. When LRRH arrives at her grandmother's her level of discounting reaches mammoth proportions — as is the wont of Victims — and she fails to notice that grandmother has been replaced by a foul-smelling, hairy creature probably slavering in anticipation of getting his teeth into her — but there we are. She even adds to the anticipatory pleasure of the wolf by remarking upon granny's unusually large ears, nose, eyes and teeth, to show the extent of her discounting abilities. Whereupon the Persecutor pounces on the Victim and gobbles her up. Very contented, the wolf falls asleep in the bed.

There are several endings to this story, according to which version you were brought up on, but we will use the one with the huntsman who happens to be passing by just at that moment. He (Persecutor/Rescuer) cuts open the sleeping wolf (now Victim) and releases the still-living granny and LRRH. They are still Victims at this point, having waited to be rescued rather than fathoming their own way out. However, they do not stay Victims for long. Soon they switch to being vicious Persecutors as they hit upon the cruel idea of putting stones inside the wolf's gaping stomach before sewing him up again. Once awake, the wolf is destined for a life of heavy indigestion and immobility — probably a very short life indeed. Meanwhile, back on the other side of the forest, we can imagine the Rescuer mother, blissfully ignorant of the bloody state of affairs at Granny's, watching television by the fireside, congratulating herself on the good deed she has done and dreaming of how much she will get in the will.

Leaving the realm of fairy tales, games may, of course, be played within counselling. A client, Mary, is complaining about the inattentiveness of her husband. She shows little emotion as she repeats the same dissatisfactions again and again (Victim). The counsellor responds with superficial reassurances and messages of sympathy (Rescuer). This continues for some time until Mary, whose hunger for greater recognition, stimulation and incident is not being met by the current transactions, switches role to that of Persecutor by turning on the counsellor, saying, "Well, I'm certainly not feeling any better. You're not being any help at all!" The counsellor, now Victim, vies for the Persecutor role and retorts, "The way you're going on, it seems to me you have no intention of being helped." Mary switches back to the Victim position, crying, "Nobody understands me," but makes a final switch to Persecutor as she leaves the room, shouting, "You're no better than my husband!" She ends the game feeling righteously indignant and confirmed in her script belief that all men are useless. The counsellor ends the game in the Victim position, feeling dejected and ineffectual, as decreed by his script beliefs. The beginning and end moves in this game are shown in Figure 17.

Degrees of Games

Comparing the story of Little Red Riding Hood with our counselling example, you may realize that games can be played to varying degrees of intensity. Berne suggested that, like burns, there are three degrees of games.

A first degree game can take place in just a few transactions and is signalled by a moment of surprise and discomfort or a vague sense of "Oh, I didn't mean that to happen." An example would be the counsellor who plays a brief game of 'Why Don't You — Yes but' with his client, in which he makes two or three helpful suggestions intended to alleviate his client's suffering, to be met by a blank look, a sigh and the comment, "Yes, I've tried all that."

A second degree game carries more intense feelings and causes enough pain to ensure an unequivocal confirmation of script beliefs. Berne said that second degree games are those

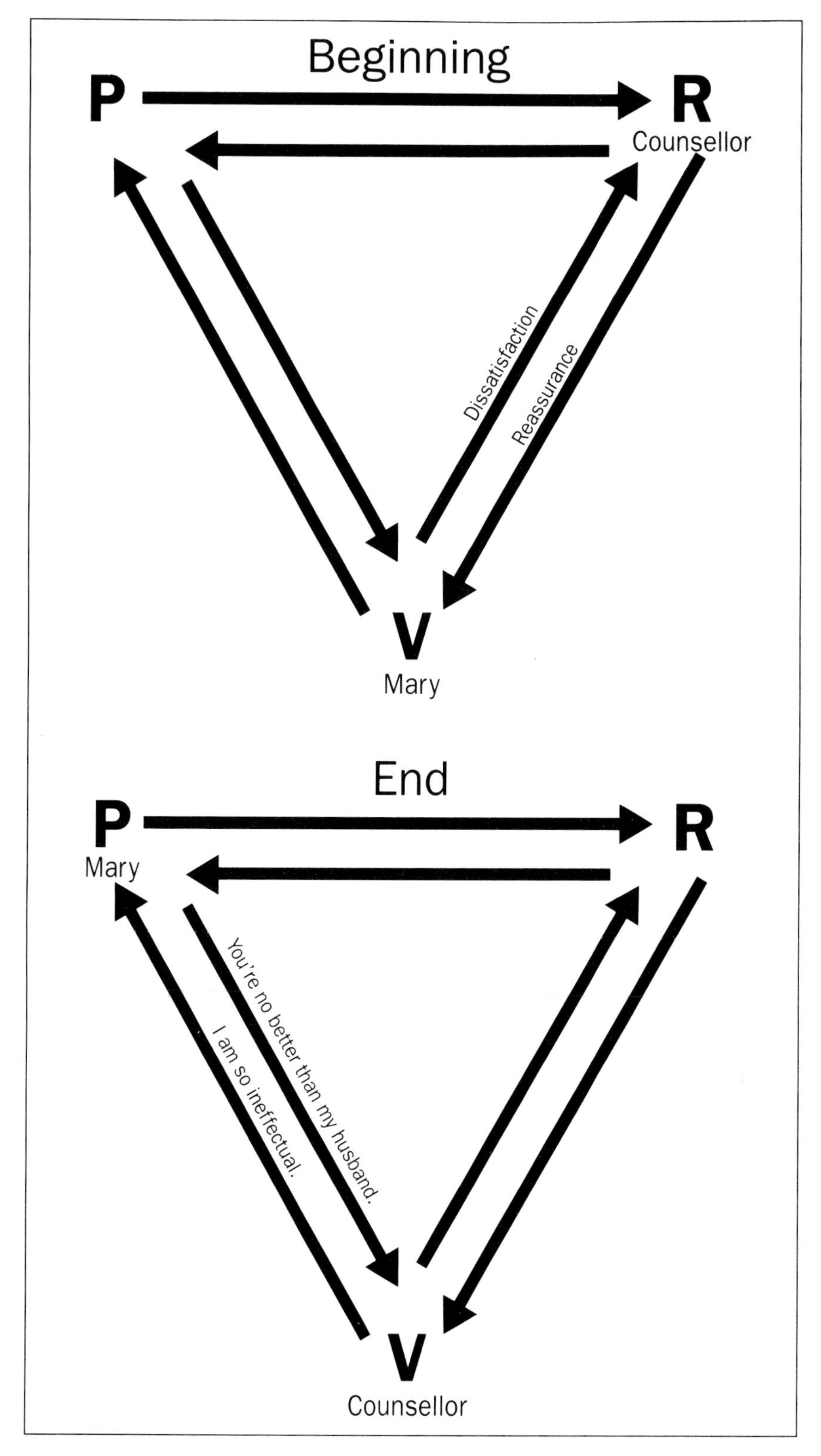

Figure 17 *Moves around the drama triangle*

which we would prefer not to play in public. An example of this degree of game is when Harry and Bill arrange to meet in the pub at 7.00pm each week. Harry consistently comes late. He always apologizes and Bill forgives him. Bill consistently suggests 7.00pm and arrives promptly himself, although it is clear that Harry is not going to get there on time. Finally, one night, Bill loses his temper and storms off. He feels abused and disrespected. Harry feels guilty but aggrieved when he later telephones Bill from the pub. He apologizes profusely but cannot understand Bill's 'over-reaction'. It takes them some months to resolve their falling out: a fact they do not mention to their friends.

A third degree game is the most serious and harmful. It ends in an irreversible situation such as a prison sentence, a divorce, a suicide or even murder. For example, a woman is frequently beaten by her husband. Her friends get to know of her situation and beg her to leave him but she always forgives him. Here is the standard Persecutor, Victim and Rescuer situation where the roles are genuine as well as part of the game in which the Victim rescues the Persecutor. However, one night, as she is preparing supper, her husband arrives home violently drunk. As he moves towards her, fists raised, she suddenly feels that she can take no more. Afterwards she cannot remember stabbing him but she supposes that she did.

Naming the Gaming

At the back of his *Games People Play*, Eric Berne lists one hundred games. This is not a fixed list; it can be added to and some in the list may be found to be substantially similar. In fact, many do not contain a switch in game role and should more correctly be referred to as 'racketeering' (Fanita English, *TAJ*, 6, 1, 1976) where two game roles are used to collect familiar strokes by complementary transactions from those roles. Some partners, for example, use racketeering as a basis for their relationship: one person always playing the Rescuer role from an Inadequate Parent mode while the other contentedly or discontentedly plays the Victim role in an Adapted Child mode. Most of the names of the games involve colloquialisms which are self-explanatory and are those words of some of Berne's patients which best sum up the essence of the game. As mentioned earlier, it is Berne's use of such 'down to earth' language that has often resulted in his work and TA being seen and rejected as being simplistic, but, as Berne says: "We prefer playing 'Ain't it awful' to 'verbalising projected anal aggression'. The former not only has a more dynamic meaning and impact, but it is actually more precise. And sometimes people get better faster in bright rooms than they do in drab ones" (E. Berne, *Beyond Games and Scripts*, ed Claude Steiner and Carmen Kerr, New York: Grove Press, 1976). Furthermore, Berne divides games into seven major categories:

1 *Life* games are often played in ordinary social situations and involve such games as 'Kick Me' and 'Now see what you made me do'. These games may colour most of a particular person's social interactions.
2 *Marital* games provide the structure for couples to remain stimulated within the relationship at those times when both parties seem unable to be straight about themselves to their partner. These include such games as 'If it weren't for you', 'Courtroom' and 'Look how hard I've tried'.
3 *Party* games are those that are played as people move from the rituals and pastimes engaged in before they 'get serious' (official and social meetings, for example) towards intimacy. We search for 'intimates' with whom our gaming strategies can *interlock* in order to create some certainty that our hungers will be met within the future, potential relationship. These games include 'Ain't it awful', 'Blemish' and 'Schlemiel'.
4 *Sexual* games develop when satisfaction of our sexual hunger is being avoided or exploited in some way. These include 'Rapo' and 'Uproar'.
5 *Underworld* games are played in particular by clients of the 'Social System' and include games such as 'Cops and Robbers' and 'Let's pull a fast one on Joey'.
6 *Consulting room* games can include all and any of the above categories. Perhaps the more prevalent counselling games would include those initiated more often by the counsellor, 'I'm only trying to help you' or 'Psychiatry (TA)', and those initiated more often by the client, 'Wooden leg' and 'Stupid'.
7 Berne hypothesizes that there are a few *good* games. They are still games because of their ulterior, exploitative and repeti-

tive nature but, in overall terms, they result in some enhancing of a situation after the switch has been made. 'Busman's holiday' and 'They'll be glad they knew me' are examples in this category.

Application

As with strokes, identifying how and to what extent clients satisfy their six hungers in their lives can be a useful way into the dissatisfactions brought into counselling. Though there is no 'right' way, or prescribed 'mix', of hunger-satisfaction, since each client will have their own individual proclivities and needs, it is often illuminating to explore the high and low satisfactions of these hungers, what may be missing, and what may be experimented with as a means for change. For example, Mary, a client who 'felt' there was something missing in her life, identified that, of the six hungers, contact-hunger and sexual hunger were by far the least satisfied in her life. She had a stimulating job through which she gained recognition, she thought her time structure was well balanced and she even had a satisfying amount of incident in her recreational hobby of hang-gliding. Though she had a sexual relationship, she recognized a lack of good contact with her partner for whom the emphasis of their sex together was orgasm. Until she learnt of her possible need for better physical contact and strokes, she had accepted that this was enough. Fortunately, her partner was willing for them to explore ways of pleasuring each other which would satisfy both sexual and contact hunger. They jointly attended a massage class, spent much more time holding and stroking each other non-sexually as well as sexually and became generally much more physical with each other.

Clearly, a similar assessment within the area of structure-hunger and the six ways of structuring time can help clients discover what is 'missing' in their lives. Are they spending enough time getting positive strokes and satisfaction through ritual exchanges, pastimes, activity and intimacy? Are they spending too much or too little time in withdrawal? Or are they attempting to meet their hungers negatively and indirectly by structuring their time in the script-bound and script-reinforcing playing of games?

What games are they playing? Which role do they take at the beginning and at the end of the games, to what degree are they playing them and how is their script reinforced by such games? These are all areas for exploration with your clients. But, having explored, how do clients stop playing games?

In answer to this last question, given that part of the definition of games is that they are played *outside Adult awareness*, by exploration, recognition and naming you are bringing them into Adult awareness. However, this does not mean the immediate cessation of game playing. Remember that games are patterns that have been repeated many times throughout our lives (often daily) and are an entrenched part of our script system (see 'The Racket System' in the next chapter). It is often only by working through our script beliefs and decisions that we are ready and willing to relinquish our most familiar games. Nonetheless, awareness is an intrinsic and important first step and, in some instances, may be enough to eliminate, transform or lessen the degree of some games. Working with clients to change any behaviour, including game playing, usually involves three stages (Petruska Clarkson, personal communication, 1981):

Hindsight

This means being aware after the event that some game has been played. This can be usefully analysed in terms of which game was being played, which roles adopted, what was being discounted, what hungers were being satisfied and which script beliefs reinforced. The game can then be looked at in terms of the options the person had as ways of avoiding future repetition of the game. What could have been said or done differently? How could that particular hunger have been satisfied more constructively (and so on)?

Midsight

At this stage, the client, now familiar with their game analysis, is also familiar with their own 'signals' that a game is being played. They may, for example, recognize their own physiological response at the point the switch is made as 'a sudden sinking feeling in my stomach' and, even at this late stage, avoid the pay-off of bad feeling they usually experience by crossing the transaction with a more Adult response. Better still, they may recognize at an earlier stage that they are playing a game as they experience themselves in their familiar role of Victim, Rescuer or Persecutor and use this knowledge to 'step outside' the drama triangle and, again, address the situation from an Adult perspective, looking at options of the moment.

Foresight

Eventually, the client becomes so familiar with their game patterns that they know how and in which situations they are likely to play them. They can pre-empt playing games by looking, in advance, at creative options for having their needs met.

In counselling, we need to become aware of our clients' game moves as they invite us to become locked into their familiar system of attracting strokes and preventing the intimate and frank exchange necessary for counselling. We also need to be aware of our own game moves towards our clients, hence the need for our ongoing supervision and personal counselling. Once you have a treatment contract with your clients, you will need to recognize and plan a counter-strategy for their game moves. Doing something, or inviting your clients to do something, *out of the predictable sequence* will interrupt the usual game pattern and may result in more direct and positive stroke fulfilment. No game can proceed if accounting replaces discounting.

With clients who have some awareness of games and a good working relationship with the counsellor, it can be effective to play the game and exaggerate the required role in order to 'tease' the client into awareness of the game. For example, a client playing 'Ain't it awful' may give an insightful laugh and move out of the game if the counsellor plays an extreme Rescuer to their Victim by saying such things as, "My word, that really is awful. In fact, I think that is the most awful story I've ever heard in my life . . . and to such a nice person too . . ." and so on. Clearly, this response should be used carefully and discriminatingly and only when such 'teasing' will be received constructively as a move out of the game and not as a Persecution.

The counsellor may also choose to play the game in order both to understand the client better, to see what the pay-off is and to what degree the client is playing games. This is most likely to be in the early stages of counselling in order to identify the game and provide useful current information that can then be analysed. The counsellor, working from Adult, can provide the client with feedback about feelings at the end of the game, what was going on at the Child level, what switches occurred, and invite similar awareness from the client. Thus, by the playing of the game, material for counselling is elicited, whether it be to then work on the game at the behavioural level of looking at options or on the script level of tracing the origins of these familiar roles and feelings. Clearly, it is important for the counsellor never to play out a third degree game with a client.

The counsellor may choose to ignore the invitation to a game to provide appropriate modelling for the client as to how not to get 'hooked' into games playing, however strong the invitation. By not playing the complementary hand and staying in Adult, the counsellor shows that the RSVP of games is not inevitable.

Exposing the game is another alternative for the counsellor. However, it is vital that this is done in an understanding and compassionate way — "This is human. This is the best way you know at present of getting something or of living" — rather than a Persecution. One way of exposing the game (or the invitation to a game) is to confront the discounting always present in games. For example, if someone playing 'Stupid' replies to a question with "I dunno", the counsellor may move them to accounting for their knowledge by saying, "And if you did know, what would you say?" which often gets a smile of recognition and a reply to the question. Similarly, grandiosity and other types of contaminations may be confronted and the game element exposed. Words like 'never', 'always' or 'impossible' can often usefully be reflected back — "What never?" — or confronted — "Wasn't there that time when you . . . ?"

Where clients are familiar with their games but are still at the hindsight or midsight stage, the exposing of the game invitations they are giving can be achieved by such questions as, "If you continue transacting in this way, how will it end?" or "What is it that you're really wanting when you do this or say this to me?" Permission to be straight about asking for needs to be met may well be served by such interventions as, "You don't have to play 'Ain't it awful', you can ask for the positive strokes you're wanting", or "Instead of persecuting, you can tell Jim just how angry you feel with him."

When a client seems really entrenched in a game and where other interventions may not be taken notice of, it may be appropriate for the counsellor to change the game or to switch roles within the game in order to heighten what is going on. For example, Samantha is again playing a game of 'If it weren't for him' (her husband). In order to emphasize the passive role she is taking and the lack of 'owning' her responsibility, the counsellor widens the game to 'Wooden Leg' by adding, "And those children of yours too and, of course, the terrible way your in-laws treat you — how on earth can you be expected to get somewhere in your life with troubles like that?" At which she begins to laugh and eventually to think. As an example of the counsellor switching roles within the game, Dave is again playing 'Do me something' — a Victim in search of a Rescuer. Rather than rescue, the counsellor chooses to compete for the Victim position by saying, "Well, I don't know what to do right now, Dave. I really think I need your help on this. I'm feeling a bit stuck. I don't know what to suggest." Dave's efforts to induce the counsellor to rescue are frustrated by this response and he soon moves into a constructive, problem-solving mode.

Exercises

Self

1 When beginning to experiment with awareness of your ways of meeting (or not) your six hungers, start by reviewing the week you have just lived. With regard to stimulus-hunger, think about or list the variety of ways you sought the following:

(a) *Visual stimulation* Perhaps it would be helpful to think of this aspect of your life in terms of (i) colour: did the environment in which you chose to spend the past seven days contain a rich variety of colours or did you mostly spend time looking at papers, books, crosswords or the kitchen? (ii) distances: how often in the past week did you give yourself the opportunity to stretch your gaze to half a mile or more? (iii) contrast of light: did you have time to use your eyes in contrasting lights — sunlight, electric light, candle-light and dull light etc? (iv) direction of gaze: do you mostly look at the world straight ahead of you or do you practise using the entire range available? (v) content: have you been aware of looking at interesting shapes, beauty, and so on? As you sit reading this book, take some minutes now to feed your eyes on some variety of colour, distance, lights and range around you.

(b) *Aural stimulation* As you remember or relive aspects of your past week, as with your use of your eyes, list or think of your awareness of the sounds that surrounded you. Do you tend to expose yourself to an overload of one type of sound, for example the radio, and have little or no response to other types such as those of nature — gurgling water, birds, insects and so on? As you read this book, a suggestion now is to stop a while and explore listening to unusual sounds, aspects of the world about you to which you do not usually expose your attention.

(c) *Tactile stimulation* How often in the past week did you let yourself touch those things in your world at which you were looking? We 'see' with our fingers, as is so well demonstrated by small children before they are socialized out of it. Can you remember the texture and temperature of the handle of your hair-brush or comb? As you sit or stand there now with this book, perhaps let your fingers feel the difference between the book's cover and its pages. Feel some of the items near you now. It will probably help to do this with your eyes closed.

(d) *Olfactory stimulation* Over this past week can you remember/resmell some of those odours which fill our world? Do you inhibit or hurt your sense of smell with the over-use of perfumes, deodorants, cigarettes, exposure to carbon dioxide fumes or the like? As you sit there reading you could experiment with smelling the arm of your shirt, blouse, jersey or the back of your own hand (this may be enhanced by licking and moistening the back of your hand first).

(e) *Gustatory stimulation* Do you remember or can you retaste any of the foods or drinks you have had over the past few days? Again review the variety of foods: have you had foods of many colours, textures, flavours and consistencies? Do you need more variety for your tastebuds, teeth and stomach?

(f) An exercise which includes stimulation of all these aspects would be to take a 'trust-walk' with a friend who leads you blindfolded to explore the garden or wherever will awaken, refresh and restimulate your hearing, sound, taste and olfactory senses. Then take the blindfold off and really look.

2 Moving on to contact-hunger, let yourself recall how often in the past week you had physical contact with other people. Look at the range you had available to you. The range might include being jam-packed against many strangers in a crowded train, shaking hands with colleagues, cradling your young baby in your arms and kissing his/her forehead, or embracing a partner. How can you improve the quality or quantity of physical contact with others?

3 With regard to recognition-hunger, at what moment in the past seven days did you feel most recognized? Was that special because of the identity of the person who did it — for example, someone you admire praised you — or was it because of the content of the stroke, or was it the way it was delivered — for example, a slow and sexy wink?

4 How have you dealt with your sexual needs in the past week — alone, with a satisfactory or unsatisfactory partner, or have you chosen to focus on some other expressive form instead, involving your spiritual growth or your creativity? How would you like this to be different?

5 Look at the way you time-structured your last week, comprising 168 hours. First, subtract the number of hours spent sleeping from the total and then apportion the remaining hours to time you spent alone (withdrawal), in rituals, chatting (pastimes), participating in some activity, playing psychological games, and being close or intimate with others. Do you feel satisfied with the results? Do you obviously need more time alone or with special others or less time working or arguing? Work out how you can change your time structure to satisfy your individual needs.

6 How did you get excited (incident hunger) over the past week? Was your life too humdrum or too exciting? What could you plan, say in the week ahead, to bring the balance you need?

7 Earlier in this book you may have identified the existential position you take up under stress: I'm OK — You're not OK; I'm not OK — You're OK; I'm not OK — You're not OK; or I'm OK — You're OK. Linked with that awareness you could now let yourself work out which position on the drama triangle is your favourite. Are you likely to be the Rescuer, taking the 'don't worry, I'll do it for you' position; or the Persecutor, taking the 'if there's something wrong I'll soon point it out' position; or the Victim, taking the 'I'm in a jam and need help out of it' position? When you have marked yours out you could let yourself know which of the six hungers this 'role' is an attempt to satisfy, albeit in a phoney, roundabout and, in the final outcome, unsatisfactory way. Perhaps by playing — and remember we all have a favourite role, and this 'playing' can be, and is usually, no fun at all — the Victim role we get some version of physical consolation, such as pats on the arm, or are recognized/seen as being 'poor old so and so'. As Rescuers we might be meeting our unmet incident needs, or as Persecutors getting to structure our time carefully. Each of us will have a different agenda in the role we most frequently adopt at the beginning of games and the role in which we end up once the switch has been made.

8 In letting yourself become more acquainted with your favourite roles and types of games, you may find it helpful to identify in which areas of your life you most often end up feeling confused, hurt or angry — is it with your partner, at work or socially? You could then find a phrase which most sums up the feeling(s) or situation you encounter time and time again. You may find something like, "I always try so hard and keep failing in that situation", or "I nearly always end up feeling trodden on or kicked in the gut by them." In essence, you will have brought to your awareness a game you use to meet some of your needs in the presence of others. They, in their turn, will be people who can use the same game for their own purposes and needs from a different role perspective. This awareness is the first step in stopping games or helping your clients so to do, as the main point, as we have already stressed, is that games are outside a person's Adult awareness.

9 Once you have an outline of the game you are playing, say 'Kick me', you can begin to hypothesize about what original needs/hungers you are trying to meet. Perhaps the repetitive moves are time-fillers or the 'kick to the gut' provides stimulus, contact and recognition, even though in a painful way. As you next identify your underlying need beneath the parody of your game, list alternative ways in which you might more positively meet your needs: for example, a very vigorous massage rather than a 'kick'.

10 See if you can discover a specific 'game package' you may be constantly playing out in service of your script. For instance, a person may begin a move towards reinforcing a script position by seeking to play, 'Gee you're wonderful, professor'. This will have intrinsic but temporary pleasure, so the person may move on to 'See how hard I'm trying' and, finally, at switch time, may develop into 'Now I've got you' or 'Kick me'.

11 Another way of bringing your usual games to awareness is to return to the exercise you did earlier in the book ('Life Script') in which you identified your early fairy story, fable, song or the like. See if you can now trace the games played in your story and, in particular, analyse the one(s) played by the character with whom you most identify.

Working with Clients

The above exercises may equally be applied to working with your clients in order to bring into awareness their hungers and how they are or are not satisfying them, the games they may be playing and the roles they may be adopting in such games. Ways of dealing with games your clients play are covered in the earlier section on application.

Chapter 9

RACKETS

'Racket' may seem a strange word to use to describe what is, in fact, an intrapsychic or internal process linked with behaviour. Eric Berne, with his penchant for colloquial terms — in this case borrowed from the criminal underworld — coined the term because of its connection with the expression 'protection racket', a system whereby a person pays in order to be allowed to preserve the relative safety of their situation. A psychological racket works in the same way. It is the means by which we protect our script. That is, we maintain the beliefs about ourselves, others and the world despite evidence to the contrary. In this way, we preserve the status quo and, in so doing, pay for it by limiting our lives.

When Berne and his colleagues first talked about a racket ('Trading Stamps', *TAB*, 3, 10, 1964) they usually described it as a feeling. This feeling may be summed up as the adapted, negative feeling which is most common to us at times when we are feeling bad about ourselves or life in general. We all have a familiar and adapted bad feeling which we tend to 'rerun' whenever we experience stress or difficulty. You have probably been in a stressful situation where you cannot understand why others are not responding with the same feeling. If your racket feeling is, for example, fear, you will respond fearfully to the situation. But others have their own racket feelings, so Bob responds to the same situation with sadness, while Judy responds with anger. These are their familiar bad feelings and they will perceive them as justifiable and appropriate to the situation just as much as you perceive your own.

Reading the above, it may seem as if we perversely choose to cling to limiting, possibly destructive attitudes and ideas, but, of course, we do not do this deliberately. Much of what we believe is not properly in our conscious awareness. It influences our lives without our realizing. There are many reasons why we might seem to want to confirm our scripts, however negative they may be. As we have already seen, scripts are decided upon under great pressure from our childhood environments and experiences. They usually seem to us to be inescapable. Furthermore, as we mentioned in Chapter 8, human beings have a great need to provide structure and order to their world and scripts fulfil this need. If we can maintain our script we may feel safer; life is more predictable and secure if we repeat the same situations again and again. At a very deep level, we can feel extremely frightened at the thought of change. A racket, therefore, is the active, internal process of feeling and thinking with external behavioural manifestations by means of which, outside our awareness, we screen out anything that does not fit our script beliefs, re-experience feelings we have had many times before and confirm for ourselves that our beliefs are true. It is the here-and-now moment by moment repetition of script experience.

Let us illustrate this with the example of John. Part of his script belief, based on his experiences as a child, is that the world is a bad place where people are out to 'get' him. When he sees someone passing his front door he feels suspicious and scared. He thinks, "I bet that man has come to check whether there's anyone in before he tries to burgle me." He spends the next few hours feeling nervous as he looks out from behind the curtain, having somehow failed to notice that the man calls at the house next door, to be greeted like the long-lost brother he actually is. In this way, John 'protects' his beliefs and feelings about others and the world and, though suspicious and scared, paradoxically, feels 'secure' by making both people and life predictable.

Mary provides another example. Her script belief is that she is unlovable and, therefore, that others do not care about her. When she receives an invitation to a party, she tells herself that no one will really want her there and ends up feeling so miserable she decides not to go. She remains at home that night, feeling unloved and uncared for. Thus, at the price of an evening of loneliness, Mary 'protects' her script beliefs about herself and others without having to risk their being confirmed or disproved by actuality.

These two examples illustrate how it is what we think and feel that determine our beliefs, not what actually happens around us. Our beliefs, in turn, create a 'frame of reference' within which we interpret what happens around us and repeat our familiar thoughts and feelings, leading to behaviour that feeds back into our frame of reference. Here is a story which further illustrates this. A man is taking a pleasant drive through the countryside away from his tense, city life where people seem to him to be purposely aggravating and unhelpful. He breathes in the clear, country air as he motors down a quiet lane, but is brought to a halt when his front tyre has a puncture. Unperturbed, he goes to the boot, gets out the spare tyre and looks for the jack. The jack is nowhere to be seen. He searches everywhere but to no avail. Just as he is beginning to feel irritated with the idiot who had forgotten to replace the jack, he notices that there is a farmhouse a few fields away, at the top of the hill, and breathes a sigh of relief that help is at hand. He sets out for the farmhouse.

As he climbs the gate to the first field, he thinks how fortuitous it was that he had the puncture here. As he strides across the field, he thinks of the farmer who will greet him at the house.

"I should think he'll be only too ready to lend a jack to me," he thinks. "Though these country folk can be a bit suspicious of strangers." As he tears his trousers on the fence to the next field, he continues pondering about the farmer.

"Despite the tear in my trousers, he'll see I'm a trustworthy and respectable man and be only too glad to help." But he adds, "I bet he lends me an old, rusty jack, just to be on the safe side." And as he trudges through the next field, getting hotter in the midday sun, he ruminates further.

"In fact, I bet he's even too mean to lend me his old, rusty jack. You know, people can be so unhelpful at times like this. They think you're scrounging and they treat you like dirt. If he did lend it to me, he'd be really resentful." Now, as he angrily climbs the gate to the farmyard, he thinks, "I've come all this way and the farmer won't appreciate the lengths I've gone to just to borrow a measly old jack. People are so thoughtless. In fact, he's the sort of man who locks all his gates just so that people will have to climb over them. I bet he's a really bad-tempered old grouch who's just too self-centred to lend anything to anyone. Well, that's how people are these days!"

Finally, puffing and shaking with anger, he arrives and knocks loudly at the farmhouse door. When the kindly farmer opens the door, he is greeted with, "You know what you can do with your rusty old jack! What makes you think I'd want it anyway?" And, leaving the dazed farmer standing in the doorway, our man stomps off down the hill, muttering something about mean, unhelpful people and how he should have called the breakdown service in the first place, though, unlike what happens in the advertisements, he probably wouldn't get a 'very nice man' anyway.

Rackets and Real Feelings

In an article entitled 'The Substitution Factor: Rackets and Real Feelings' (*TAJ*, 1, 4, 1971) Fanita English added considerably to our understanding of rackets. She describes clearly how a person might learn to choose any particular feeling as a racket. She suggests that in every household there are some feelings that are allowed and encouraged and others that are forbidden. Gradually, the child will be trained to feel the ones that seem acceptable. Different feelings may be encouraged or discouraged in girls and boys even within the same family. For instance, Bill in his highchair throws his food on the floor in a rage. His parents smile and say, "Oh, that's it, Bill, show it what for!" However, when Bill falls down, hurts himself and cries, his parents say, "Come on Bill, big boys don't cry." If this sort of thing happens often enough, Bill will learn to feel anger whenever there is a difficult or stressful situation and crush his sad feelings. He is likely to maintain a 'Be Strong' driver by substituting anger for sadness.

Sally, on the other hand, receives lots of cuddles and stroking for crying. "Come on, come and sit on daddy's knee. Daddy's little girl is sad, poor little thing," says her father. But it is a different matter when she is angry or shouts for what she wants: "That's not nice," she is told. Thus Sally learns to feel sad as a response to any difficult or stressful situation, even when anger would be more appropriate. This gender-bound scripting of feeling rackets is common. You probably know men who find it difficult to show if they are sad and several women who, when they start to be angry, seem inexplicably to dissolve into tears.

Another way of developing a racket as a substitute is through the sort of attributions we talked about in Chapter 7. Whenever

Nigel showed strong feelings as a boisterous three-year-old, his parents said, "He's tired." Often they would put him in his room for a rest. His mother often complained of being tired — and no wonder when you think of all the energy she was putting into not showing her feelings either. Nigel grew up having his experience labelled 'tired' and he began to label himself as 'tired', too, whenever he felt upset about something. Pretty soon he really started to feel tired. Now he is the man who often gets on your nerves by answering your question, "How are you?" with the inevitable, "Absolutely exhausted at the moment."

Fanita English's article therefore highlights the way racket feelings can be learnt to replace what she calls 'real' feelings. Of course, racket feelings are real, too, and hurt every bit as much. What Fanita English means is that we do not express the original feeling but cover it with a more acceptable familiar feeling. So how can we tell the difference between racket feelings and original feelings? For instance, what is the difference between real sadness and racket sadness? There are some clues. The 'real' original feeling will be associated with something that is happening (or has just happened) in the present. This may seem an obvious thing to say, but, if you think about it, you will realize how much time we spend feeling about things from the past or the future rather than feeling what is happening in the present. Racket feelings are almost always associated with a thought that links our present moment to the past or future. That thought will go something like, "Oh, I expect it will all go wrong", or "Here we go again", or "Why am I always so . . .", or "It just goes to show that . . .", or "I wish that . . .", and so on. The original or 'real' feeling is not associated with any thinking other than an awareness of an event: for example, "Tom isn't here this evening and I feel sad", or "Patrick forgot to buy the sausages and I feel cross." On the other hand, a racket feeling might be associated with thoughts such as "Tom isn't here this evening. I expect he doesn't want to be here 'cos he thinks I'm boring. I feel sad because nobody likes me"; or "Patrick forgot to buy the sausages. You can't rely on anybody to do things for you. Nobody will ever look after me. I feel cross."

In these two examples, the racket feeling is the same as the 'real' feeling, but the *quality* of the feeling is different. A 'real' feeling is usually felt quite intensely and, once expressed, dissipates as the person moves on to the next present moment of living. This is not to say that feelings only last for one moment. If somebody I love dies, I will be sad quite frequently for, perhaps, the next two years. However, this sadness will come in waves as I think about the person and how much I miss her. I will feel sad, cry for a while and then feel better for a while, until the next time. Racket sadness, however, seems to 'drizzle on' and is not relieved by its expression. Your client who comes along to the session and weeps quietly from beginning to end is very probably demonstrating racket sadness.

Another indication of a racket as opposed to a real feeling is the response of others. In the case of real feelings, witnesses feel relief as they observe these feelings being expressed, whereas, in the presence of another's racket feelings, they may well end up feeling manipulated and/or frustrated. Anger as a 'real', here-and-now feeling will be clear and probably quite brief, while racket anger will tend to be associated with ongoing resentment, bitterness, bullying or blaming. Similarly, 'real' fear will be connected with the moment and bring about action to face and deal with the danger, while racket fear may take the form of anxiety, depression or nervous exhaustion and persists for long periods.

As a rule of thumb, 'real' feelings tend to be wetter and hotter than racket feelings. When a person is experiencing real sadness, tears flow, their body temperature rises, their face colours and they often have a runny nose. Racket sadness, however, tends to leak out damply in a much cooler way. Similarly, 'real' anger tends to be hot and sweaty, with an increase in saliva, while racket anger may take the form of cold resentment devoid of any noticeable rise in temperature or wetness.

Happiness, of course, can also be a racket. If it is developed in the same way as any other racket, a person can learn to 'look on the bright side' of any situation and deny their sadness, anger or fear. Pollyanna is a classic example of someone with a happy racket. 'Real' joy is, as with the other feelings, related to something in the here and now and often manifested in heightened skin colour and other physiological signs, such as a brightening of the eyes. It also tends to be infectious. A racket happiness may seem just as loud and expansive but has an empty quality. When it is being used to 'rise above' something, it will be accompanied by many rationalizations and platitudes: for example, "Everything is for the best in the best of all possible worlds", as Pangloss assures Candide.

Again, this is not to say that what the person is feeling does not feel very real to them. The term 'racket' should not be used accusingly or pejoratively but as a means of understanding to help clients get to grips with their 'real' feelings. Clients may need to have their racket feelings heard and understood before they are ready to risk uncovering the 'real' feeling that was not allowed in their family when they were young. This, of course, is our eventual aim and a vital part of the process if the client is to get 'out of script'. It thus becomes important to ask, "Which feeling might this be replacing?" and find ways of safely encouraging and allowing that original feeling to be expressed.

Stamps

Eric Berne writes of collecting racket feelings like emotional 'trading stamps': he likens the collecting of racket feelings to the stamps given at shops or petrol stations. As with actual trading stamps, the idea is that, for a certain amount spent, a stamp is collected and stuck in a book. When the book is full it can be exchanged for a small gift, or many books full of stamps can be collected for a larger one. Berne suggests that we have a similar psychological book or collection of books. Every time something happens in life that we feel upset by, we repeat the script-associated beliefs to ourselves and collect one racket feeling to hold on to like a trading stamp. When our psychological book is full, after days, months, sometimes years of collecting, we can 'cash it in' by doing something that will really further our scripts and invariably hurt ourselves.

As in shops, where the sooner you exchange, the smaller the pay-off, so it is with psychological trading stamps. A few stamps may be traded in for an argument or a sulk, whereas volumes being cashed in may result in divorce, suicide, insanity or murder: in other words, our final script pay-off. Stamps may be cashed in with the major source of them or might be deflected onto an unsuspecting victim. For example, a husband may have collected many angry and resentful stamps from games played with his wife, yet, having had a further row with her over breakfast that day, cashes them in by having a shouting match with the traffic warden who has booked his illegally parked car.

Other examples of the saving and cashing-in of stamps include those of Henry and Dolly. Henry had a belief that to be angry was 'wrong'. When he was a child, his mother sent him to his room for hours any time he was cross or demanding. He would sit in his room feeling resentful and abused but he soon learnt to be outwardly compliant. Later in his life, at work, his boss frequently undermined his position by contradicting him in front of the staff and by making decisions over his head. Each time this happened Henry thought, "I'd better not make a fuss" and experienced his racket feeling of silent resentment. After this had happened 50 times and Henry had collected 50 stamps of smouldering resentment, he 'cashed them in' by losing his temper with his boss, shouting at him publicly and calling him abusive names. He was fired instantly, which confirmed to his own satisfaction that he should not express his anger as this leads to punishment.

Dolly's racket was guilt, which helped to support her script belief that she should never get her needs met as others' needs were more important. Thus she never asked for what she wanted from her partner. This meant that she rarely got to choose the film they saw, the food they ate, the furniture they sat on, and so on. Each time she put up with something she did not want, she felt a moment's crossness but then felt guilty for being so mean and selfish. After a year of collecting guilt stamps she was ready to 'cash in'. In her case, it was for a depression.

Clearly, there are many different rackets and many different ways of 'cashing in'. For one person it may be having a row, for another, a sulk and for another an anxiety attack. A really big 'cash in' could be leaving a relationship or getting ill or even committing suicide. Again, it is important to remember that we do not do this deliberately and consciously. Our drive to confirm our scripts is not in our awareness. The task of counselling is to bring into awareness the means by which we may be maintaining our script, our racket feelings and the stamps we may be collecting, in order that we may make more autonomous and life-enhancing decisions.

The Racket System

Richard Erskine and Marilyn Zalcman developed a way of understanding how people maintain their rackets in an article entitled '*The Racket System*' (*TAJ*, 9, 1, 1979). We have made additions to Erskine and Zalcman's original theory which are included in Figure 18. This illustrates in diagrammatic form the way in which a person, in script, enters into a self-reinforcing, closed system of beliefs, feelings, perception and behaviour.

On the left of the Figure are listed the beliefs and decisions formed in childhood and at later, stressful moments in life. At the bottom of this column is written 'Repressed feelings/needs'; we think that it may also be a whole experience that is repressed, including thoughts, feelings, needs and actions. The arrowed line shows the self-reinforcing nature of this part of the system, the beliefs maintaining the repression and vice versa. As a result of these beliefs, a person thinks, feels and behaves in a particular way at any moment, shown in the central column as observable behaviour, reported internal experience (feeling and sensation) and scripty fantasies (of what will happen). From this position, the person is likely to bring about a real or imagined repetition of the original experiences which caused them to take on these beliefs in the first place. But even if the person does not have the reinforcing experience, they can achieve the same effect by remembering all the times in the past when they did. These 'reinforcing memories', including those misinterpreted by discounting, are shown in the right-hand column. The arrowed line around the diagram shows the self-perpetuating nature of the whole system.

So when does a person get into their racket system? We are not, after all, in script all the time. However, when something happens in our lives which touches on the 'forbidden area' of denied feelings, thoughts or memories, we can escape from the forbidden into the familiar and permissible area of the racket. We can then stay in our racket system until something happens to interrupt or interfere with it. In counselling we are, more awarely, aiming to interrupt or interfere with our clients' racket systems in order to help them out of their script. We will now, in the section on application, look at ways in which a counsellor

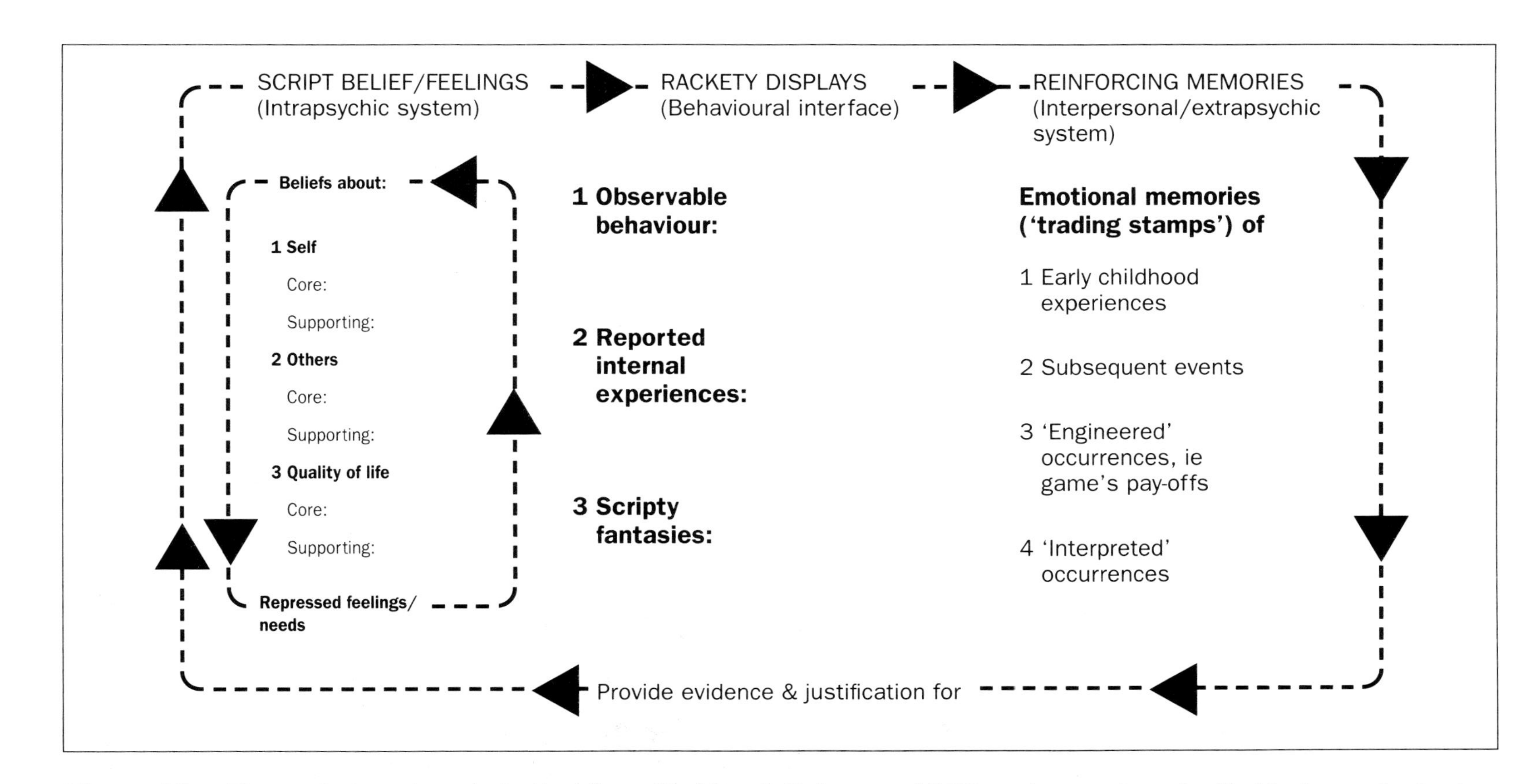

Figure 18 *The racket system (adapted from Erskine & Zalcman, 1979 and reproduced with kind permission).*

can help a client interrupt their racket system in order to live more autonomously.

Application

One of the encouraging aspects of working with a client's racket system is that changing just one element of the system can have an effect upon the whole. Consequently, there are many ways of intervening in the here and now, at any point in the racket system, which can invite clients to change the way they are experiencing their lives. This may bring about a change in their script. However, to ensure script change, a person must actually change the beliefs about self, others and the world and, for this, deeper work is sometimes necessary. This section firstly outlines some ways of intervening; in the second part, some work with a client will be described in which the origins of the racket are explored as a means to more profound and lasting change.

As you start to be aware of your own and your clients' rackets, you will notice that different people tend to emphasize different parts of the system. For instance, when they are 'in their racket', some people are most aware of the emotion they are feeling, while some are more aware of fantasizing about what is going to happen or remembering similar past occasions. Some experience most strongly a body sensation like a sinking feeling in the pit of their stomachs. Others are first alerted to their racket by noticing a typical behaviour, such as pacing, increased smoking, withdrawing and so on. Different people respond to different approaches.

Often the most useful place in the racket system to intervene is not that which is currently the focus of the client's attention. Those who are most aware of their emotion — sadness, anger and so on — may be best helped by being asked to think about what their feeling means and what they need to do about it. Those who are aware of a bodily sensation or a typical behaviour can be invited to plan ahead. What outcome do they want? How will they be when they have achieved it? How can they get there? People whose racket is experienced chiefly in thinking about what has happened may be most usefully invited to be aware of their feelings. For example, they may be asked to breathe deeply, notice their sensations within their body and to express the feelings of which they become aware. Those who are fantasizing about the future may need to be brought back to the present. For example, they may be asked what they are doing right now to bring about the situation and what they could be doing differently. They may be asked to sit differently or act differently at that moment. For example, the floor-pacing client may be invited to lie down on the floor and think from this position. We invite the reader to be flexible in finding ways of intervening, always remembering that the system can be altered by a change at any point. With all clients, it can be useful to draw up a simplified version of their racket system with them in order to better understand their contribution to the present circumstances and invite them to choose which element they could, in the first instance, most easily change.

The following extract shows a counsellor working with a client to explore her racket system and underlying feeling. Some 'traceback' work, where the racket is traced back to its childhood roots was also undertaken.

Liz withdraws in the group and loses touch with the other group members. When questioned about this, she says that she thinks everyone is cross with her and she does not want to take up their time. Everyone reassures her that they are not cross and ask her why she thought such a thing. She explains that earlier on she had made a comment to which no one responded. She had immediately started to tell herself that she had 'taken too much time' and that they were cross. She cheered up at the reassurance and started to join in again. However, this was not an isolated incident. Liz's withdrawal became a regular occurrence. Liz began to understand that it was a pattern. The triggering factor was her not receiving attention when she wanted it. Very often, this was when she had not said or done anything to indicate that she needed something. The counsellor began to explore Liz's internal process with her by gentle questioning.

COUNSELLOR: What are you saying to yourself when you withdraw like that? (Here, though the counsellor could have started to work with any part of the system, she first explores the thought process behind the rackety display.)

LIZ: I'm not thinking anything . . . yes, I'm saying, "I'm not here."
COUNSELLOR: And how do you feel saying that?
LIZ: I'm empty, I'm . . . I'm not feeling anything. Somewhere over there is someone that feels (*points away from her*) but I don't. I'm empty. I don't feel anything. I'm dead inside (*her eyes fill with tears as she contacts, quite spontaneously, a repressed underlying feeling*).
COUNSELLOR: You look as if you are very sad about feeling dead inside.
LIZ: I am . . . (*cries*).
COUNSELLOR: You're hurting so much that you have to go dead inside.

Liz cries for some time. She is already interrupting her racket system by expressing her really sad feelings and not replacing them with numb withdrawal. It is only later that the counsellor continues the exploration.

COUNSELLOR: So we have learned that, when you withdraw like that and think that people are cross with you, you are really deeply sad.
LIZ: Yes, I'm astonished. I thought I was empty and out of touch but I realize that I really hurt when I think people want me to shut up.
COUNSELLOR: You think they want to shut you up?
LIZ: Yes, I'm a nuisance. I'm in the way.
COUNSELLOR: So you believe you're in the way. And what about other people, what do you believe about them? (Exploring beliefs.)
LIZ (*long pause; eventually, in a monotone*): They hate me. They wish I wasn't here. I take up too much time.
COUNSELLOR: So what do you decide to do when you're thinking all that?
LIZ: Nothing. I do nothing. I just go dead.
COUNSELLOR: Have you ever felt like that before — dead and empty, not looking at anyone, not moving? Do you remember being like that when you were little? (Exploring the reinforcing memories.)
LIZ: (*stares at counsellor*): I've always been dead.
COUNSELLOR: But when you made yourself go dead . . . can you remember times . . . ?
LIZ: So often . . . so often . . . I say to my mother . . . but she is so . . . she says, "Get out . . . shut up", she says, "Oh, go away . . . do just go away" and she is so sad . . . I say, "I'm sorry mummy, what can I do for you? I want you to be happy (*Liz cries*) . . . What can I do?" (*cries deeply*).

COUNSELLOR: And mummy?

LIZ: She's angry. She says, "I SAID GO AWAY DIDN'T I . . . I TOLD YOU . . . GO AWAY!" (*she begins to tremble, then stops*). So I go.

COUNSELLOR: You go. You leave quiet and empty.

LIZ: That's right. That's what I did. That's what I do now. When I want something, when I want someone to like me, I just switch off and think that I shouldn't be here or, sort of, that I'm not here. And I go dead and empty.

COUNSELLOR: When really you feel very sad.

LIZ: Yes.

COUNSELLOR: So do you think you could do something different in those moments when you start to switch off?

LIZ: (*pause*): Well, I guess I could speak to someone.

COUNSELLOR: That would be different. Will you do it? (*Contracting for behavioural change.*)

LIZ: Yes, I will.

Clearly there is more work to be done. Liz needs not only to speak to someone, but also to ask for the attention she needs, to believe that she is wanted and that her needs are welcomed by others. She also needs to change the decision to 'go dead and empty' which she made at the time of her mother telling her to go away. However, this was a very important piece of work for her and the start of major changes in her relationships. At a subsequent session, Liz drew up her racket system (*see Figure 19*). The work linked directly to an analysis of her script matrix where the injunction 'Don't exist' from her mother produced the decision by Liz to act as if she was dead in terms of attracting attention and seeming acceptable.

The concept of stamps was not used in the work with Liz but was very useful to another group member. Henry was asked by a group member if he would give her a lift home. He agreed. On several further occasions, he gave group members lifts and seemed happy to do so. One day, one of the members was asking for contributions to buy a birthday cake for Chris. Henry refused and, rather pointedly, said that he spent all his money on petrol. The group confronted him immediately on being mean. Henry became self-righteous and the group ended on an uncomfortable note. The following week, the counsellor explored with Henry his agreeing to give people lifts. He revealed that he actually appreciated the time on his own after groups but that his script belief

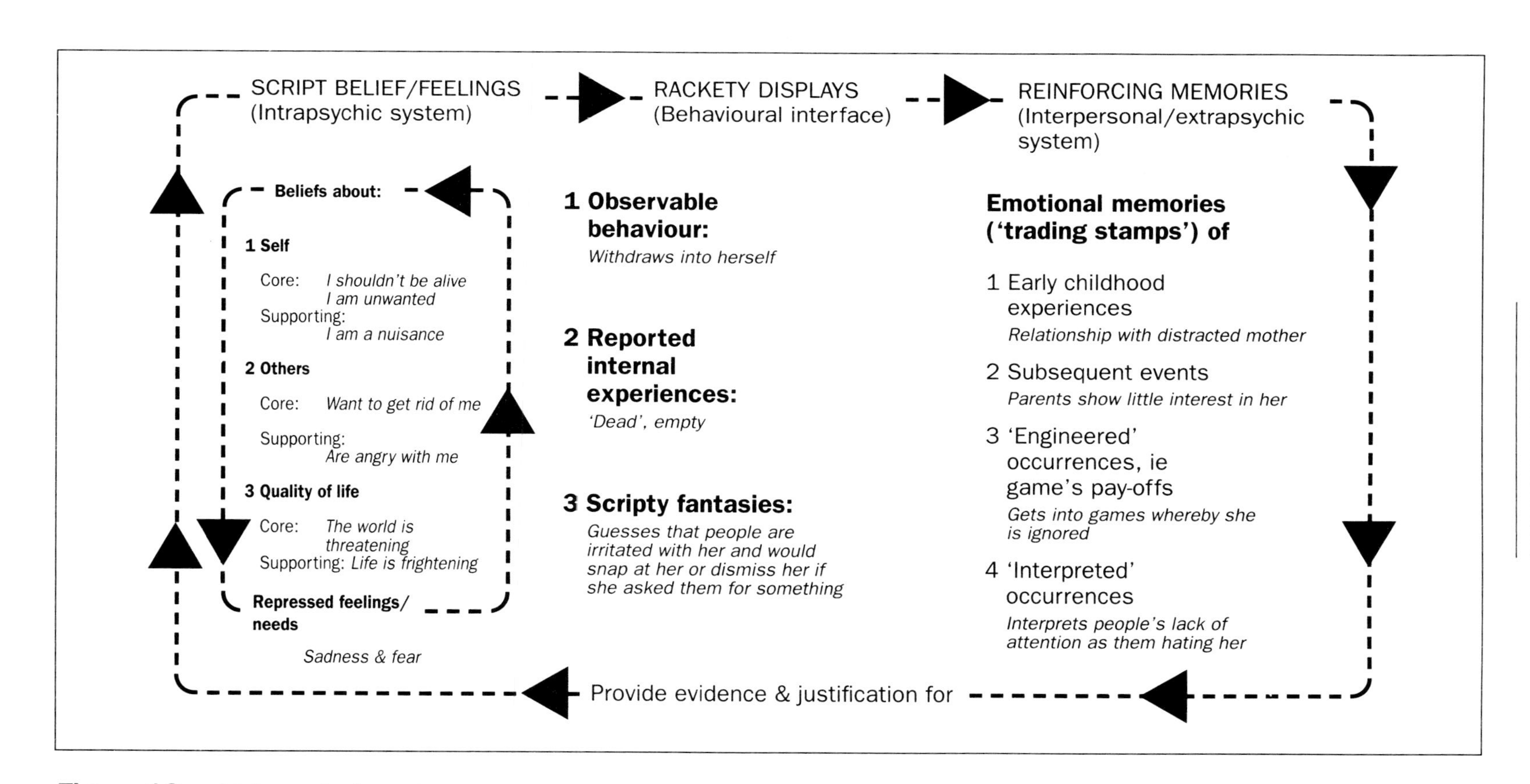

Figure 19 *Liz's racket system*

was that he should not have something for himself when others had wants too. His mother always told him to 'Please People'. So he had agreed to the lifts and, each time he had done so, he stuck a 'Hard done by' stamp in his book and ignored his own need. After the tenth (or the twentieth or the thirtieth) time, Henry had filled a complete martyr's book of stamps and felt justified in being 'mean' with his money. This realization helped to identify the work Henry needed to do in the group on his scripted 'Please People' behaviour and its associated thoughts and feelings, particularly concerning the origins of such behaviour in relation to his mother. However, a mid-term solution was agreed upon in the group by Henry contracting to take time to think whether he really wanted to do something for someone else before responding.

Exercises

Self

1 Stamps: remember a time recently when you held back from saying what you were really thinking and feeling.
What would you have liked to say?
What did you say or do instead?
What reason did you give yourself?
What feeling did you have as you told that reason to yourself?
After you have collected enough of those feelings, how might you 'cash in' your stamps?
How might you justify doing it?
Now work out what you need to do differently to avoid 'stamp collecting'.

2 Racket feelings: imagine that you are looking for a gift for a close friend whose birthday is tomorrow. You have been searching for some time for that special gift. In the window of a shop that sells hand-made articles, you see something you know this friend would really enjoy. It is expensive but, as it is such a perfect gift for your friend, you decide to go ahead with the purchase. The shop has just shut, but you have so fallen in love with this birthday gift that you are determined to return tomorrow, as soon as the shop opens, which will still leave time for you to wrap it and take it to your friend's birthday breakfast. The next day, there you are hurrying to the shop and, now you have arrived, you go inside. The article is still there. You lift it up to see it more closely. On the back of the article is a label saying, 'Sold to M. Smith. To be collected'.

How do you feel? Do you have another feeling later? If you had two feelings, it is likely that the first was your natural, spontaneous feeling that was quickly repressed and replaced by the substitute racket feeling. Was this second feeling one that you commonly have when things 'go wrong'? Notice how this feeling is accompanied by thoughts and bodily sensations. What do you say to yourself about life, about other people, about yourself? What do you do?

Using the blank racket system framework (Figure 20) at the end of this chapter, see how much of your racket system you can complete from the answers to these questions.

3 Further exploring: remember a recent time when you believed the worst about yourself and imagine yourself there. How do you experience your racket most vividly — by a feeling, thoughts, bodily sensations, actions or fantasies? Go through the following questions and let yourself know which you find the most useful when you are in this racket:

(a) What are you doing to contribute to the situation?
(b) What could you do differently?
(c) How are you feeling (emotions)?
(d) What do you need?
(e) How could you get what you need?
(f) What has been helpful to you in the past that you could use now?

Working with Clients

1 Explain to your client what a stamp is and invite them to do the first exercise above.

2 Choose a client you have known for some time. What is their racket feeling? (You will probably be able to answer this quite easily.) If it is appropriate, next time they are feeling it, invite them to remember when they have had the feeling before. Can they remember feeling it when they were a child? What are they

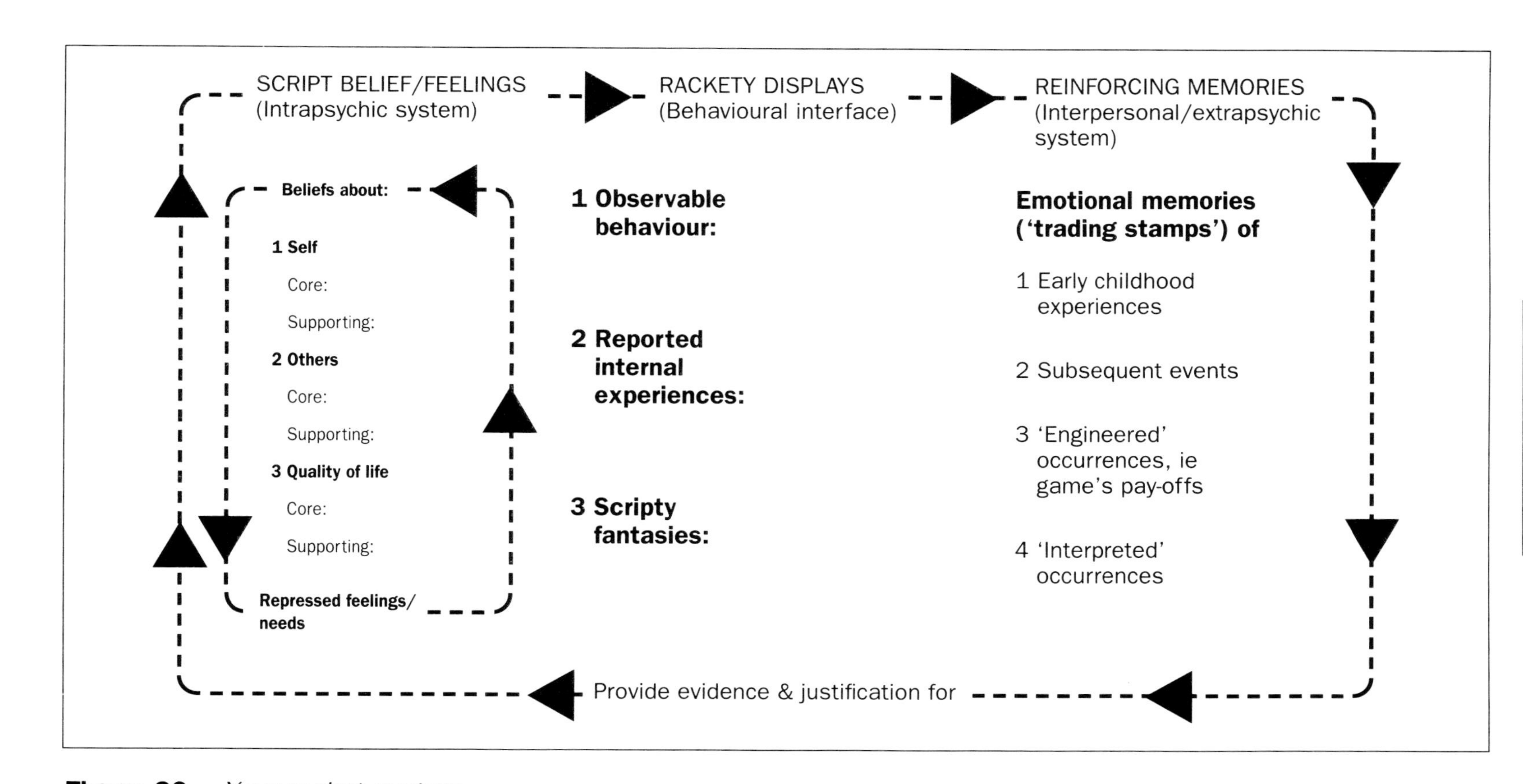

Figure 20 *Your racket system*

believing about themselves when they are feeling it? Gently ask the questions that will elicit the racket system and help the client to notice the reinforcing nature of the pattern. It may be appropriate to draw a diagram of the racket system.

3 Experiment with the list of questions in the third exercise above.

Chapter 10

ASSESSMENT AND THE PROCESS OF CHANGE

In this chapter we will first look at general considerations of the assessment of clients' problems and the process of change and then, more specifically, address these issues from a TA perspective. When clients come for counselling, they usually present problems which fall into three main categories of disturbance: confusion, conflict or deficit (Clarkson & Gilbert, in '*Individual Therapy*', 1990, ed Windy Dryden). Though one of these may be the major focus for the client, it is common for all three to be playing a part in the client's problems. It is important, however, to make an assessment of where, how and to what extent these areas of disturbance are prevalent in order to help the client make changes. Let us take a general look at these areas.

Confusion

Many clients present themselves for counselling not really knowing what it is they are wanting from the situation. They may know that something is not right or clear in their lives, or areas of their lives, but have little idea of what the problem is or where or how to begin to address the situation. They may also be distressed and additionally disturbed by having only a vague notion as to why this may be so.

"I have a good job, a loving relationship, a busy social life but I feel so unhappy and I don't understand it," says one client. "I know there's something wrong but I don't know what it is," says another. Many clients are confused by the strong feelings they are experiencing: intense anger that seems unrelated to the situations they are describing, deep sadness that seems to have no cause, or severe anxiety that is way out of proportion to current events. Others are disturbed by recurring thoughts which seem muddled and out of step with the actuality of their everyday lives.

For these confused clients, the area of focus, at least in the initial stages of counselling, will be understanding and clarifying their states of confusion. In general terms, this may be accomplished through forming a trusting relationship with the client, providing a safe and protective environment, accepting the client's thoughts and feelings and allowing time and space for exploration.

Conflict

There are two types of conflict which clients may present, interpersonal and intrapsychic, closely interlinked. Here clients often know of the dilemmas, arguments, pros and cons of the situation but seem stuck and indecisive within themselves or 'locked' in unresolved conflict with another person.

"I want to stop having rows with Jim about the house being untidy but I keep nagging him like I'm his mother," says one client. "I know I can keep a job longer than I have but I seem to screw it up every time," says another. Many clients are aware of conflicting internal dialogues that go on relentlessly without resolution: "I wanted to meet her on Saturday but then I thought she'd think I was too pushy. I told myself she might like me being more spontaneous but then I thought I'd better wait and see 'cos she might feel it as a pressure. But then again . . ."; or "Part of me felt so sad but another part kept telling me to pull myself together."

These clients are experiencing either internal or external conflict (or both) and, clearly, the area of focus in the counselling situation will need to be a resolution of these conflicts. These conflicts, the feelings and thoughts that lie beneath them and the purpose they may be playing in the client's life will need to be explored. Two chair techniques either to role-play the external dialogue or to clarify the internal dialogue may be useful here in bringing about a resolution.

Deficit

Many clients may appear to be neither confused nor experiencing conflict yet still have difficulty in making changes in their lives. They often know what they want and they are motivated to do something about getting it, but somehow they are not succeeding. "I want to make more friends and I've been socializing much more, yet I don't seem to make friends easily," says one client. "I've decided to be more assertive at work but I'm just being ignored," says another. Something is missing. That 'something' may be information, skills, experience or permission. It may be that the person wanting to make more friends is lacking social skills, the experience of being close to people and the permission to do so. The person wanting to be more assertive may be lacking in information as to how people can be assertive without being aggressive, as well as the skills and experience of assertive behaviour. Somewhere in their development there has been a lack of adequate teaching, modelling, permission or direct experience of the intended new behaviour. Counselling can be used to make up for this deficiency. To this end the relationship between client and counsellor can be used reparatively by providing a protective environment for exploration and experimentation, skill learning, the provision of information and permission to do things differently.

We believe that, indirectly, all three areas of confusion, conflict and deficit — which, of course, interweave and overlap — are likely to be generally addressed by the counselling relationship. For many people, the opportunity to talk, to be listened to and to be respected by another is, in itself, likely to facilitate clarity, resolve conflicts and be a reparative experience. However, making a more direct and aware assessment of client needs in these three areas provides a useful diagnostic map for facilitating the work with clients and can assist greatly in the process of change. While it is not always the case, and movement across and between these areas may often be important and necessary, it is generally likely that work will proceed from addressing confusion, through conflict resolution to repairing the deficit. Many clients, for example, avoid experiencing their internal conflicts by becoming confused. It is only in the course of addressing the confusion that these conflicts may be clarified and worked through. It is often in the working through of these conflicts that the developmental deficits may come to light. TA provides specific concepts which enhance the assessment and process of change in these three areas. It is to these concepts we now turn.

TA and Confusion

TA provides us with two important concepts of confusion. One is the confusion brought about by the interference with one ego state by another, the working through of which is known as *decontamination*. The second is the confusion often found within the Child ego state, the working through of which is known as *deconfusion*. Decontamination usually precedes deconfusion.

Decontamination

To write of a process called decontamination clearly implies that there must be a state of contamination. This may not seem a very pleasant description but it certainly captures the essence of the concept. Contamination suggests impurity caused by mixing something with something else, and this is certainly what is meant when the term is applied to ego states. It is the Adult ego state which can be contaminated by either the Parent or Child ego states or, more often than not, both. When Introjected Parent feelings, thoughts and behaviours interfere with the purity of the Adult ego state, we speak of a Parent contamination. When Archaic Child feelings, thoughts and behaviours interfere with the purity of the Adult ego state, we speak of a Child contamination. If both sets of historic ego states are interfering simultaneously, we speak of a double contamination. Figure 21 shows these types of contamination, the overlapping of the circles indicating the contaminated areas.

When we transact internally or externally from a contamination, we consider ourselves to be in Adult. We may make statements about ourselves or others *as if* they were Adult statements. For example, Jane's first words to her counsellor are, "I'm sorry I'm late. I really am incapable of doing anything right." Jane, at

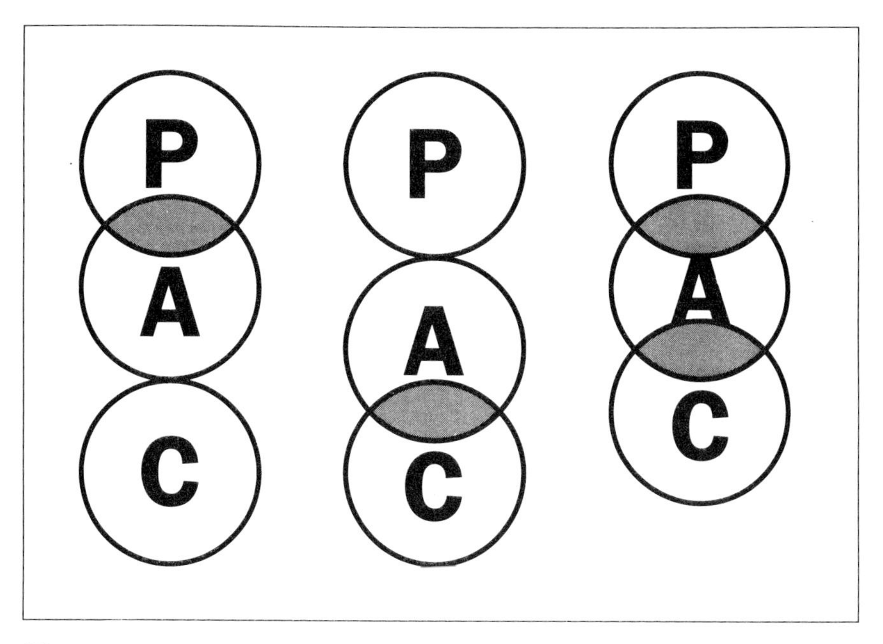

Figure 21 *Contaminations*

this moment, believes this to be a statement of fact. It is as if this is a here-and-now reality of the Adult ego state. Jane is, in this instance, responding from a Child contamination of the Adult. Tom begins his counselling session by saying, "I know counselling's a bit of a self-indulgence . . .", as if this is an indisputable statement of reality. In fact, this is a Parent contamination of his Adult ego state. He is repeating the exact words of his father.

We all have contaminations. We are unaware that some of what we are saying, thinking, believing, doing or feeling comes from historic ego states. Many of our prejudices towards other people or about certain aspects of life have their roots within the area of Parent–Adult contamination. For example:

- All red-heads are quick-tempered.
- The [particular race or minority group] are stupid.
- Keep yourself to yourself.
- Never trust a stranger.

Many of our delusions and fantasies about ourselves, others and the world have their roots in the area of Child–Adult contamination. For example:

- I'm really hopeless.
- I'll never come to any good.
- I can't stop drinking.
- I just get in people's way.
- Spiders/cars/people/ are frightening.

Understandably, when clients first come to counselling, they experience their feelings, thoughts and behaviours as, "This is me. This is who I am. This is my experience of myself." And, of course, this is still true. Historic ego states are a part of ourselves, but while they remain outside our awareness they are likely to be interfering with our effective Adult functioning in ways which may not be useful or appropriate, supporting and reinforcing our script beliefs.

The process of decontamination is the identifying and separating out of historic ego states from the Adult ego state in order to allow for more autonomous choice. As we have mentioned in previous chapters, we may actively choose to draw upon historic ego states in order to enhance the present moment. While the present moment is contaminated by historic experiences perceived as Adult reality, this is not possible.

Application

Decontamination is clearly an ongoing process which begins in the early stages of counselling and continues throughout and beyond it. Once clients are familiar with their ego states, the concept of contaminations can help to make sense of their experience of themselves, their beliefs, thoughts, feelings and behaviours. Gradually, by identification of particular ego states and their contents (structural analysis), the clients separate what is here-and-now reality from what is there-and-then experience masquerading as a current reality. Many opinions, for example about themselves, others and the world, are discovered to be outdated and outmoded beliefs from childhood. Similarly, behaviours and feelings seen to be inevitable responses to current situations are rightfully placed back in history where they belong. Script, game and racket analysis are all part of the process of decontamination. In the course of following the exercises with clients at the end of previous chapters, you have largely been facilitating your clients in the process of decontamination.

Let us take a closer look at the way in which decontamination may be facilitated in counselling. Hal is having problems in his relationship with Julie.

HAL: I'm just so anxious all the time. I want to do things right.
COUNSELLOR: What does it mean to 'do things right'?
HAL: Well, to please her, I suppose. You know, to do things for her.
COUNSELLOR: And if you do things for her to please her, what then?
HAL: Then she should know that I love her and she'll be happy.
COUNSELLOR: It sounds like you're saying that loving is doing things to please people?
HAL: Yes, that's right. But it's not working.
COUNSELLOR: Have you had other experiences of trying so hard to please someone and it not working?
HAL: Oh yes, I could never get it right for my mother.
COUNSELLOR: In what way?
HAL: I tried so hard to make her happy. She was always wanting me to do things for her. She said that I didn't love her if I didn't.
COUNSELLOR: You must have felt very anxious a lot of the time trying to prove to her that you loved her.
HAL: I can't remember not feeling anxious around her. She was never satisfied so I had to go on trying. And I kept failing and getting more and more anxious.
COUNSELLOR: So you tried and tried to please her. In the process you denied your own needs and, what's more, it didn't even work and you felt you failed.
(*Pause*)
HAL: I shouldn't have had to prove that I loved her. I shouldn't have had to keep doing things for her. That's not love.
COUNSELLOR: Will you say that again?
HAL: That's not love! No, that's not love at all. Love is being with someone and enjoying them. It's giving and taking, not just one or the other. I don't have to keep on proving that I love Julie. It gets in the way of our really being together.

In this example, in a few transactions, the counsellor has helped Hal to separate the historic ego states from Hal's Adult. The belief that love is doing things for someone else belongs both to the Introjected Parent, his mother who told him this, and his Archaic

Child, the young boy who believed her and acted upon this belief in a constant state of anxiety. Hal's Adult is now more able to make his own decisions about what constitutes love in a relationship and can choose to act upon these decisions.

Deconfusion

In the process of deconfusion we are dealing mainly with the Child ego state. The term 'deconfusion' means allowing the Child to express the feelings, thoughts and behaviours that were not allowed expression during childhood and sorting out the confusions brought about by such repression. This process is made clearer after decontamination has been achieved, so that the Child ego state can be easily distinguished from the Adult ego state. However, there may be times when deconfusion must come first as it may be an essential part of the decontamination. For instance, in the example in the section on application after this, Deborah needs to feel and express her Child's anxiety about upsetting her mother before she can fully understand just how she has been quashing her anger.

As we have already seen in previous chapters, our current transactions, strokes, games and rackets are all influenced by our childhood experiences. These experiences and the decisions arrived at through them are replayed from our Child ego state, most often with the reinforcement of our Introjected Parent. These decisions about ourselves, others and the world were the best possible decisions we could make within the influence of our particular childhood environment. In the course of deconfusion, we are encouraging our clients to get in touch with and express their feelings, wants and needs freed from their dysfunctional beliefs. In this sense, deconfusion can be seen as expressive decontamination within the Child ego state, the original needs having been contaminated by interference from the childhood environment.

The expression of repressed feelings — catharsis — and the discharge of these feelings through bodily expression, such as weeping, shouting, hitting cushions, wringing towels, allowing the body to shake and so on, is an accepted and important part of TA clinical practice for many practitioners.

Application

The application of the process of deconfusion is here illustrated by the example of Deborah, who entered counselling because she had been depressed for as long as she could remember. She had no close friends and spent most of her time working or reading. In the course of counselling, Deborah talked about her childhood experiences in a middle-class family where feelings were frowned upon and not expressed by anyone except her mother, who suffered from 'nerves'. If Deborah expressed her feelings in any way, including her delight or excitement, her mother would get upset and take to her bed, whilst her father responded to her with a rejecting, stony silence. Deborah spent most of her time alone in her room in the safe company of books on technology — she still does. As a grown-up, Deborah, not suprisingly, held many Parent and Child-contaminated beliefs about feelings. She saw no place for feelings: they were selfish, upsetting for others and could only lead to rejection. By ego state identification and structural analysis, Deborah separated her Parent and Child ego states with regard to feelings from her Adult. We join her now in a session where she is showing her first signs of anger.

DEBORAH: I don't seem to be getting anywhere. All this explanation doesn't seem to help. I'm just as depressed as I ever was.
COUNSELLOR: Right now, you seem to be angry about that.
DEBORAH: No, no, I'm just depressed by it all. There's no point feeling angry.
COUNSELLOR: What would happen if you felt angry?
DEBORAH: I don't know. You might get upset.
COUNSELLOR: And then I might take to my bed and leave you?
DEBORAH: No, I know you wouldn't do that.
COUNSELLOR: But it sounds like your Child might think that. It's exactly what your mother did. How about letting her speak directly to your mother? Would you be willing to do that?
DEBORAH: I don't see much point but I'll talk to her.
COUNSELLOR: OK, just let yourself be little and talk to her (*indicates mother's symbolic presence on an empty chair nearby*).
DEBORAH (*to mother*): I don't know what I want to say to you. You never listen to me anyway. You're always talking about your 'nerves'.

COUNSELLOR: And when she's talking about her 'nerves'?

DEBORAH (*to mother*): There's no room for me.

COUNSELLOR: Tell her how you feel about that.

DEBORAH (*to mother*): I don't feel anything 'cos I know you'll get upset.

COUNSELLOR: So you're responsible for how she feels? Do you want to say that to her?

DEBORAH (*to mother*): No, I can't be responsible for how you feel. I'm a child. You're the grown-up. You're meant to look after me!

COUNSELLOR: And you feel . . .?

DEBORAH (*to mother*): I feel angry. Yes, that's right, I don't feel depressed, I feel angry! I feel so angry that you can't deal with your own feelings, let alone mine. You just put yourself to bed. You go away from me and leave me alone as if I didn't exist. (*Shouting*) Well, I do exist, do you hear, and I do have feelings! You may not like them but that's your problem, not mine. I exist in my own right and I have feelings!

COUNSELLOR: And just because she gets upset is no reason for you not to show your feelings.

DEBORAH (*to mother*): No, I look after you by getting depressed. That's how I stop feeling things. Well, that's not right. You should be looking after me and my feelings. I have feelings and I need to show them. And I've just done it!

COUNSELLOR: Yes, you did, and very forcibly too.

In this example, the process of deconfusion begins with decontamination. The counsellor recognizes that Deborah's perception of the current situation is contaminated by her Child ego state. By separating the Child ego state from the Adult (though Deborah initially replays her childhood experience with, for example, "I don't feel anything 'cos I know you'll get upset") she eventually expresses her anger, which has been 'depressed' for so long. Further, she realizes that her depression of her feelings has been protecting her mother to the detriment of her own natural expression of feelings, that, in effect, she has been 'parenting' her own mother, whose responsibility it was to look after her. Deborah is likely to need to do more decontamination and deconfusion work in the area of feelings and their expression, notably in respect of her father too. She may then be prepared to make a new decision which will liberate her feelings and bring an end to her depression. This process of *redecision* will be addressed in the next section, 'TA and Conflict' (page 168).

Exercises

If you have been following the exercises in previous chapters, you have already started the process of decontamination. You may be well aware of many thoughts, beliefs, feelings and behaviours which you had previously assumed to be appropriate responses to here-and-now reality but which you are now questioning and identifying as intrusions from Parent or Child ego states. You may have noticed that, more often than not, there is a double contamination. For example, a contaminating Parent belief that 'pride comes before a fall' may be echoed by a contaminating Child belief that, "If I express my excitement at my success, I'll regret it", and the consequent suppression of excitement and self-stroking. The following exercises may be used to further identify such contaminations and help to decontaminate your Adult ego state.

Self

DECONTAMINATION

1 Write down a list of the sayings and mottoes that were common in your family. Add to this list the things your family said about money, sex, sexuality, race, work, duty and relationships.

2 Consider the possibility that some of these may be contaminations. Go through the list and pick out any of these beliefs or attitudes that you may have taken in as statements of fact.

3 Against each of these, write down the concomitant, contaminating Child beliefs. You will probably find that many of the contaminating Parent beliefs are prefixed by 'You' and the contaminating Child beliefs prefixed by 'I'. For example, "You can't trust foreigners" (contaminating Parent) and "I cannot trust anyone from another country" (contaminating Child).

4 Work through these contaminations, question their validity from your Adult ego state, and decontaminate by writing down your reality-based beliefs. For example, you might write, "Big boys/girls don't cry" (contaminating Parent) with "I'm a baby if I show my sadness" (contaminating Child), followed by "Children and grown-ups feel sad at times. Sadness is an appropriate and healthy response to loss or hurt. I can cry and get comfort in healthy ways" (reality-based belief).

DECONFUSION

The process of deconfusion belongs within the safety of the counselling relationship and setting. Becoming aware of thoughts and feelings not expressed in childhood requires the sensitivity, support, permission and protection of the skilled counsellor who can act as an important ally to the Child. Therefore we do not suggest exercises for you to do for yourself but recommend you work through this process with your own counsellor or psychotherapist.

Working with Clients

DECONTAMINATION

The task of the counsellor in the ongoing process of decontamination with clients is to listen for those thoughts, feelings and behaviours which the client passes off as Adult statements of fact, inevitable feeling responses or inevitable behaviour responses, and to question and challenge them. This does not mean aggressive challenging or persecution but that the counsellor, from an empathetic position, assists the client in reassessing those aspects of their script which are interfering in the here and now. Such questioning may include:

1 Questioning the origins in order to distinguish and separate the three ego states.
Who was it that used to talk of you so dismissively?
Did any of your family behave in this way under stress?
How was anger dealt with in your family?
Did your parents believe that hard work is the most important thing in life?
So what happened if you got excited as a child?

2 Questioning the validity.
Is it true that people always reject you for showing your sadness?
If others are scared, do you label them as weak too?
Can you think of an alternative way you might have responded?
Have you had experiences of being close to people who didn't take advantage of you?
How do you know that others are thinking that about you?

3 Using previously shared information to decontaminate the present (confrontation).

That's what your father used to say about you.
This sounds similar to the way you felt when your mother scolded you.
You were spontaneous when you played with your brother and sister.
I remember how angry you said you were when your teacher was absent.
That's how your father behaved when things went wrong.

4 Three chair work: using one chair for each of the three ego states, the client moves from one to the other expressing the thoughts, feelings or behaviours that may be contaminating the Adult. For example, the client may explore the belief that they are 'stupid' by moving from chair to chair and separating historic experiences from the current reality. On the Parent chair, they may recall direct remarks and attributions of being 'stupid' from parents. On the Child chair, they may get in touch with their decisions that they were stupid when they experienced themselves as failing. On the Adult chair, they may update this belief by acknowledging their skills, intelligence, creativity and success in their grown-up life.

DECONFUSION

As already indicated, the task of the counsellor in the process of deconfusion is to provide a safe and protective environment which will enable the Child of the client to express feelings, thoughts and behaviours that were not allowed expression in childhood. This can only be done within the developing relationship between counsellor and client where the genuineness, understanding and potency of the counsellor is responded to with the confidence and trust of the client. There are no techniques to be employed here. We are talking of a developing relationship between one person and another. However, once this relationship has been established, as shown in the example of Deborah, the technique of setting up a dialogue between the Child ego state of the client and the relevant Introjected Parent is a useful vehicle for deconfusion. In this process, the client may be encouraged to express those feelings, thoughts or behaviours which have been repressed, reach an understanding of the decisions they made as children and discover how and why they are maintaining these decisions. This is likely to clarify the internal conflicts and lead to the necessary, new decisions to which we now turn.

TA and Conflict

We have mentioned earlier that conflict may be seen externally as between two people or internally as between two parts of the person. Of course, there will always be conflicts between people as part of healthy disagreement. However, when two people seem to be locked in a pattern of conflict that is familiar to one or both parties, we believe that this is usually the external manifestation of an internal conflict. In previous examples we have seen that the perceived opposition of a partner can be the result of the projection of a Parent ego state onto the other. In such cases, the conflict that really needs to be resolved is that between this person's internal Parent and their Child ego states. It is this internal conflict which we will now address.

Impasse Theory

Bob and Mary Goulding, well known for their book *Changing Lives Through Redecision Therapy* (New York: Brunner/Mazel, 1979), use the word 'impasse' (from Gestalt therapy) to describe the stuck point a person reaches when two ego states are at odds with each other. As we described in Chapter 7, under the pressure of the environment and of parental messages, children will make decisions about who they are and how to live their lives. Sometimes these decisions will involve a wholehearted acceptance of the parental command — for instance, to work hard and achieve academic success. Sometimes the decision will be a compromise based upon the balance between an injunction and the natural drive to grow and blossom. An example is that of the child who perceives father's attitude to contain a 'Don't succeed' messsage. Naturally, the child also has the instinct to grow and achieve. To satisfy both sides the child may decide to be successful only in areas that do not compete with or threaten father's self-esteem. An example with even more serious possible consequences involves the child who takes in a 'Don't exist' message.

Here the compromise between obedience and survival may be the child's decision to be depressed and thus 'dead' in affect.

As long as these decisions remain firm, and the person manages to function relatively adequately, they experience no sense of conflict. But, as a result of having worked through decontamination in counselling or as a result of life changes, the person begins to experience natural needs and feelings which go against the creative script compromise. As the Adult strengthens, the person allows the needs of the Child to become stronger and, as a result, the inner tussle becomes more vivid. Ultimately, the impasse needs to be broken and a new, healthy decision made. This is called a *redecision*. This requires accounting for the actual needs and feelings of the Child, tempering them only with that part of Parental influence which is appropriate to the current life of the person. There are three types of impasse.

Type 1 Impasse

The conflict here is between the Child ego state and the Parent ego state. The Child is expressing natural needs and is met by a social level message from the Parent which tells them how they ought to be behaving. For example, experimentation, noise and sensitivity are respectively thwarted by such 'advice' as "It's important to do your best", "They won't like you if you're noisy", "Be a brave little soldier". These are social level messages (drivers) about how to get on in life by being strong or pleasing or hardworking and the like. The Child responds to these demands either by compliance or by rebellion, both of which are adaptations and neglect the natural wants and feelings of the child.

Type 2 Impasse

The second type of impasse also involves conflict between the Child and the Parent. However, here we are dealing with the psychological level messages, the injunctions in their purest form, which were incorporated by the child at an earlier age than the Type 1. Though these messages will, for the most part, have been communicated non-verbally, they may have been embedded, or be perceived to have been embedded, in such statements as "Get out of my sight!" (Don't exist), "Oh, don't be such a baby" (Don't be a child) or "Stop whining!" (Don't feel). In exploring these impasses, a client may experience their parents as being all-pervasively prohibiting, even though, for the parent, their attitude may have been specifically contextual. In these cases, it is the client's experience that is important. They incorporated these messages at a time when their parents seemed very powerful giants to them and they did not have enough information to understand the total context of, for instance, mother's stressful day or father's tendency to get angry when he was worried. Type 2 impasses are likely to have a much stronger attendant feeling component both in the Parental message and in the Child response of desolation, rage or powerlessness. Fear of annihilation, harm or abandonment is often attendant upon the perceived injunction.

Type 3 Impasse

The third type of impasse is different from the first two types of impasse in that the emerging conflict is between two parts of the Child ego state. Using the concept of functional modes the impasse within the Archaic Child ego state is between a part of the Adapted Child and a part of the Natural Child. The Natural Child has been so successfully repressed by adapted behaviour that certain spontaneous emotions and sensations seem almost non-existent.

Type 3 impasses are the result of decisions made at so young an age and so deep a level that it seems strange to call them decisions. They are made at a time when our powers of thinking and reasoning are not yet developed. This means that the 'decision' is more of a bodily assumption of a state of being that anything that can be said to have been decided upon. Many of our bodily holding patterns originate from the time of such 'decisions'. There is often no awareness of any particular instruction or message from outside the self. There is simply a feeling of having 'always been this way'. For example, a client told his counsellor, "I just don't really feel very much, I never have. I've always been quiet." We might guess that this person may have had a mother who, for some reason, needed her child to suppress natural feelings. This could have been due to her own discomfort with feelings, her level of stress at the time, or many other reasons. In fact, the person who said these things was born in a cellar in 1956 in Hungary to a mother who was in the process of escaping during the revolution. From the moment he was born, it was imperative that he remain quiet. But this man was not aware of any internal pressure. He merely experienced himself as a quiet, even person.

Application

Even when the processes of decontamination and deconfusion have been worked through and the impasses exposed, making new decisions in the Child ego state (redecision) is not likely to be immediate or necessarily achieved in a one-off 'piece of work'. These decisions have been made to please parents, to maximize strokes and, in some instances, to ensure survival. The Child, even with reassurance from the integrated Adult, may be tentative in relinquishing such once-important and necessary decisions. It may take time, several repetitions and explorations, much strengthening of the Adult to provide the nurturing that was not available at the time and a great deal of practising of the new behaviours resulting from the redecision before permanent change is achieved.

We will go on to describe some techniques which may be used to facilitate your client in making redecisions. However, it is our experience that clients can and do make many redecisions in the course of counselling without such techniques. In the safety and trust of the relationship between counsellor and client, developed over time, clients may make new and far-reaching decisions, not only in their Adult ego state but also in their Child ego state. For example, a client with an injunction not to feel may express their feelings and have them received with acceptance and understanding by the counsellor. Over time, the client's Child learns to trust that it is safe and appropriate to express feelings within and outside the counselling setting and makes a redecision to this effect.

Redecision Technique

Whichever impasse is being worked through, the redecision technique requires the client to be in one of their Child ego states while simultaneously being aware of the resources now available in their Adult ego state.

Both Type 1 and Type 2 impasses can be approached in the same way. In practice, we find that, after a Type 1 impasse has been resolved, a Type 2 is usually revealed. (Frequently, a Type 3 will also emerge but, needing a different approach, this will be addressed later.) Broadly speaking, the stages of impasse resolution for these two types involve:

1 an experience of dissatisfaction in the present;
2 the identification of the impasse;
3 the location of the impasse in childhood;
4 the re-experiencing of the childhood situation, including the painful feelings and the decision made, with all its implications — the benefits, the drawbacks and so on;
5 the awareness by the Child that he or she can survive changing the decision and 'defying' the Parent;
6 the redecision;
7 the integration of the new decision into the client's current life.

This simplified list of stages seems to imply that profound change can take place according to a format. Of course, this is not the case. In practice, as we have emphasized, the redecision process will be subtle and take place over time, possibly many months, with much retracing of steps in order more fully to explore, understand and bring about the redecision. Nonetheless, while bearing the above in mind, it may be useful to take a closer look at these stages with the example of Hal from the previous section.

An experience of dissatisfaction in the present: Hal, you may remember, is constantly anxious in his relationship with Julie because he is wanting to please her all the time. This is his current dissatisfaction.

The identification of the impasse: In the course of decontamination and deconfusion, Hal has identified a Type 1 impasse between his Parent and Child ego states. His Parent, the mother he has introjected, is saying, "Please me to show you love me." His compliant Child — which up to now has said, "I'll do my best to please you because then you'll know I love you and you'll be happy" — is now saying, "I don't want to have to please you all the time." This created the impasse at the root of his dissatisfaction in his relationship with Julie. Recognizing the impasse, Hal decides to stop automatically pleasing others and to look to his own needs. This, however, is not enough. He experiences a great deal of discomfort with this new behaviour and a 'pull' to revert to the old pattern, despite his resolve. Now, a Type 2 impasse is identified, which involves the Parental injunction, "Don't have your own wants and needs", which until now has been complied with by Hal's repression of such wants and needs in the service of pleasing others. Tentatively, through his fear of abandonment if he should defy his mother, Hal is now saying, "I have my own wants and needs." Here we see why just the Adult recognition of this fact, reached during decontamination, may not be enough to ensure a redecision. Similarly, working through the Type 1 impasse and making a new decision to please himself rather than others, Hal still felt anxious as he came up against the Type 2 impasse where he is instructed not to have his own needs and wants and is threatened with abandonment if he does. Both impasses will need resolution if Hal is to make the changes he wants to make.

The location of the impasse in childhood: Tracing back, from his current situation into the past, Hal remembers the persistent messages from his mother to please her, to do things for her, to look after her, messages which were a continual and all-pervasive 'background' in his childhood experience, and recalls his constant anxiety in his attempts to please her. These are the components of the Type 1 impasse. Further, he recalls a particular scene at an early stage in which his mother had asked him to 'be a good little boy for mummy' by staying in and sitting with her rather than going out to play with the neighbouring children. Hal remembers feeling torn between his excitement at the thought of playing with the children and his anxiety at the thought of his mother's disapproval. He had hesitated and this mere hesitation had been responded to with a look from his mother. Though she said nothing, this look, to Hal, held sadness — for which he felt responsible — and rage. When the counsellor asked Hal what words he associated with the look, he said, "If you desert me, you'll regret it. You dare to leave me and I'll leave you, you bad boy." As he spoke of it in the session, he could feel his stomach churning with anxiety. In the event, all excitement gone, he sat with his mother, whose face now showed benign contentment. These are the components of the Type 2 impasse through which Hal will need to work.

The re-experiencing of the childhood situation: In recounting the childhood scene, Hal is already re-experiencing many cf the feelings he had at the time. The counsellor invites him to 'go into' the scene and 'be there'. Talking now in the present tense rather than the past, Hal more fully 'relives' his experience of the scene: his feeling torn, his excitement and his anxiety, indeed his terror, at his mother's almost demonic look, his acquiescence and the dissipation of anxiety once his mother seemed content. He ends by saying, "I feel better now. My mother looks happy. I know she will not go away. I think of the children playing outside but quickly push aside my feelings because I mustn't be a bad boy."

The awareness that the Child can survive changing the decision and 'defying' the parent: While still in the Child ego state, the client has access to the grown-up self which can draw upon qualities, skills, information and experiences that could assist the Child in changing the present experience of the past situation. The counsellor helps Hal to be aware of this in the following extract.

COUNSELLOR: What do you want to say to your mother when she looks at you like that?

HAL (*to mother*): I'm really scared. I want to do what I want but I'm scared you'll leave me.

COUNSELLOR: That is scary for a little boy. If you call upon the resources of grown-up Hal, what can you experience differently as little Hal?

HAL: I don't feel so scared.

COUNSELLOR: And if she leaves you?

HAL (*to mother*): I know I don't need you around. You can look at me like that as much as you like but I know I don't need you. You don't give me much anyway. It's me that does all the giving, all the pleasing.

COUNSELLOR: And if you don't please her?

HAL (*to mother*): That's too bad. If I go on trying to please you, I'll be doing it forever! And for what? I've got nothing to be scared of now. I've got nothing to lose.

The redecision: You can probably 'feel' that Hal is about to make a redecision in the above extract. Indeed, it is often the case that, having reached this point of harnessing the grown-up resources in aid of the Child, the Child moves into the redecision spontaneously. Notice that Hal has stayed in his Child ego state throughout this work. The counsellor has spoken to the Child and not invited him out of this ego state, knowing that his redecision needs to be in Child if it is to be effective. Here the counsellor facilitates Hal in making a clear and positive statement of his new decision.

COUNSELLOR: So you could go on for ever pleasing her?

HAL (*to mother*): Yes. If I stay scared of you leaving me I could go on and on. But I'm not scared. I'm really not scared any more. I'm not going to get in a state trying to please you any more. I've done enough of that.

COUNSELLOR: Will you tell her how you're going to be different?

HAL (*to mother*): I'm going to take notice of what I need and what I want, mum.

COUNSELLOR: And when you've taken notice?

HAL: I'll do something about them. I don't have to hesitate any more. I don't have to feel anxious. I know I can still give to people but I can take as well.

COUNSELLOR: So will you tell her what you'll do about your needs and wants?

HAL (*to mother*): I'll look after my needs and wants and I'll tell people what they are and get them met.

COUNSELLOR: And how do you feel when you say that?

HAL: I feel really released. I feel really clear and relaxed.

COUNSELLOR: You look it, too! Your whole body looks relaxed. Is there anything more you want to say to your mother?

HAL: No, I've finished with her. I'm going to go out to play!

COUNSELLOR: That's great!

Notice that the counsellor checks whether Hal has more to say to his mother at the end of the work. This reduces the possibility of Hal coming out of his Child ego state with a feeling of incompleteness, which may dilute the redecision.

After spending any length of time in a Child ego state, it is vital that, before the end of the session or at the end of work, the client is brought back to the here and now and does not leave, for example, to drive home while still in Child. It is therefore important that the redecision work be scheduled within the session with enough time left towards the end for reconnecting with Adult. This process may be assisted by the counsellor asking the client the time, day of the week and date, what they are planning to do in the week following or by asking them to focus on something in the room and describe it. For example:

COUNSELLOR: Do you think you're fully back in the present?
HAL: Well, almost.
COUNSELLOR: What time is it now?
HAL (*looks at watch*): It's quarter to four.
COUNSELLOR: OK, so a few more minutes before you go. Is it your day to pick up Julie?
HAL: Yes, she's on an early shift, so I'll meet her from work. I'm really looking forward to seeing her.
COUNSELLOR: Any plans for the evening?
HAL: I think a meal in town and then a disco. Two grown-ups going out to play!
COUNSELLOR: Sounds like fun. Enjoy yourself.

The integration of the new decision into the client's current life: However potent the redecision made by the client may seem, if it is to be effective and enduring it will need to be integrated both cognitively and behaviourally into the client's life. The counsellor may have done considerable preparatory cognitive work with the client prior to the redecision, for example, structural, script or racket analysis, or a combination of all three, as well as addressing the desired behavioural outcome. It is still important to discuss and integrate the client's understanding of what they have been dealing with in the redecision process and to find ways of practising and monitoring the resultant new behaviours.

In Hal's case, the counsellor reviewed with him the script matrix they had drawn up earlier. Hal identified the social level and psychological level messages from his mother — "Please me to show you love me" and "Don't have your own needs and wants", respectively — and the early decision to please her (and everyone) in order not to be abandoned which involved negating his own needs and wants. He understood his early need to make such a decision but was now quite clear about his new decision to look after his own needs and wants and get those needs and wants met. For Hal, the most important area in which to practise and monitor his new behaviour was in his relationship with Julie. He contracted to be aware of his needs and wants in his relationship with her and to tell her what they were as he became aware of them. Each week he would monitor his change in behaviour with his counsellor. Once this new behaviour was established and Julie was responding positively to the new 'give and take' of their relationship, Hal contracted to practise this new behaviour with friends and colleagues too.

In this last stage, the client often needs a great deal of ongoing support and encouragement from the counsellor. It is important to remember this and not just move on to something else or relax the focus. After the sometimes dramatic and intense experience of the redecision work, putting new decisions into effect in the outside world can be difficult. Clients are sometimes disappointed by the response of their friends to their new behaviour and need to bear in mind that friends may have a lot of investment in them remaining the way they were — after all, they chose them as friends because of how they were. In Hal's case, he discovered that some of his friends did not like him asking for things for himself. They had been quite happy with him pleasing them all the time. Over time, he let go of such one-sided friendships and maintained those old friendships that could accept the new reciprocity. He then made new and mutually supportive friendships.

Let us now take a look at the Type 3 impasse, which is approached differently from the other two. The difference of approach is necessary because, as we said before, the 'decision' is made at such a young age and/or at such a deep organismic level that there is no conscious memory of adapting to an outside force or repressing a natural part of the self. On the contrary, the Adapted Child mode of the Archaic Child is experienced as the 'real me'. Sometimes, as the counselling progresses, clients come to realize that there may be ways of being which would enhance their lives, even though they seem currently unavailable to them. For example, Jemma, whose contract is to enjoy her life, would love to be 'the sort of person who goes out dancing'. Her friends go dancing and have great fun but Jemma says she has always been shy and awkward and does not go out dancing. In this case, there were a number of stages in the redecision which were spread over many weeks. The first was for Jemma to heighten her sense of being aware of the conflict between two parts of her self. She did this by enacting a conversation between these two parts — one shy, the other fun-loving and gregarious. In this initial dialogue, Jemma's sense of her real self came from her Adapted Child mode, 'I'm shy'. The other polarity felt very odd and unlikely to her. However, it was the beginning of a possibility.

It is interesting to notice the difference between this Type 3 impasse dialogue and those involved with a Type 2 impasse, in which one side, the Parent, tends to be telling the other, the Child, what he or she should or should not be doing or must not do — 'You must be brave' or 'Don't have your feelings' and so on. With the third type, both sides are talking about 'I', as in 'I don't feel' and 'I want to feel'. Of course, as we explained earlier, the taking of a decision at this level will originally have been in response to outside pressure. No baby is conceived in the womb feeling shy or unfeeling, depressed or unlovable. Somehow they take on that attitude as a result of their early experience, but so early (even in the womb) that there is no conscious awareness of a Parental message. Therefore the conflict is between the Free and the Adapted Child modes of the Archaic Child.

Shortly after Jemma had begun to identify this Type 3 impasse she had a dream about a tigress walking lithely along the streets of a village. There were people about who watched, not in fear but in awe, as the tigress began to run, low to the ground and effortlessly, through the village and into the country, covering the distance at amazing speed. When she explored this dream, Jemma identified the tigress as a powerful and passionate being who could do as she liked. She also stressed how striking she was, and that the villagers had thought her beautiful and arresting. At the suggestion that the tigress in her dream was in fact a part of herself she giggled and blushed, then dismissed the idea. However, minutes later the counsellor noticed that Jemma was stretching on her chair with slow, sensuous and 'cat-like' movements. She chose not to comment at that moment but knew that she was purposely smiling and nodding in admiration in the hope that she was duly playing her part of a villager.

As the weeks went by, the counsellor noticed some tiny and subtle changes in Jemma's manner and appearance. She was dressing in a livelier way. She talked with more vigour. She changed her hairstyle — a sure sign of a change of mind. The counsellor commented on these changes from time to time and

Jemma acknowledged them. Then she dreamed about the tigress again, this time playing with other animals in a park. At the following counselling session Jemma agreed to explore the dream by talking as if she was the tigress. On this occasion — feeling protected somewhat by the symbolism — she threw herself into the part, saying, "I am handsome and impressive. I am playing with the other animals. They like being with me. My skin is beautiful and I am proud of it." This time, in response to the suggestion that the tigress was a part of herself she giggled but her eyes sparkled and she did not disagree. At about this time, Jemma was becoming increasingly aware of the negative and destructive things she repeatedly said to herself (injunctions) about her abilities, whether people would like her and what would happen if she 'put herself forward'. She did some Type 2 impasse work in which she began to understand that, whenever she started to do something, she would say to herself, "You won't be able to do this", then immediately feel hesitant and foolish. Jemma had been the youngest in the family, and she realized that besides her parents her siblings too would have said those sorts of things to her.

Meanwhile, the work at the Type 3 impasse level was continuing. One day Jemma reported another dream about walking on a beach with a little girl who was splashing and paddling in the waves. She cried as she recounted the dream. She said she felt both happy and sad. Then she did another 'two chair dialogue' between the Free and Adapted Child modes of her Archaic Child. From her Adapted Child she spoke about how much safer she felt staying on the sand: the waves could be dangerous and in any case she was 'shy'. She did not like a lot of noise and mess and wetness. She liked calm and staying at home with a book. Her Free Child, from the heady heights of the waves, replied, "But I love to play — I love to splash and get wet and laugh and dance in the waves" and then exclaimed, "I want to dance with my friends." In her Adapted Child, Jemma wept again and said, "But what about me?" She felt as if, having discovered a new part of her, she would have to lose the 'me' she knew. A negotiation started between the two 'selves', aided by the Adult, in which a compromise was reached. Jemma decided that she did not need to be shy any more but she could be quiet sometimes and she could certainly make sure she was safe. However, she could also be boisterous, beautiful, noisy, exciting and fun to be with. And most especially, she could dance.

After this, the changes that had been gradually happening over the last weeks and months began to be more evident. Jemma first joined a dancing class. Then she joined a club. Then she and some workmates started going out regularly to have fun and dance. Jemma, initially, said she felt a little awkward at these gatherings, but she got into the swing of them surprisingly quickly. Recently, she and a friend started going to flamenco dancing classes. It was the counsellor's turn to say to herself, "I think I might like to become as zippy as that!"

We would like to stress that the work outlined above in relation to the Type 3 impasse is not intended to suggest a format for resolving this type of impasse. We believe that there is no such format. The different 'pieces' that Jemma brought to the counselling situation and worked through show the way that the impasse unfolded for her. Everyone is different. The example is given merely to illustrate one approach that can be taken. However, the true resolution of any Type 3 impasse is less a result of TA and more a result of the counselling relationship in which the counsellor seeks to know, value and accept the client in their entirety and thus invites the client to do the same for themselves. It was in Jemma's willingness to see, to understand and to embrace that split-off part of herself that the healing lay.

Exercises

Self

1 Imagine a situation that you faced recently when a difficult decision had to be made, a situation where it was not easy but you eventually decided what to do. Close your eyes and feel yourself there at that difficult time before you made the decision. Think about the dilemma. Feel the discomfort. Now imagine your mother standing on one side of you and your father on the other. (If you were not brought up by your mother and father, choose two people who were around when you were about seven.) What advice does your mother have for you? What advice does your father have for you? Listen carefully to the voices you hear internally.

Now remember what in fact you did decide to do. Did you follow your mother's advice or your father's, or did you make a compromise between them? Perhaps you made an autonomous decision based on here-and-now information. Whichever you did, it is likely that in that difficult situation you would have been facing an impasse and the exercise could have 'thrown' up some social-level messages that highlight a Type 1 impasse.

2 Stop reading now and listen to the voices you hear internally. Listen carefully. It could be that you are having some Adult opinions about what you are reading. However, along with those opinions, there may be a series of introjected messages in your Parent ego state. Are they about what you are reading or about you? If you pay close attention you may easily become aware of a Parental message undermining you. These internal voices may be reproaching you for all the things you have not done. They may be telling you that reading books is not going to help *you* become a counsellor because . . ., they may be telling you that you are stupid and will not remember all this or they may be reminding you that your friend has not called and maybe she does not like you any more. If you cannot hear any voices, that is fine. Breathe in and out and be aware of how you are fully in the here and now. If you can hear internal voices, congratulate yourself on your fine awareness, and tell the voice you are not going to listen any more. If you feel anxious, depressed or hopeless at that thought, you may have reached a Type 2 impasse. You may want to take it to your own counsellor.

3 Put two chairs or cushions opposite each other. Sit on one side and say "I am . . .", followed by an attribution that you have carried all your life that you know is somewhat limiting. (Examples: I am quiet, noisy, clumsy, late, dirty, hysterical, bad, slow, speedy, polite, confident, fearful, and so on.) Reel off a few "I ams" to get into the frame of mind of letting yourself know yourself. Then choose one "I am . . ." that still causes discomfort for you. As you say the adjective, let yourself sit and hold your body in a way that suits the word, a way with which you are familiar. Exaggerate a little. Let your voice tone reflect the word. Be aware of how you feel 'being' that word.

Now switch onto the opposite cushion. Choose the word that is the complete opposite of your attribution. Say "I am . . ." whatever that opposite is. For example, where you said, "I am cowardly", now experiment with "I am brave". Change your body position so that it reflects the new word. Change your voice tone. How do you feel? It may feel very strange indeed. Would you *like* it to be true of you? If not, move off the chair. If, however, you would like to get to know that part of you, you could research ways of building up such an attribute. You may begin dreaming about it, both as daydreams and at night.

Working with Clients

1 Next time your client talks about part of them feeling like this and part like that, invite them to explore those two parts, talking from one side and then from the other. This could be done using two chairs. It can also be done without moving but just mentally exploring the two parts. Some people literally use their hands to denote the two sides, speaking as if now on the one hand, now on the other.

Encourage the client to explore fully the thoughts and feelings of each side. Notice if one side says, "You are" or "You should" instead of "I am". Sometimes, even when it is a Parent message, the person says "I". However, you may notice from the tone of voice a critical, scornful or disapproving attitude. On these occasions you can invite the person to say "You" instead. Later, the client may be able to identify who was the original sender of the message. This should be quite easy if it is a first type impasse message as the words used will probably be the same or similar to the parent or teacher who used them first. If it is a second type impasse message, it may be harder because parents do not usually actually say the things we say to ourselves — we perceive and experience them that way.

Also many people feel loyal to parents and do not want to let themselves know how they have been hurt: perhaps, as a small child, they even preferred to believe themselves 'bad' and therefore deserving of ill-treatment rather than face the frightening implications of seeing their desperately needed parent as cruel. It may take some time before clients gradually allow themselves to understand themselves and what happened to them. During this time the counsellor can help the process and give permission for such growth by their accepting attitude of I'm OK — You're OK.

2 If a client is talking in an animated fashion about something and then seems to interrupt their flow with a 'but', invite them to explore what happened in that interruption, and what message was being repeated. Highlight the impasse with an enactment of their earlier experience. Invite the client to identify patterns in the way they interrupt themselves.

3 If the client talks about a current situation in which they have repeatedly behaved in a way that has left them feeling 'bad', experiment with going through the steps for making a re-decision which were outlined in the application section. Remember that they do not all have to be achieved on the same day, and sometimes the working through of a major impasse can take weeks, months or even years.

TA and Deficit

The word 'deficit' is used in this context to mean some lack of necessary experience — or lack of appropriate timing of that experience — within our development as human beings. An analogy can be made between our development from conception to death and a traveller's journey. Before undertaking a significant journey, various plans need to be thought through. En route, stock needs to be taken of progress. The end of the journey requires anticipation and new journeys require forward planning. So it is with the upbringing of children: their needs warrant anticipation and forethought. Without these, key foundation stones are missed or mislaid, so that many later difficulties may emerge.

Another requirement prior to setting off on a voyage is that of packing. If you set off without certain essential things, as soon as a need for them occurs, for example your passport at passport control or payment for a train ticket, then you have to interrupt your journey to find a way of regaining or replacing the missing item(s). This may mean retracing your steps and returning home to find what is wanted. It may mean waiting where you are until someone can forward the needed thing(s) or it may mean going through the procedure of replacing or borrowing the item(s). Whichever of these alternatives is used, what is common to all of them is that the journey cannot be continued as originally meant until these missing pieces are available to the journeyer. So it is in our journey of life. If factors conducive to normal development — physical, psychological and social — are missing, then the human organism may not be able to continue growing to its full capacity. With certain physical deprivations, for example severe malnutrition, these may result in permanent impairment of the person's body. From a TA perspective, psychosocial deficits, even very severe ones, can be compensated for and creatively adjusted to at later times in the process of development, depending on the circumstances in the life of the person concerned.

At this point it is worth highlighting some of the essential needs that should be met at crucial times in the psychosocial development of a human being. If these developmental tasks are not fulfilled at the time, the person concerned will attempt to fill those gaps as adequately as possible given their present circumstances. Sometimes they may find unusual — and often deemed 'sick' — ways of compensating for the deficit. If the needs of earlier stages remain unmet, the needs of later stages will be detrimentally affected. Pam Levin (*Becoming the Way We Are*, Berkeley, CA: Pam Levin, 1974) a transactional analyst who has written widely on the cycles of human development, extrapolates six major developmental themes linked with specific periods in the growing child's lifetime. We here describe these stages, with additional material from the psychoanalyst Erik Erikson (*Childhood and Society*, New York: Norton, 1950/63).

The Stage of Being

In this first developmental stage, from birth — and, we would suggest, from conception — to approximately the age of six months, the infant requires from the world (and at this stage the world's major representative is usually mother) recognition, support and affirmation for being alive. This is communicated by the way in which the infant's body and bodily needs are handled, how the caretakers socially relate to the child and each other, and how they feel about themselves. The latter will be a result of the way the carers in turn were treated as infants. Even tiny babies introject: that is, absorb their caretakers' feelings as if they were their own. So if, for example, a parent feels severely depressed and destructive towards themselves, their baby may well absorb these feelings and then experience them as though those difficult feelings were in fact their very own. These are often the experiences at the heart of the Type 3 impasse mentioned in the previous section. If babies are treated with care, respect and love, they will stand more chance of growing up with a healthy sense of worthiness in being alive than if their bodies and beings are abused, invaded, or inadequately cared for in major ways by parents or other guardians.

Erikson extends this stage to approximately the age of 18 months and defines its primary developmental task as developing *trust* as opposed to *mistrust*. Infancy is a decisive time for resolving the 'psychosocial crisis' in deciding that the world, mostly represented by mother, is either basically trustworthy or to be mistrusted. In other words, during this stage infants will or will not acquire the psychosocial strength of *hope*. Infants require somatic, Natural Child conviction that responses to their basic needs will be forthcoming and, if they internalize such experiences, they will develop a fundamental sense of appropriate trust and hopefulness about self and others on which they can more positively face their future developmental tasks.

An adult person who has adequately met these earliest developmental tasks will probably have, amongst other attributes, an intrinsic acceptance of their needs, a sense of belonging and a sense of security and optimism. They will feel accepted and accepting of their gender and will demonstrate trust in self and others. A person who, in infancy, has experienced deprivation, unresolved trauma, inadequate modelling, lack of permission or been brought up by emotionally or psychologically disturbed parents will probably exhibit unhealthy behaviours in their adulthood. Some of the ways in which these might be seen are: homicidal, psychotic or suicidal tendencies, addictions, eating disorders, disgust of their gender, fears of sudden changes and of separation or engulfment and the use of suffering to get their needs met. Such people may experience feelings of dissatisfaction and believe that they will never get enough. They may worry interminably or experience chronic anxiety. These inadequacies may be generally observable or they may emerge during those periods of an adult's life which most approximate infancy. Such times might include the start of processes such as a new course or a different job, times when they are sick, vulnerable, weary, stressed or hurt, or during traumas such as bereavement or when they are taking care of a young infant.

The Stage of Doing

From approximately the age of 6 to 18 months babies are very involved with developmental needs concerning *acting and doing* things in the world. They require modelling, support and approval of their explorations and experimentations, their proactivity and their curiosity. If the caretakers affirm their children's need to explore, they are likely to develop into adults who have a capacity for uninhibited creativity, motivation and interdependence. If these exploring needs are thwarted at this stage in life — and remember that, although trust issues were super-relevant in the first six months, they are still relevant here and in later stages — as adults such people may exhibit problems such as over-adaptation, lifelessness, passivity, being easily bored, solving difficulties with fight, flight or freeze responses, or being unaware of bodily needs or feelings; they may frequently injure themselves or experience racket fear where anger may be more appropriate. These difficulties, if not regularly in evidence, may develop at specific times during adulthood, such as when taking care of a baby or toddler, as part of a creative process or when learning new skills.

As mentioned earlier, Erikson includes this stage with the first one as the stage of trust versus mistrust.

The Stage of Thinking

This third stage stretches from the age of about 18 months to 3 years and has as its major focus affirmation of the child's capacity to think. Children meet this developmental task by receiving permissions: to sometimes think things out for themselves, to disagree, to make mistakes in the course of learning and experimenting, to socialize and to experience firm boundaries.

Erikson defines this stage in human development as the *autonomy* versus *shame and doubt* phase. He sees this stage as decisive in the growth of the child's goodwill and will power. If children at this stage have these psychosocial needs met, they will grow up to have a personalized sense of identity and respect for others; will have their memory and thinking ability functioning at an appropriate level for their innate capacity and will be able to exercise healthy self-control. However, if they are shamed, over- or under-controlled, competed against by adults or older siblings, or spoon-fed with regard to problem solving then the adults who emerge at the end of adolescence may be negative, oppositional, over-controlling, over-compliant, obsessive, competitive, fearful or passive. Some of the times when these deficits may be most noticed could be when looking after a young child, needing to think through an emergency, taking a personal stand on something, ending a long-standing relationship, or when learning new information.

The Stage of Identity

During the fourth phase of human development, from approximately 3 to 6 years of age, besides reinforcement of their previous developmental tasks, a child's sense of their power and identity needs encouragement, stimulation and recognition. They need guidance and modelling in such things as the ability to think, feel and act simultaneously and appropriately, having their needs met without 'acting' ill, peculiar, confused or stupid, being assertive and knowing what comprises reality and what is realistically achievable as opposed to magical and fanciful.

Erikson names this the 'play age'. Here children will develop their sense of *initiative* or develop learnt feelings of *guilt*.

Children whose parents are consistent, patient and have respect for their own and their children's thoughts, feelings and attitudes will gain a healthy sense of their own power, will have social skills and will demonstrate a healthy and active imagination. On the other hand, if children have inadequate parental guidance at this stage of their lives, for example if they are made responsible for their caretaker's feelings, thoughts or behaviour, encouraged always to please others above themselves or made to feel guilty or inept, they may well, as adults, show symptoms of phobias, manipulate others to take control of their lives, shoplift, find self-stimulation and creativity blocked, keep trying to make recompense for wrongs they have done or find difficulty in co-operation and in healthy competition.

Problems concerned with developmental deficit at this stage will be more noticeable when an adult is caring for children of this age-group, developing a new role, when seeking a new job or partner or when negotiating a social contract.

The Stage of Skilfulness

Around the ages of 6 to 12 years children are engrossed with the developmental tasks concerned with skilfulness. Here they need affirmations concerning learning without suffering and with enjoyment, developing personal, integrated ways of doing things, starting and completing tasks, asking for and using positive and negative conditional strokes, receiving and absorbing positive, unconditional strokes and exchanging 'have tos' with 'want tos'.

Erikson sees children in this school-going age-group as involved with issues of competency, in his words, *industry* versus *inferiority*.

Now a real sense of the technological ethos of their culture develops. If parents/caretakers are not too pushy, dominating, competitive or uninterested, if they are not obstructive of, or inadequate in responding to, the requirements of this developmental stage and continue to support the tasks of the previous stages which will require practice and nurturing, children are likely to grow up able to take pride in their achievements. They will envisage, begin and complete tasks with satisfaction and feel competent with the technology of their culture (for example, in the 1990s this would include use of computers). However, if children's progress is blocked or traumatized, they could, as adults, experience achievement anxiety, self-criticism, a sense of personal inadequacy, obsessionality or somatizations with regard to expectations from others.

Deficits in the development of primary school-aged children will not only negatively affect the next phase, adolescence, but might be particularly noticeable when, as adults, these people need to take responsibility for managing aspects of their technological world, deal with figures of authority, argue and judge, or take care of school-going children.

The Stage of Regeneration

The final stage to be traversed in childhood is that of the teenage years. During these years, recycling of earlier stages is particularly noticeable. At one moment an adolescent seems an adult and at another acts like a small child. Youngsters now particularly need affirmation with regard to regeneration. They are learning how to move gradually towards becoming separate from their family while experiencing the sanctuary that home can provide. They also become very concerned with their own individuality and with moving away from parental stereotyping in order to experiment safely with who they are, as different from the older generation yet conforming with certain groups or cliques of their peers. Sexuality becomes increasingly important and requires straightforward and frank addressing without shame, confusion, excitement or disgust on the part of the caretakers.

Erikson describes adolescence as being concerned with developing and integrating a sense of *identity* as opposed to suffering *identity diffusion*.

At this stage, teenagers seek a set of values which they can stand by and, without compromising their essence, live by. It is the stage of developing and confirming fidelity to self and to significant others so that one moves towards self-actualization, autonomy, spontaneity and heightened self-awareness.

The caretakers of teenagers should maintain their adequate support throughout this sometimes turbulent and revolutionary stage. They should allow their children to separate from them while maintaining unconditional, positive regard for them. If these requirements are met by the caretakers, then the adolescents stand a fine chance of entering the world of chronological adults. They are likely to have a sound sense of individuality, yet with an ability to be interdependent, an internalized value structure, the ability to maintain mutually satisfying relationships and a sense of fulfilment in the way they choose to structure their time. On the other hand, if adolescents are turned free too early or are overly suppressed and protected, they may exhibit such behaviours as escalated game-playing to have needs met, sexual problems, addictions, regression, depression or extreme anti-socialism. Deficits experienced in one's teenage years may flare up in later life, especially if one is the parent of adolescents, ending a process such as a relationship or a job or, on the other hand, starting a new process such as a sexual relationship or career.

You may have noticed that, throughout these descriptions of the childhood developmental stages, it was suggested that children *might* develop into healthy adults as a result of good-enough parental guidance or *might* exhibit disturbed behaviours if such guidance was inadequate. The reason for such uncertainty stems from two elements: one is the degree of psychological and emotional resilience a person may inherently possess; the other is the essential element in all scripting — that of personal choice. Whatever parental influences and life-experiences a child is exposed to, he or she makes an individual choice as to how they are going to cope with those experiences. There is the story of the constantly overwrought mother who used to harangue her four children with the statement, "You'll all end up in a lunatic asylum!" As adults two of them became psychiatric patients and two became psychiatrists.

Stages in Adulthood

Adulthood, like childhood, has certain readily observable developmental stages. Just as counsellors will need to observe the childhood developmental deficits in clients, they will also need to take cognizance of their clients' present, chronological adult developmental stage. According to Pam Levin, the six childhood stages are revisited in adulthood in similar cycles, spanning approximately 18 years. However, Erikson, further to his first five developmental stages, delineates three adult psychosocial stages.

He notes that young adulthood is a time of consolidation of the ability to *love*. This is a stage involved with developing *intimacy* instead of *isolation*. Parental caring is replaced by mutual caring for another or others. Sex is no longer part of identity confirmation but should now be part of genital maturity and sexual partners selected out of an aware choice and not compulsively, in response to introjected decrees. Full adulthood or maturity is that stage in our lives when we are faced with our sense of *generativity* versus *stagnation*. Here we are involved, or not, with *care* of and for the generation to follow. This may involve producing and nurturing children or it may mean being involved in different aspects of making any creative contribution to one's ecological and/or psychosocial world. The eighth and last of Erikson's stages of life, old age, is seen by him as a time concerned with *wisdom*, 'a detached and yet active concern with life in the face of death' (p609). Here one encounters *integrity* versus *despair*. If the previous life stages have been well integrated, we can face death as the essential boundary that it is while looking back with a sense of satisfaction and appreciation. If the earlier stages still hold serious deficits, a person might face the last years of their life in depression, hypochondria, paranoia or the like.

Application

The major way in which clients make up for their developmental deficits in counselling is through the ongoing *relationship* with their counsellor. Having a predictably consistent, dependable, good-enough and caring person involved with one's life is in itself a reparative opportunity for all aspects of developmental pathology. Research projects involved with comparing the success of different orientations of psychotherapy conclude that usually the most competent counselling and psychotherapy practitioners, no matter what their particular approach to therapy or counselling, have more in common with one another and help evoke more curative change than do the least effective practitioners within their own schools of practice. Furthermore, the major healing tool common to these effective therapists is that of the relationship between the therapist and the client. This is why it is essential that the first counselling sessions, like the first weeks and months of life, concentrate on the building of trust in the relationship between counsellor and client.

Where a counsellor, within the developing relationship with the client, diagnoses certain specific deficits in their client's psychosocial development, they will need to include within their treatment plan some contingencies for correcting or replacing inadequate caring that occurred during those stages or for offering experiences which were absent during crucial times in their client's development. The careful timing of such interventions is essential and must only take place once decontamination has been effected, otherwise the counsellor could, for example, be reinforcing a form of magical thinking in the Child who is still waiting for someone to come and take care of her.

Extreme or severe deficit requiring major structural changes and more intensive techniques may need the help of an outside agency such as a psychotherapist or psychiatrist specializing in regressive approaches. It is important that, through their training, ongoing supervision and personal counselling or psychotherapy, counsellors can accept and operate within their areas of competency and refer out as necessary. However, simple deficit healing can be achieved by the sensitive and experienced counsellor using the TA techniques which follow. We will first describe them and then provide an extended client example of the use of the deficit model including each of the four techniques.

Self-reparenting

Self-reparenting is a process developed by Muriel James (*It's Never Too Late To Be Happy*, Reading, Mass., Addison-Wesley, 1985). With self-reparenting a person selects and then adds a new Parent to their existing Parent which can be drawn upon by the integrated Adult in response to here-and-now needs. This new Parent has qualities of which the client deems themselves in need and which are not already a part of their existing Parent

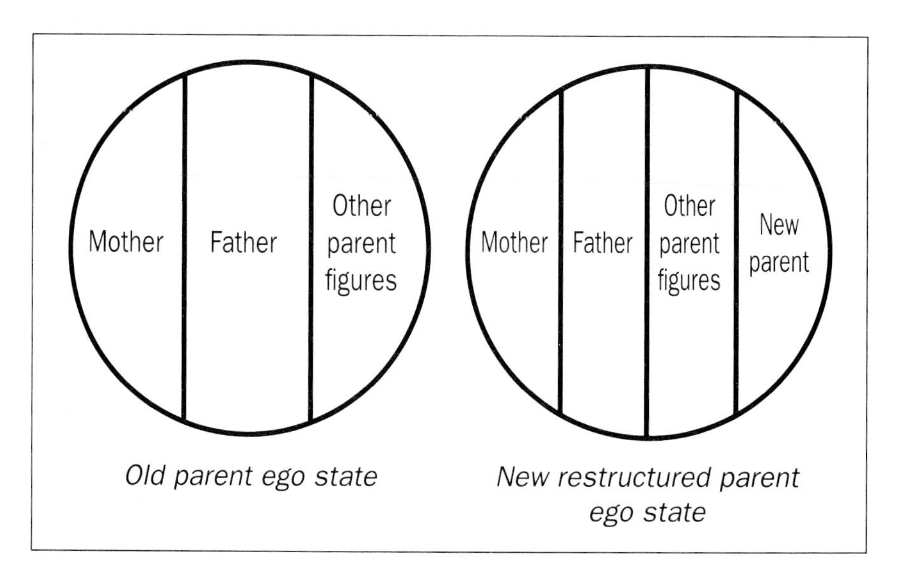

Figure 22 *Before and after self-reparenting*

Adapted from **Muriel James,** *It's Never Too Late To Be Happy,* © 1985 by Addison-Wesley Pub Co. Reprinted by permission of Addison-Wesley Publishing Co Inc, Reading, MA.

ego state. Figure 22 illustrates how the contents of a person's Parent ego state may be represented before and after the self-reparenting process.

The stages of the self-reparenting procedure are as follows:

1 Develop awareness of the need for change and for a new Parent and of what is missing within the Parent ego state.
2 Note and become educated in the commonality of parenting/caretaking styles and the responses to these.
3 Analyse own parent figures: in other words, make an historical diagnosis of each childhood parent figure.
4 Become aware of own Child needs and how these could start being met by a new Parent.
5 Decide what is possible and who could assist.
6 Clarify the collated data and mobilize your inner resources in order to realize what you want.
7 Learn to make life-enhancing contracts and to practise the new behaviours, drawing upon the new Introjected Parent behaviours in service of the inner child.
8 Recognize and celebrate the new parental caring behaviours, so that conscious caring can become automatic.

In essence, the counsellor is assisting the client in examining how they would be different if they had had more suitable parents, in learning what would comprise ideal parents, in designing and implementing an internal adequate Parent and then in practising using him or her.

Spot Reparenting

The next TA technique used for work on developmental deficits is that of spot reparenting, as developed by Russell Osnes (*TAJ*, 4, 3, 1974). He suggested using this as an alternative to the more intensive, long-term, restructural, psychotherapeutic process called reparenting, hence its inclusion here as an appropriate and useful technique in counselling. Spot reparenting comprises giving the client a necessary piece of appropriate parenting at the moment that the client's Child meets a previously experienced inadequate form of caretaking. The spot reparenting procedure is as follows:

1 The client contracts to connect with a certain Child ego state or, in the course of their counselling time, has already become 'little'.
2 The client relives that Child experience to the point of the negative parenting.
3 The counsellor gives the missing parenting.

We suggest an additional and important fourth stage:

4 The client 'grows up' and integrates the new experience.

The Parent Interview

The third TA method to be described in this chapter is that of John McNeel's parent interview, (*TAJ*, 6, 1, 1976). A parent interview takes place when the counsellor talks to one of the internal parents in the client's Parent ego state with a view to helping the client to experience that part as really separate from themselves. The procedure is as follows:

1 A 'two chair' dialogue is set up between the client's Child and Parent.
2 The counsellor talks to the internal Parent as if this Parent were a real person.
3 The counsellor asks questions which will elicit the Parent's Child ego state.
4 The counsellor facilitates the Parent in expressing those feelings and experiences which are triggered by the needs and requests of the client (the real son or daughter).
5 The client is assisted in experiencing viscerally the Parent from an Adult position and thus seeing the parent as separate.

To be effective for, and protective of, the client, the Parent interview needs to be conducted from the frame of reference that the original parent acted from a threatened and not a malicious position. For this reason, we recommend the use of the Parent interview only when the counsellor feels certain that the parents were not actively abusive or malicious and feels sympathetic to their acting from fear or from their own unresolved issues.

Rechilding

In this fourth method of addressing deficit we move from the Parent ego state to the Child. The concept of rechilding was introduced by Petrūska Clarkson and Sue Fish in their article, 'Rechilding: creating a new past in the present as a support for the future' (*TAJ*, 18, 1, 1988). Though, as the article proposes, the full rechilding process should be practised in workshops over several days by qualified and experienced psychotherapists, we suggest that 'spot' rechilding can and does take place within more regular individual and group counselling.

Just as new ego states can be added to the reservoir of Parent ego states, so too new thought, feeling and behavioural experiences can be added to the reservoir of Child ego states. Reparenting work naturally affects the Child in providing the support and nurturing that was originally lacking. Rechilding work, however, directly addresses the Child ego state. The intention is to give the Child new healthy experiences which, once in place, can both support and stabilize the Adult, particularly in stressful situations.

For example, Jim, as an only child who had been tutored at home, had little experience of playing with others. In his adult life he did not enjoy 'having fun' socially. He did not know how. Any attempts to join in were spoilt because he felt awkward and out of place. He found such situations extremely stressful. In counselling he did some rechilding work whereby, at various ages and stages of his Child, he played age-appropriate games with the counsellor over several sessions, including a five-year-old's pillow fight and an eight-year-old's paper plane-making session. Eventually, Jim was able to draw upon these new healthy experiences of playing when in the company of other grown-ups having fun. He became not only an enthusiastic 'Charades' player but also a spontaneous inventor of improvization games. In this example, as is often the case with rechilding experiences, the work was not accompanied by reparenting. The counsellor played a child role rather than a parent role in Jim's rechilding work. (Please note that it is important that the counsellor choose to use a positive child ego state and one older than the client's, monitored by their Adult, to ensure a safe and constructive experience.) In group counselling settings, other group members often take on the roles of siblings or peers and, just as in childhood experiences, 'parents' may not be present.

The rechilding procedure is as follows:

1 Following decontamination, deconfusion, redecision and work on the Parent ego state, the client identifies difficulties or disturbances in Adult functioning that may need the support of new Child experiences.
2 The needed Child experience at a particular developmental age is identified.
3 The client contracts with the counsellor (and, where applicable, the group) to regress to the appropriate developmental age for a specific time-limited period. We would suggest that 10 minutes within the first half of a 50-minute counselling session allows enough time for the next steps in the procedure and provides appropriate protection for the client. The conducive roles required of the counsellor and/or group members (if any) are also identified and contracted for at this time.
4 The rechilding experience takes place for the agreed amount of time. Clearly, whatever role he is adopting in the rechilding, the counsellor should remain responsible for the time-keeping and other necessary safety boundaries.
5 The client and any other participants in the rechilding return to Adult and the client cognitively integrates the experience by comment and discussion. Further aspects of deficit may be identified and noted for future work.
6 The client, in Adult, practises drawing upon the supportive new Child ego state by experiencing situations within and/or outside the counselling setting where the original difficulty was experienced and behaving differently.

An example

Let us take a look at the way in which use of the deficit model and the above techniques played an important part in the counselling of a particular client, Samantha. When Samantha first sought counselling, she introduced herself as a 'frumpy, boring, old housewife who feels miserable and pessimistic most of the time'. Actually, she was a good-looking, 46-year-old woman who had devoted the past 24 years to the upbringing of four healthy and creative children.

During the course of counselling, the following developmental issues emerged. At 46, Samantha was *chronologically* still engaged in her life stage concerned with generativity versus stagnation. Having fulfilled her procreativity in terms of raising a family, she was faced with the dilemma of time structuring now that her children no longer needed her. Her major model as a child for this stage of her life had been her maternal grandmother who had "rather pathetically, sort of haunted the family, trying unsuccessfully to make herself important to us with no other outside interests at all".

Besides various other *childhood* developmental deficits that Samantha had experienced, for the sake of this example the inadequate parental care she received in her fifth year should be described. At this time her two-year-old brother contracted leukaemia and, after a long illness, died. During his illness, Samantha experienced long periods of time deprived of her parents' presence, especially that of her mother. She was taken care of by a distant aunt. Whereas her mother had very actively and creatively pursued stimulating ways of being with Samantha, this aunt had occupied her by having her amuse her toddler cousins. She was not given any sensible information about the situation. She was told, "Mummy and Daddy are trying to make Trevor better because he is a bit sick. If you pray very hard and wish with all your might he may get well again and everybody can get back to normal." She started school for the first time without much preparation for it and with very little support on her first days there. Once her brother died, she was told that he had gone to sleep for ever and now lived in heaven with God.

As can be understood from the above, at a time in her childhood when Samantha needed developmentally to be facing, with the support of her caretakers, the task of confirming her identity in the larger world and experimenting with initiating and being powerful, the family was suddenly faced with a trauma during which Samantha's needs were very inadequately met. Children can adjust creatively to even terrible traumas if they are given the space and attention to express their thoughts and feelings about them. They need to be guided through the reality of the painful situation while attention to reconfirming and reintegrating their earlier developmental stages receives special consideration. But the tragedy of Samantha's brother's death was that it was not worked through. She was not given the space, modelling or encouragement to talk about her brother's illness and death. She was not helped to understand some of the facts involved in childhood illness and death: for example, that such a serious illness is unusual and that she could not catch it; that death and sleep are different, and so on. Nor were space and understanding provided for her natural regression to a younger age which occurs in order to reconfirm the underpinnings of previous developmental tasks — in Samantha's case, rediscovering her own capacity to think for herself and experience some degree of autonomy. Her parents did not wilfully mistreat her but were caught up in their own script issues when faced with such a tragedy.

While working with Samantha the counsellor kept in mind Samantha's present adult developmental journey and, when appropriate, helped her to appreciate the generativity she had already exhibited in her successful raising of 4 children. He also supported her creative thinking around ways in which she could expand her horizons of productivity. When her mother grew infirm and died and Samantha thought she should take a break from counselling, he pointed out how script reinforcing that could be. It could reinforce her belief that "when things get tough I must do everything on my own", so Samantha decided to stay and used their relationship to build a very different experience with respect to death and dying.

An example of some spot reparenting work done with Samantha to address a specific area of developmental deficit is illustrated in the following extract. Samantha had frequently referred in her counselling sessions to her loneliness and despair while staying with her aunt. She vividly remembered one evening in particular. In previous sessions she had expressed her feelings about it and in this session she and the counsellor had contracted that she would re-experience that night, but that this time it would proceed differently and the counsellor would intercede on her behalf.

SAMANTHA: I'm in bed. Auntie Phillipa is downstairs watching TV.

COUNSELLOR: What are you feeling, Samantha?

SAMANTHA (*beginning to cry*): I'm very sad. I want my mummy. (*Cries*) I want to go home. Auntie Flip doesn't love me. Nobody wants me any more. (*Weeps.*)

COUNSELLOR: Let yourself imagine that I'm also downstairs, Samantha. Will you do that?

SAMANTHA: Yes, you've just come in the front door. (*Cries loudly.*)

COUNSELLOR (*taking on the role of an able caretaker in that situation*): Oh dear, I can hear little Samantha crying and crying upstairs. Flip, you should not be ignoring her and watching the TV when a small child sounds so very sad and lonely. (*Raising his voice*) I'm coming, Samantha. Oh dear me, here's a very sad little girl indeed. (*Samantha cries deeply while the counsellor waits, making empathetic sounds.*) Do you want to tell me what's happening, Samantha?

SAMANTHA: I want to go home 'cos Auntie Flip doesn't . . . isn't nice.

COUNSELLOR: I'm sorry, Samantha. What else?

SAMANTHA: Mummy and Daddy don't want me anymore.

COUNSELLOR: Oooooh.

Samantha proceeds to tell her counsellor (good-enough caretaker of her five-year-old) all about her thoughts and feelings with regard to the tragedy through which the family is living. He listens to her version of the story without contradiction or interruption. After she has finished, we hear him helping her with some of the details.

SAMANTHA: No one, even Mummy doesn't want me any more.

COUNSELLOR: Mummy is sad and busy with Trevor, that's true, and even while she's doing that she still knows you are the little girl she loves and she sometimes misses you, too.

SAMANTHA: I wish and wish that Trevor was all better but God won't listen to me.

COUNSELLOR: I think it's great that you send loving and get-better thoughts to Trevor, but when people are very ill as he is they need certain special medicines and to be looked after in certain ways and many people are involved in trying to help Trevor get better, aren't they?

SAMANTHA: Mmm.

COUNSELLOR: And usually that help succeeds and the person gets better, but sometimes the ill person or little boy or girl is so very, very sick that they can't get better and that is nobody's fault.

SAMANTHA: So then they go to sleep forever and ever.

COUNSELLOR: Then they die and that is very different from sleeping. Can you work out a way in which they are different?

SAMANTHA: Ummmm, when mmmm, when you go to sleep you are still there in the morning and you can get up and eat your breakfast but if you are dead you can't.

And so the session proceeds until Samantha returns to her present age and integrates her experience.

An example of self-reparenting can also be drawn from Samantha's counselling journey. Both before and after the session as described above, Samantha had become increasingly aware of the deficits in her Parent ego state. With the help of the spot reparenting she did with her counsellor (as above and on other occasions), appropriate reading and film-watching of material illustrating healthy parental caring and observing parental techniques in the world around her, Samantha built up a profile of what constitutes a good-enough parent. This work was linked to the analysis she did of her own parent figures and of her childhood needs. She reached the point where she could design herself a new Parent. She could start practising these new parental behaviours under Adult vigilance until such effective behaviour became automatic and she and the counsellor knew that it had become part of her Parent ego state which she could draw upon from her Adult where necessary. In this extract we hear Samantha describing to her counsellor an incident where she was practising her new parental behaviours.

SAMANTHA: Well, I attended my first French class last Wednesday.

COUNSELLOR: Yes?

SAMANTHA: And when I first walked in, I nearly turned round and ran all the way home because all the other students looked like children to me and I felt out of place and ancient.

COUNSELLOR: You *nearly* left.

SAMANTHA: But then I remembered that work we did around my first day at school and I imagined an encouraging hand on my shoulder . . . and it was like . . . yes, just as though it was really there and I said to myself, "Come on now Samantha, relax and slow down, this could be exciting."

COUNSELLOR: Hey, well done.

SAMANTHA: I even managed to say to myself that, in the sense that all of us there were ignorant about French, we were all, knowledge-wise, the same age and I felt braver. I sat next to another student and started chatting. I even told him that I was nervous and, guess what, he was also scared 'cos he said he was terrible at languages and had to do the course for use in his job.

COUNSELLOR: You seem to have settled yourself in there very effectively.

SAMANTHA: And I later doodled on my pad . . . "Go there, kid!"

To illustrate the Parent interview here is an extract from another of Samantha's counselling sessions. Samantha is moving between a chair which represents her Child and another which symbolically represents her mother.

SAMANTHA (*from the Child chair*): You are always criticizing me. Whatever I do or say, you come chipping in telling me how it's just not good enough or how I should be doing it. Why are you never satisfied with me . . . oh, what's the use?

COUNSELLOR: Swap over.

SAMANTHA (*from the Parent chair*): It's just for your own good, my girl. You need me there. Someone has to look after you, don't you know?

COUNSELLOR: Change over.

SAMANTHA (*from the Child chair*): Please leave off nagging me. (*Swapping herself over*) That's right — call 'caring' nagging!

COUNSELLOR: Can I talk to you a while please, Mrs Williams?

SAMANTHA (*continues as mother*): All right, but I want you to know that I don't believe in all this counselling stuff. A lot of self-indulgence if you ask me. Samantha would be better off playing a game of tennis or going for a long walk somewhere.

COUNSELLOR: Yes, those are certainly ways of relaxing — did you walk or play tennis at all?

SAMANTHA: Oh yes, especially at Samantha's age.

COUNSELLOR: From what I heard earlier, it seems to me that you worry a great deal about Samantha.

SAMANTHA: Oh yes indeed. I don't think that she takes enough care in life.

COUNSELLOR: I see, and how do you feel when she seems not to be being careful enough to you?

SAMANTHA: I . . . (*hesitates*) . . . I . . . well, to be quite honest with you . . . I am terrified that I'll lose her.

COUNSELLOR: You are terrified she could die?

SAMANTHA (*crying*): Losing one child was torture . . . an absolute nightmare for years and years . . . and I only just managed, and really only for the sake of Sam, to pull myself back together again. I think that I'd only want to die if I had ever to face that again. (*Weeps.*)

COUNSELLOR: I understand. That period of your life sounds unutterably awful. I am sorry.

SAMANTHA: You know, my father died when I was eight and to this day I can't imagine how my mother seemed to carry on as usual.

Some time is given to helping Samantha's mother's Child release some of her pain. Later the counsellor concludes the session:

COUNSELLOR: So in a way you show your love for Sam by nagging her?

SAMANTHA: I suppose so, although I do also buy her presents to show her how much she means to me too.

COUNSELLOR: Could you think of any other way in which she might like to know you care?

SAMANTHA: I could try and tell her but there's seldom time in her busy life for saying such things.

COUNSELLOR: You do find time to nag and choose presents to give her. Would you be prepared to take a few minutes now to tell her?

SAMANTHA: Yes, I will. Sam, honey, I probably won't say this properly but I do want you to know that I really, really (*cries a little*) love you very dearly . . . you are very precious and I'm sorry that I nag you so.

COUNSELLOR: OK?

SAMANTHA: Was that enough?

COUNSELLOR: It seems a fine start to me. Thank you for talking to me today despite your initial reservations.

SAMANTHA: Thank you, too.

COUNSELLOR: Samantha, would you go back to the other chair now?

SAMANTHA (*from Child chair*): Gosh, I never knew (*laughs*), although of course I must have known to say it all, but I never really took on board just how sad and scared my mother was.

Rechilding was employed later in the counselling when Samantha referred to her tendency to be entertaining to others at the expense of her own enjoyment. This was identified as being partly due to her experiences while staying with her Auntie Flip and being required to amuse her toddler cousins. She contracted with the counsellor to regress to the age she had been while staying at her aunt's. The counsellor, in turn, agreed to play with her from his Adult-monitored Child ego state in a way which allowed Samantha the experience of 'amusing herself' while playing with another child. She chose to play with the doll's house and together they arranged all the furniture, with all the agreement and disagreement that was entailed in deciding where things should go, before making up stories between them about the characters in the house. The mutuality of this experience was a first step for Samantha towards not only amusing herself but really enjoying herself with others.

Exercises

Self and Working with Clients

With regard to Self-reparenting you might want to explore some of the following exercises for yourself and your clients.

1 List positive aspects of yourself and then alongside them list which styles of parenting probably contributed to eliciting them. For example:

POSITIVE ASPECTS OF MYSELF	PARENT CONTRIBUTION
• I am attentive to my own and others' needs.	▪ Modelling healthy interdependence and non-rescuing care to me.
• I am loving to my friends.	▪ Physically, demonstratively loving to each other and to me.
• I am persistent in my endeavours.	▪ Permission to take time, be patient and tolerant of mistakes, encouraging.

Similarly, list those parts of yourself which limit actualization, fulfilment, satisfaction and so on, and which types of parenting accompany them. For example:

LIMITING ASPECTS OF MYSELF	PARENT CONTRIBUTION
• I hide my anger.	▪ Equating anger with being 'bad'.
• I don't have enough fun.	▪ Too much emphasis on work and achievement at the expense of leisure.
• I rush my food at meal-times.	▪ Similar to above. Hurry up to get back to work. Eating is an interruption rather than a pleasure.

2 Note how you parent yourself in situations of stress, challenge, pleasure, and so on. If you find some inadequate self-parenting, suggest alternatives for yourself. For example:

SITUATION	SELF-PARENTING
• Wife's illness	■ Take good care of myself with weekly massage and asking others for help.
• Giving a speech	■ Keep questioning my ability; internal pessimism. Suggest I remind myself of successful past speeches and do some visualization of the next one.
• Playing tennis	■ Encourage myself when serving badly and suggest different techniques.

3 Read about childhood needs and development, and about creative parenting.
4 Take time to be with children of different ages. Observe which developmental tasks a child is involved with and note which caretaking styles promote the child's fuller actualization and which dampen his or her innate individuality. Also spend time in the supermarket, on a train, in a park or at the cinema watching how parenting styles differ.
5 Gently encourage your Child to list his or her needs and wants while being vigilant not to let a punitive Parent interfere in the process. For a while your Adult will need to be responsible for vetting all negotiations between your Child and the beginnings of a new Parent to protect the Child from the old Parent. It is sometimes helpful to create a composite picture or collage in your mind's eye comprising different aspects of different models showing good-enough parenting. You could choose to do this with paper and pens or pieces cut from various magazines so that you can actually refer to and see depictions of caring parents as needed.
6 Have your Adult set you simple experiments to do each day or week which will promote the caring you require in areas of

deficit. An example here could be that you had agreed to give yourself an encouraging remark at least three times daily, so you might now be saying to yourself something like “It's great that you are reading and using this book. Well done, Mary.” In any form of interaction, whether external or internal, a person's name and tone of voice can be used to emphasize the caring nature of the transaction.

7 Identify your own areas of deficit in childhood experiences and contract with your counsellor or psychotherapist to do some rechilding. Do the same with your client, following the outlined procedure.

Chapter 11

A CLIENT EXAMPLE

The Initial Contact with the Client

Ernestine came to see the counsellor at the suggestion of a friend who was concerned about her. Smallish, plumpish, very pretty, with a tumbling mass of wavy brown hair, she was aged 21 but looked younger than her years. She wore long, full skirts in pretty Indian fabric, with an eye-catching blouse and floppy beret. She had rather a 1960s look about her. The counsellor asked her about her name and she said she preferred to be called Ernie, which seemed to encapsulate her feelings about herself and her attitude to the world: confused, defiant, struggling — and young. The eldest child in her family, she had a sister of 14 and a brother of 12, and still lived at her parents' home. Since leaving school at 17, she had had a succession of short-term jobs, mostly below her potential and all ending unhappily. She found personal relationships difficult and puzzling both at work and in her social life, which mainly consisted of folk-singing and folk festivals.

The Presenting Problems and Contracts

At the first interview, Ernie said that she was generally very unhappy and had a drink problem, often getting drunk both in company and in the isolation of her room at home. She also said that she was worried about work, where she was threatened with disciplinary proceedings for being generally unsatisfactory. She could not get on with the other staff and did not like the job, but did not want to lose it for financial reasons and because she was desperate to improve her job record. Through her reading, Ernie had learned a lot of psychological jargon which she used to her own disadvantage. She told the counsellor that she was 'manipulative' and 'played games'. The counsellor asked why Ernie had told her that and she replied that it was so that the counsellor would know about it and not let it happen. This seemed to the counsellor to be both a reasonable expectation and also an invitation to a game of 'Do Me Something', a Victim–Rescuer game which she continued to play for a long time.

The counsellor concluded that Ernie's two main driver behaviours were Try Hard and Be Perfect: constantly hearing a very negative, introjected Parent with a corresponding Child ego state which complied, yet was very resentful of parent figures.

The Business Contract

Ernie and the counsellor agreed to meet on a weekly basis for an hour and agreed upon a fee. Ernie's father was willing to pay for her counselling but, shortly after starting counselling, she came to an agreement with the counsellor to pay part of the cost herself. The counsellor thought that this indicated both her continued dependence and her wish to be independent. They also agreed on confidentiality and arrangements for cancellations and holidays.

Initial Treatment Contracts

When the counsellor asked Ernie what she wanted to get out of counselling for herself she said that she wanted to find ways of improving her work and her relationships with colleagues in order to keep her job. She was also afraid that she might give the job up of her own accord. She said that she wanted to stop playing games (this was her own phrase, not necessarily as defined in TA). They therefore agreed on two contracts: (1) to stay in her job until she gained a better one; and (2) to learn how to ask straight out for what she wanted and then do so.

As Ernie had been depressed for several years and had even attempted suicide, the counsellor asked her to make a contract not to harm herself or others. She would not do so on a long-term basis at this point but agreed to make it for a week (or until the counsellor and Ernie next met if they were delayed in meeting for any reason). This keeping safe contract was renewed carefully and consistently for some months until Ernie could make one for longer. In order to have reasonably accurate information on which to decide how to tackle her drink problem, the counsellor asked Ernie to keep a record of all the alcohol she drank in the coming week and she agreed to do so.

History

Ernie was the first child in her family. Her mother worked in a GP's surgery and her father was a bank manager. When she was 3, a sister was born who was sickly from birth, occupying much of her mother's attention, so that Ernie was sent to stay with an aunt for a lot of the time. When she was about 5, the sister died. Subsequently, Ernie was deemed by mother to be 'a difficult child' and taken to a child psychiatrist. Ernie did not remember these sessions clearly, but they do not seem to have been useful, for she was unhappy and unpopular throughout most of her school life, in spite of her parents' attempts to encourage her artistic talents.

She reported always feeling confused as a child — confused about what people wanted and about the meaning of what they said, confused about how she was meant to behave and about what result her actions might have. A friend, to whom she had been close but from whom she had later become somewhat distant, died of cancer when Ernie was 15 years old. She felt very upset and wanted sympathy from her mother, but she did not get much and was not permitted to go to the funeral. The counsellor surmised that she had not properly mourned either of these early losses and that the unresolved feelings arising from them continued to trouble her. When she was 17 she attempted suicide and was subsequently referred to a psychiatrist.

Ernie had never had a boyfriend although, at a week-long folk festival, she had formed a romantic attachment with a much older man. This had subsequently petered out and she now felt 'embarrassed at the thought of it'. She said she did not want a sexual relationship until she had 'sorted herself out' but would definitely hope then to find a boyfriend. Consequently, this did not become a focus within the counselling sessions. The counsellor judged that this might happen naturally enough when that time came. The counsellor felt a genuine liking for her client which she found helpful in counselling someone as 'challenging' as Ernie sometimes proved to be.

Assessment

Discounting

It was clear to the counsellor that Ernie and her mother were in an unhealthy relationship in which Ernie discounted her own ability to look after herself and to think for herself. She would say, "I feel I'm only half a person. Mum fills the other half." She had an obvious investment in staying in Child as her mother cooked, cleaned and tidied up for her from an Inadequate Parent mode. The 'price' of this on her part was to carry her mother's unexpressed grief and rage at her second daughter's death by being unhappy and behaving 'badly'. Though the counsellor positively stroked Ernie's clear thinking and expression during the sessions, she would discount herself by saying, "I can only do it when I'm here; I can't do it on my own."

The Script Matrix

In the course of the first few months of the counselling, Ernie's script matrix was drawn up by the counsellor and Ernie. Father was always a rather vague figure, almost mother's shadow. His contribution to Ernie's script was to model passive behaviours in which he gave in to and agreed with Ernie's mother. His very distance was probably received by Ernie as a 'Don't be close' injunction. Mother provided more active messages which were clearly influential to Ernie's decision-making and script formation. The counsellor soon recognized Ernie's 'Please People' driver in addition to the others noted earlier, and the principal injunctions from mother: Don't feel, Don't succeed, Don't leave me, Don't cross me or I'll get you, Don't think for yourself, and plain DON'T. It is immediately obvious how many of these injunctions are involved with the overall instruction not to be a separate person, with separate feelings, thoughts and needs.

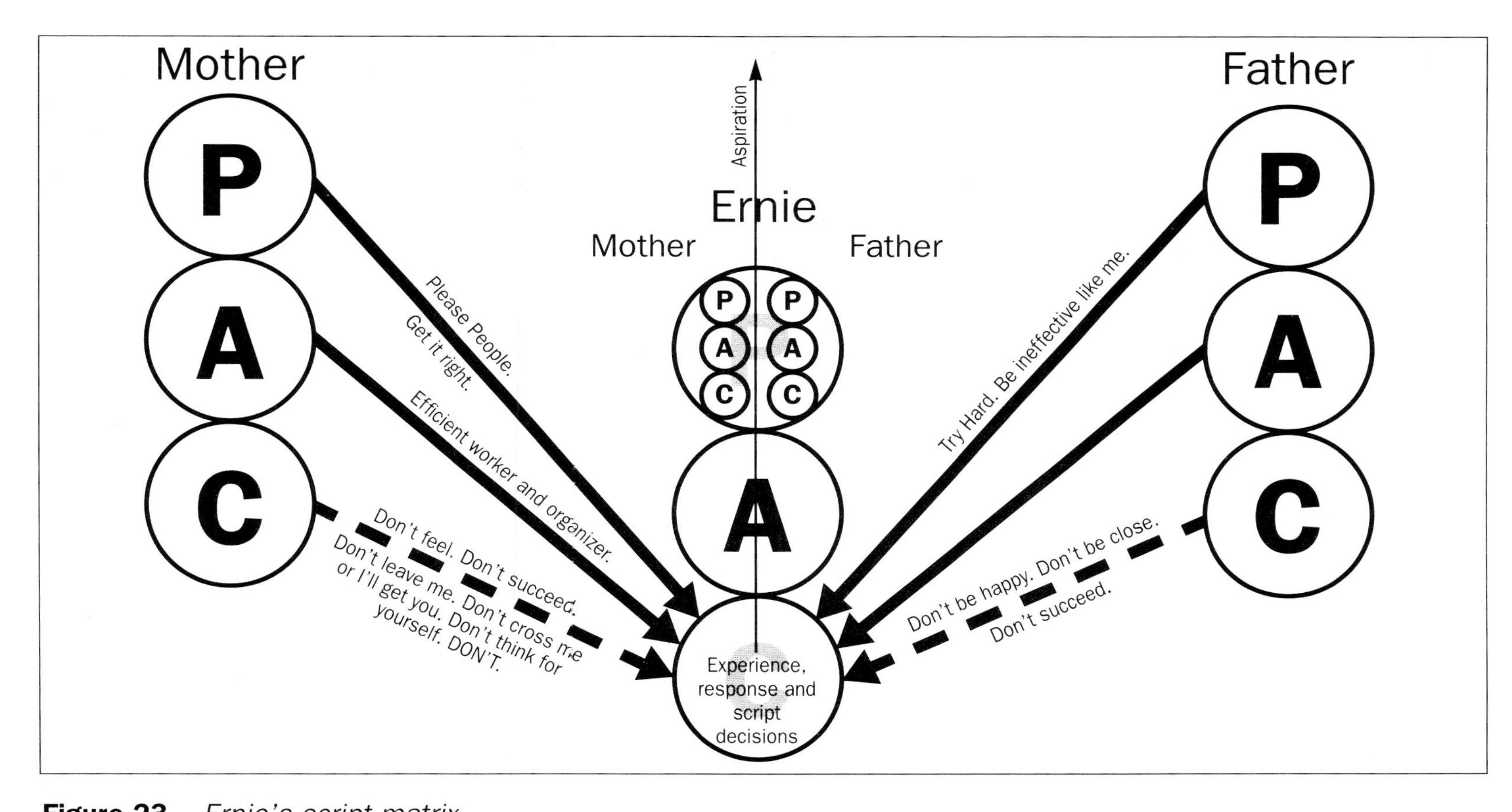

Figure 23 *Ernie's script matrix*

Ernie spent much of her time obeying the social level messages she received, trying hard to get things right and to please other people both in her work and in her hobby of weaving rugs to order. When her Child got tired or rebelled, she stopped getting things right and failed to please and so lapsed into the psychological level of her script, feeling guilty and scared. At such times she could not think what to do in her work and got way behind with her weaving and everything else that she 'should' be doing. Eventually, she would try to catch up and make amends, following the social level messages and believing "I'm OK if I get it right and please people." From this scripting, Ernie had decided early in her life that anything bad that happened was her fault. This was reinforced by her family's election of her as the 'identified patient' from the time of her sister's death. She would need to change this decision before she could achieve what she wanted in her life.

Taking all this into account, the counsellor's overall impression of Ernie was of a young girl struggling to grow up. In terms of Pam Levin's developmental stages, it seemed that the main deficits were at the stage of what Levin calls Thinking which concerns developing autonomy, (18 months to 3 years of age), and this had prevented her from fully completing the tasks at later stages of development which would ensure a true sense of identity in early adulthood. Consequently, her presentation was more that of an adolescent than of a mature, young woman. She needed help to separate from her mother and achieve autonomy in order to discover who she really was and what she wanted to do with her life. The counsellor did not think that she would have difficulty in achieving her contracts, in spite of the early traumas, once she had reached the point of separateness.

When she first came, Ernie simply wanted to stop being so unhappy, but about six months later she began to recognize her difficulty and expressed it in the following manner: "I'm like a chameleon. I try to give everyone what I think they want, so I'm different depending on who I'm with. I'm never just myself. I don't know who I am. I don't know what I'm really like if I stop being a chameleon." At this point, the initial social contracts concerning keeping her job and learning to ask for what she wanted were reviewed and revised to include a contract specifically addressing the issue of Ernie's existence as a separate being.

Counsellor's Thoughts on the Likely Process of Counselling

ESTABLISHING THE RELATIONSHIP

It was important that Ernie build up a feeling of trust and confidence in order to be able to use the counselling sessions. During this period she would tell her story and she and the counsellor would begin to understand it together and make contracts for the desired change. The counsellor thought that the relationship between herself and Ernie would be of great importance, since the difficulties in her earlier relationship with her mother lay within her failure to develop sufficient basic trust in order to move towards autonomy. She needed to experience a relationship appropriate to that early stage — one which would contain and set boundaries as well as nurture and respect.

CONFUSION

The counsellor assessed that Ernie's process of becoming a separate person would need to start with decontamination and strengthening of her Adult. For this she would use the classical analyses of TA: structural analysis, transactional analysis, game and racket analysis and script analysis. Ernie urgently needed to free herself from her very critical and negative Inadequate Parent, so the counsellor decided in the early sessions to teach her functional analysis. She responded very well and from the beginning made good use of this, structural ego state analysis and transactional analysis proper. Extensive decontamination would lead on to the treatment contract for deconfusion of the Child involving the building of internal supports to permit the expression of previously inhibited feelings and needs.

CONFLICT

Ernie would then be in a position fully to experience and resolve her impasses, leading to eventual redecision. She clearly needed to change early decisions about her own badness ("When anything goes wrong, I feel it's my fault") and to deal with the injunctions Don't be happy and Don't succeed. Her goals came to include finding who she was and leaving her family in order to live an independent life.

DEFICIT

As mentioned above, the counsellor thought that what had been missing in Ernie's development was a parent who had supported and encouraged the growth of her individuality. She needed to be in a relationship with someone who would care about her and be with her while accepting her differences of opinion, her negative feelings, her difference. In this sense, therefore, the counsellor would work in the deficit model right from the start of the counselling, as she encouraged Ernie to make her own decisions and 'grow up'.

INTEGRATION

At this stage of counselling clients often experience a time of feeling quite lost and vulnerable as well as excited as they begin to realize the opportunities open to them. They may need to learn new life skills for the changes they make. During this stage, Ernie might need to take time to adjust to the world as it would be seen through eyes unclouded by script beliefs.

TERMINATION

This would be a time of actual as well as psychological separation for Ernie and the counsellor. Attention would need to be paid to addressing the feelings and thoughts that would arise.

The Process of Counselling

The following is an account of Ernie's journey with the counsellor. The above phases are included, not as separated stages, but as they are found in a real relationship, interweaving and blending. The counsellor began the first phase — that of establishing the relationship — by making it clear, in every way she could, that she was taking Ernie seriously and thought her someone with whom it was worth working. This was important to Ernie because she had felt brushed off with pills and platitudes by psychiatrists in the past. So the counsellor used all the counselling skills of listening, reflecting and clarifying while also beginning to teach her about ego states. They agreed on a contract to work weekly together until the end of the year (about nine months ahead) although the counsellor indicated that she would be prepared to work with her for longer if required. She continued to use empathic transactions all through the course of the counselling, firstly to build a good relationship, and also to facilitate redecision.

It was very interesting to see how effective this proved in tackling Ernie's drink problem. Having asked her to keep a count of her drinking for a week, the counsellor checked with her in the second session, when she reported having consumed about 40 units of alcohol (the recommended safe limit for women in one week being 14 units). She then went on to say that she thought she did it because her being a 'drunkard' made people sorry for her. Clearly, she needed an alternative source of strokes. The counsellor began to teach her about the stroke economy, which she quickly grasped. They also talked in this session about strategies to help her keep her job, especially avoiding going in with a hangover every morning. Ernie widened her 'No harm' contract to include causing harm to herself in any way by drinking. The following week she reported that she had reduced her intake considerably and made a contract to drink only 'a sensible amount'. This apparently 'soft' contract was sufficient for the drink problem to reduce considerably. The counsellor believed that the attention Ernie now felt sure of receiving from her was enough to replace the strokes she had gained through drinking and winning her friends' concern.

When discussing her difficulties within the family and at work, Ernie invited the counsellor into games of 'Poor me' and 'Yes But', invitations to which, initially, she sometimes responded. On reflection, the counsellor thought that simple contracts for behavioural change might be effective, with Ernie choosing one thing at a time that she would like to do differently. The first one was to finish by the end of the month all the outstanding weaving orders which she had undertaken. They discussed whether this was realistically feasible (it was, provided that she stick to the task), how she might sabotage herself (by forgetting) and avoid the sabotage (by a note on her mirror), and finally how she would reward herself for succeeding — by buying herself another weaving tool that she wanted. In the event, she completed the contract but discounted herself and refused strokes because 'it was easy' to carry out. She was feeling despairing at this point, fearing that she would never change because there was so much to change and time was short — short because her temporary contract at work was due to end or be renewed within six months; also because her internal Parent told her Child that she should have sorted herself out by now.

The counsellor responded with understanding to her feelings of despair and panic, and nevertheless kept on with the 'change one thing at a time' plan. In this way Ernie began to deal with what she perceived as her 'over-the-top' way of transacting with most people. This was because of her constant anxiety about how to do it correctly. They looked at how she needed to think about exactly what she wanted to convey, how she could listen intently to other people for short spells, how and with whom and for how long she could practise these new skills. She became aware that family rituals for everyday transactions were very rigid and had to be 'got right'. She felt uncertain of procedures, conventions and expectations outside the family. For example, she had difficulty in accepting a stroke, finding it hard to say 'thank you' for it because she was not sure whether that was correct. Here indeed was an 'adolescent' in need of straightforward social education.

At the same time, her real underlying problems with her mother were beginning to emerge — reluctantly on Ernie's part. She started to talk of feeling angry with her mother who criticized her for not behaving responsibly and then frustrated her attempts to do so by taking over. Before attempting any work with Ernie on her underlying feelings and decisions, the counsellor kept to the plan of initiating behavioural change, and suggested that she choose one thing for which she was prepared to take responsibility. She wanted to be left to change her own bed-linen so that her mother would not 'tidy' her room while changing the sheets and interfere with all Ernie's scattered pieces of craft work. It took Ernie several weeks to establish this satisfactorily, disciplining herself to do it regularly so that her mother had no cause for complaint, and using the 'Broken Record' assertiveness technique (*When I Say No, I Feel Guilty*, Manuel J. Smith, Bantam Books, 1975) to help her scared Child stand up to her mother's resistance. This technique involves acknowledging what the other person is saying while repeating the request firmly and clearly. It was during this period that she spoke of being only half a person and began to recognize her own investment in staying a child. By both acting to change behaviour patterns and talking about her beliefs and feelings underlying them, Ernie was clearing her Adult of Parent and Child contaminations and discovering a freedom to act from that Adult if she chose.

That was the positive side. The 'downside' was her frequent despair and being disheartened by the apparent enormity of her task. There were many areas of her life in which she wanted change to 'happen'. This, of course, was the real snag. Like most people, she secretly hoped that others would change — her mother would love her, her colleagues stop misjudging and criticizing her — a satisfying career would materialize, and a boyfriend would appear on the scene. At the same time, she was beginning to acknowledge that her mother (and perhaps her shadowy father) had never really loved her as she wanted to be loved: for herself. In painfully acknowledging this, she began to mourn it, and to let go of the hope that somehow, one day, it might be different. As she worked further, Ernie began to disclose violent and unpredictable behaviour on her mother's part: verbal attacks would sometimes become physical and Ernie at times feared for her own safety. About three months after beginning counselling, she came to a session in despair, feeling very uncared-for by her family. At this point she extended her weekly no harm contract and made a 'no suicide contract' for three months. The counsellor thought that the underlying question was whether she herself would care for Ernie and support her struggles to be herself. Ernie seemed to her to be giving herself a chance to find out if this was enough. She no longer played 'Poor Me', since the counsellor had stopped joining in. She still sometimes played 'Yes But', although the counsellor avoided giving her the opportunity as carefully as she could.

At this point Ernie expanded her creativity. As a child, she had painted and drawn a good deal but she had had to struggle with her frustration at her child ability not matching her vision of what she wanted to create. She was blamed for 'bad temper' and 'having a do' about making things, and her creativity waned. She had not painted a single picture since leaving school but now she was considering starting to paint again. The summer holidays now arrived and they broke for a month with some degree of optimism.

When they returned, they entered a new phase. Ernie had had a good summer, enjoying folk festivals and a camping holiday with like-minded friends. She now began to focus on her wish to leave home and live independently (which she had tried and failed to do once before). She knew that she was not yet ready to do this, neither emotionally nor practically, and she wanted to change her feelings about her mother which she found difficult to voice, saying that she both resented and needed her. She also felt disloyal talking about her. At this point, she was very discouraged and said that she thought she would give up counselling because she was getting nowhere. She was tacitly implying that the counsellor was no use, and inviting her to 'Do Me Something'. The counsellor side-stepped and invited her to talk about anything good in her life. She was pleased because she had now embarked on her Art 'A' level, and enjoyed writing short pieces and reading interesting books. They discussed that a little. The counsellor wondered if this 'chatting' was really helping her counselling but decided that engaging her Child in this way helped to free the block. The next session began with her saying that she was afraid that she might tell things inaccurately and be unfair to her mother. When the counsellor emphasized that it was the mother-in-her-head that they were dealing with, rather than the real person that she actually was, Ernie launched straight into her story. She told of how very much she feared criticism if she failed to please, just as at home she feared physical retaliation. She sought to avoid attack by using placatory behaviour; she was very aware of the difference between herself and her sister, whose attitude was open defiance. However, if her mother attacked too heavily, Ernie would fight back, both verbally and, when necessary, physically. Her father did not attempt to stop her mother's violence or even remonstrate. Ernie thought he feared that the attack would turn on him if he did so. Saying that she had "always felt different", Ernie could not explain in what way this was so. The counsellor hypothesized that she knew that she came from a 'different' and crazy family.

The counsellor did not attempt to go any further in that session, as it had required such an effort for Ernie to get that far. But, at the very next session, Ernie started by saying that she was fed up with being a chameleon, putting on masks to give others what she guessed they wanted to hear or see. She talked here about work which, after various confrontations, she had finally had to leave when her employer declined to renew her temporary contract. She had handled the situation well from Adult, even while feeling upset by it, and had found a new job before leaving. She was now worried that she would repeat old patterns with her new colleagues, seeking to placate and somehow only succeeding in antagonizing them. Now began a new phase, one of "Who am I?" Describing herself in turn as caring, artistic, and very 'tuned in' to all aspects of Nature, she began to feel her way into her own identity, a process which went on for many months. For the rest of that year, Ernie alternated between Adult realizations and Adapted Child helplessness. In one memorable session, she reported that she was doing better than before in her Art course, but that she was "fed up with the world". She reiterated that if things went wrong it must be her fault but, paradoxically, she did not really accept responsibility, playing the helpless Victim: "People are the trouble." Using ego state analysis, she began to recognize that there was constant internal dialogue between her very negative Parent and her Child (an impasse of the first type). The Child believed and submitted to her Parent, while bitterly resenting this and projecting her frustration onto 'the world'. The question was how to raise her Natural Child and Good-enough Parent modes to support her Adult. She resented any challenge or suggestion from the counsellor, hearing it as more criticism from the Parent, and she played a hard game of 'Yes But' — even with herself. The counsellor needed all her own Adult awareness and skills to stay out of Rescue or Persecution. It was important for her to make all transactions from Integrated Adult, helping Ernie to continue thinking and nurturing herself.

So began the next year, with Ernie feeling overwhelmed by the magnitude and multiplicity of her problems, still shackled by her belief that if anything bad happened it was her fault. Clearly, she needed to make a redecision and change this belief. It seemed to the counsellor that further decontamination was necessary because her contaminated Adult seemed to support her Child belief. The counsellor's problem at this point was that Ernie was against any more of this kind of work: "I understand in my Adult but it doesn't do any good. It doesn't change anything." (In spite of behavioural change, her feelings were so far unaffected.) The counsellor was concerned that, if she persisted, Ernie might stop coming to counselling and that if she did she might end by killing herself. In supervision, the counsellor recognized her own helpless feelings as reflecting Ernie's — a typical 'parallel process'. She confirmed her judgment that decontamination was both needed and helpful, in spite of Ernie's feelings about it. She assessed that their relationship was strong enough to hold Ernie. In the next few weeks, they concentrated on three chair work, which Ernie proved to use brilliantly. Her Adult supported her Child and she fully understood how her family's thinking had been distorted. When her sister had died, her mother had 'got on with life' and Ernie was made the repository of all bad feelings, especially sadness and anger. Every time she had expressed strong feelings the response was to send for the doctor. Ernie's sadness and anger, being invalidated, became despair. She remembered feeling lonely and unhappy and wanting to die at the age of 10. Now she knew how important it was to clarify her thinking but voiced her difficulty: "I can do it while I'm here but when I'm back there I get all confused again."

It seemed that Ernie was experiencing the counsellor's Adult as a parent who was stronger than the Parent in her head. However, she still sometimes pulled away and played 'Yes But' and she was becoming aware of how much she did that in the world. During one session, she suddenly said, "Do I really push everything away?" When they subsequently analysed the game of 'Yes But', Ernie realized that she felt confused when trying to decide upon a course of action and was afraid of getting it wrong. It was safer to hedge and be uncertain than take this risk. She also said that she felt as if something stopped her thinking and she now realized that it was her fear of getting hurt by discovering something she did not like about herself or her family. Yet her Parent accused her of wasting time and money if she did not make the fullest use of the sessions — 'damned if you do, damned if you don't'. She did some three chair work about this issue:

ERNIE (*Parent*): I know what's right. I know better than you.
ERNIE (*Child*): I don't think you do. Why should you know better than me?
ERNIE (*Parent*): That's the way of the world.
ERNIE (*Child*): (*Says nothing, nods, accepting it.*)
COUNSELLOR: That's not true. Parents don't necessarily know

better than their children. They don't know everything.
ERNIE (*Child*): (*Looks up, smiles.*)
ERNIE (*Adult to Child*): I know what we can do; you can do the work you need to do and I will say stop if it gets too painful for you and you need support.
ERNIE (*Child*): Agreed.
COUNSELLOR: Agreed.

Deconfusion and conflict work: They had begun now to build the internal supports which Ernie needed in order to express her feelings fully. In spite of this, in the next session, Ernie was reluctant to work, inviting the counsellor to take responsibility for her, even to the point of wanting to be bullied. The counsellor had to stay alongside her in her despair. The next week, Ernie bounced in full of energy, declaring that she had definitely decided to leave home. This was following a row in which her mother had become physically violent and bitten Ernie, who was outraged. They explored her feelings about all her relationships within the family, the possible consequences of her leaving and any obstacles to her doing so. It was also very important for her to plan how to keep herself from physical harm. They now had a real treatment contract, with Ernie purposefully directing her energies to achieving separation.

Over the next few months they worked with her internal process and with her practical needs. On the one hand, there were some very moving times during which Ernie shared her feelings of delight in "discovering my soul", as she expressed it, and of deep sadness at her baby sister's death as she recognized for the first time the possible effects on her 5-year-old self. She was gaining insight all the time into her own process, on one occasion commenting on her increasing use of her Adult and Good-enough Parent mode to support her Child and direct her actions. In another session, after describing feeling isolated and misunderstood, following an incident with folk-singing friends, she commented: "If you feel isolated, it's very easy to get into a situation where you are a bit shut out" — a neat description of a racket. The counsellor's part in her becoming aware of this was to suggest that she should relate the incident from all 3 ego states in turn, with Adult coming last and achieving the insight.

Most of the time now, the counsellor's interventions consisted of providing Ernie with a suggested framework for tackling the difficulty, leaving her to do it her own way within the framework and find her own solution. This is always, of course, a desirable way to work if a client has enough energy and commitment, and doubly so when the issue at stake is achieving separation and independence. At a practical level, they planned how Ernie could achieve financial independence instead of having a running loan from her father. They talked of career options, buying a car and making sure she could cater and cook adequately. Almost all of one session was spent discussing her fears of 'house-sitting' with a friend in a third party's house, doing her share of the practical chores while keeping a good relationship with the friend. After the event, she returned delighted with herself for how well she had managed. Her friend had found Ernie's cooking very tasty and, in consequence, she was questioning her old belief that 'everything I do or am is crap'. She was clearly open to learning from experience, which was heartening for both of them. She now gave evidence of growing self-value, being aware of a changing perspective on the company she was used to keeping. Her feeling that others treated her as an inferior she now recognized as largely a projection of her own feeling of inferiority, and she was increasingly able to put it aside.

Having built internal supports and expressed many buried feelings, Ernie was now beginning to complete the work with her Child by making redecisions, even without any specific 'redecision scenes'. It was rather akin to a religious belief, in which a person may experience growing conviction rather than sudden conversion. She demonstrated this in an unequivocal manner when she walked into one session and announced straight away that she had made a decision about her name: "I've always told people, 'My name is Ernestine and I like to be called Ernie'. Now I've started to say, 'My name is Ernestine and I like to be called Tina'." The picture of an attractive, vibrant, even elegant young woman which this name conjured up for the counsellor was borne out by her appearance, altogether a more grown-up one. She was excited by many observations which she had noted during the week, especially of having very frequent 'paranoid fantasies' of people thinking ill of her, and of her own Adult putting aside the fantasy with "They may not be thinking that at all, and in any case what does it matter?" She was beginning to use her new attitudes and behaviours more readily.

Tina now moved into a phase of integrating the new decisions and learning ways of supporting them and dealing with the 'backlash' of old script patterns which re-emerged under pressure. Ironically enough, her inadequate Parent now nagged her to monitor herself and assiduously practise the new habit of thinking. Tina showed no sign of 'Yes But' as she took in and used the counsellor's suggestions for dealing with this by such ploys as switching into physical activity, raising her Natural Child mode by doing something for fun (she chose to paint T-shirts for sale at craft fairs) or visualizing some image containing her vision of herself. At times she found it difficult to experience a sense of self and keep an image in visualization. She was grappling with the dilemma of how to dare to be herself and become adult, and yet remain safe. She was in a transitional phase and felt it to be so. This was reflected in the reactions of other people to her now, especially to her change of name: some willingly used the new form, others grumpily resisted, some ignored it and yet others managed it some of the time. Gradually, she learned how to deal with old patterns if they emerged, by not trying too hard to contradict each one, but to explore it or ignore it and go on. There had twice been a fortnight's gap between sessions because of circumstances, and they now agreed to make that the regular interval, as Tina was managing very well with this frequency. This also gave her a little more time, as coming to a therapy session took virtually a whole evening, with over an hour's travel each way, and she was now enjoying helping with a Brownie pack.

Tina said that she felt no pressing need at this point to go to college to escape from work, which she found quite manageable and even enjoyable; neither was she worried about finding a boyfriend, as her social life was pleasantly full. However, she really did want to move out of her parents' house. She needed more space for all her art and craft projects and she now felt prepared, with all the necessary skills. Although aware of losing the comforts and security of home and a little fearful of being lonely, she very much wanted to take the plunge and prove that she could manage it, as she believed she could. After several weeks of searching and inspecting, she finally found a large room in a shared house, chosen carefully to meet her needs for space, companionship, easy access to work and so on. Now she faced an initial period of feeling strange and rather lonely in new surroundings. Tina dealt with the ensuing despondency by reminding herself that it was probably to be expected in the circumstances, and she did not fall into depression. Instead she concentrated on organizing herself and making reasonable relationships with the other occupants. In fact, she can be considered to have remained 'stable under stress', the acid test of real change. Soon she was feeling good again, happy with work and leisure activities. She was now temporarily in charge at Brownies in the absence of the Brown Owl and bubbling with enthusiasm over all the activities which she initiated for the girls. Shortly afterwards she was asked to take over as Brown Owl, a well-deserved compliment to her ability. The week after she had moved, she said that she felt she had turned over a page in her life, the last page of the chapter entitled 'Childhood', and was now beginning a new chapter, 'Adult Life'.

The counsellor and Tina now judged that Tina would soon be ready to leave counselling: they should not end abruptly but rather spread out sessions over longer intervals so that she could continue to feel support while spreading her wings. There was, of course, a parallel with her leaving home. She had entered a whole new social circle of young people meeting at the local pub, and had noticed that she was occasionally inclined to slip into old patterns of drinking to attract attention. Thinking that she could do without that, she realized that what she really wanted now was a boyfriend, and that there was plenty of opportunity in this new milieu.

In the same session, Tina reported evidence of her change from external sources. "It's funny, you know, now I've left home Mum's different. When I pop in to see her she treats me like anyone else — we just talk Adult to Adult in fact." She went on to relate how her mother had offered to help with typing or anything else in Tina's Brownie work because she was bored with nothing but routine family chores. The counsellor wondered privately whether mother was trying to regain control, but Tina said cheerfully that she planned to invite her mother to test Brownies for 'interest badges' such as Hostess and House Manager. What a beautiful reversal of roles! She also mentioned that an older woman at work who had previously been very defensive and unco-operative towards her was now a good colleague, sharing the work amicably. The environment was surely changing in response to Tina's change. A friend had summed it up at a New Year party: "You've really changed since you changed your name; changing your name must really make a difference." Tina grinned in full appreciation of the irony as she related it to the counsellor. At the end of that session, they agreed to meet monthly. The counsellor also asked her permission to use her as the subject of a case study and she was delighted at this further demonstration, as she felt it, of her value.

Tina has now fulfilled all her contracts. As described earlier, drinking ceased to be a problem almost as soon as she started in counselling, when she contracted to drink only a sensible amount. Having finished her 6 month contract at work, she found herself a better job and has stayed in it for 18 months, longer than in any previous employment. While the clerical work is not in itself very stretching or satisfying, it has provided a useful context for Tina to develop relationship skills with colleagues. She plans to stay there for another year or two while she consolidates her personal growth, her job record and her finances. Seriously considering a career in teaching after that, she now looks forward to going to college as a mature student with no parental contribution towards her maintenance grant. Her other original contract was to learn to ask in a straight way for what she wants. This did indeed require to be learnt, since she had no pattern of doing so from either parent. She now mostly does ask straight, and is quickly aware when she does not.

The autonomy contract which finally became the focus of all the later work was to achieve separation and independence, in fact to be herself. This Tina has demonstrably achieved, leaving home to live independently and finding new friends and interests as well as continuing with former ones. The counsellor's own goal in the counselling was to help Tina meet these contracts. She checked her achievements against the original assessment. She considered Tina in terms of symbiosis, redecision and script. She believed that Tina had resolved the symbiosis, having tested and proved her ability to look after herself; she has left home and no longer looks to her mother for approval or direction. She has also given up her belief that any bad happening is her fault and, paradoxically, is then willing to take responsibility for her share in any unsatisfactory state of affairs, and for putting it right. As far as script is concerned, she no longer lives in fear of displeasing her mother, but gets on with her own life; she has become aware that from time to time she wants to please and to 'get it all right', and then reminds herself that there is no need to do so.

Starting now from a basic trust in herself and others, she has worked through the other stages postulated by Levin and Erikson and developed a real sense of her own identity. The counsellor now has a definite 'feel' of Tina as a lively young adult, very different from the troubled adolescent who presented herself two years ago. The outside world appears to see her in a similar way. They have worked through the different phases of counselling, including confusion, conflict, deficit work and relationship building. Of these the relationship has been of primary importance, both as an essential foundation for counselling and as the vehicle for the other phases.

Tina has spent many months integrating new beliefs and behaviours into her life, and at the time of writing she is continuing with this and at the same time moving into the termination stage of counselling. She will continue to meet the counsellor monthly while she practises her new life style and extends her own support network. When she is ready for the final break, it will be in the knowledge that she can 'check in' for further help if she needs it in the future. They will part with mutual feelings of respect and satisfaction.

A Final Word

We have greatly enjoyed writing this book together. We have had many amusing moments as well as stimulating discussions and new insights into our own understanding of transactional analysis and how we use this approach in our counselling.

We hope you have enjoyed this introduction to transactional analysis and have found it useful for yourselves and your clients. We would welcome your views and comments; please write to us at the Winslow Press address.

We include here a recommended reading list and some addresses to enable you to extend your interest if you so wish.

Recommended Reading

Berne E, *Transactional Analysis in Psychotherapy*, Grove Press, New York, 1961, 1966.

Berne E, *The Structure and Dynamics of Organizations and Groups*, J. B. Lippincott Co, Philadelphia, 1963; Grove Press, New York, 1966; Ballantine, New York, 1973.

Berne E, *Games People Play*, Grove Press, New York, 1964; Penguin, Harmondsworth, 1968.

Berne E, *Principles of Group Treatment*, Oxford University Press, New York, 1966; Grove Press, New York, 1966.

Berne E, *Sex in Human Loving*, Simon & Schuster, New York, 1970; Penguin, Harmondsworth, 1973.

Berne E, *What Do You Say After You Say Hello?*, Grove Press, New York, 1972; Corgi, London, 1975.

Berne E, *Intuition and Ego States*, TA Press, San Francisco, 1977.

Clarkson P, *Transactional Analysis Psychotherapy: an integrated approach*, Tavistock/Routledge, London & New York, 1992.

Goulding M & R, *The Power is in the Patient*, TA Press, San Francisco, 1978.

Goulding M & R, *Changing Lives Through Redecision Therapy*, Brunner/Mazel, New York, 1979.

James M, *Techniques in Transactional Analysis*, Addison-Wesley, Reading, Mass., 1977.

James M, *Breaking Free: self-reparenting for a new life*, Addison-Wesley, Philippines, 1981.

James M & Jongeward D, *Born to Win: transactional analysis with gestalt experiments*, Addison-Wesley, Reading, Mass., 1971.

Steiner C, *Scripts People Live*, Grove Press, New York, 1974.

Stewart I, *Transactional Analysis Counselling in Action*, Sage, London, 1989.

Stewart I & Joines V, *TA Today: a new introduction to transactional analysis*, Lifespace Publishing, Nottingham, 1987.

Woollams S & Brown M, *Transactional Analysis*, Huron Valley Institute, Dexter, 1978.
Woollams S & Brown M, *TA: the total handbook of transactional analysis*, Prentice-Hall, Englewood Cliffs, 1979.

Addresses of TA Organizations

The European Association for Transactional Analysis
Case Grand-Pré 59
1211 Geneva 16
Switzerland

The Institute of Transactional Analysis
BM Box 4104
London WC1 3XX

The International Transactional Analysis Association
1772 Vallejo Street
San Francisco
California 94123
USA

metanoia Psychotherapy Training Institute
13, North Common Road
Ealing
London W5 2QB

metanoia Psychotherapy Training Institute is a member of the above organizations and offers, among other programmes, introductory and advanced training and supervision in transactional analysis as well as individual and group counselling and psychotherapy. It is also a member of the United Kingdom Council for Psychotherapy.

Index of Major TA Concepts

A

B

C

D

E

F

G